The Concept of Sin in Judaism, Christianity and Islam

Key Concepts in Interreligious Discourses

Edited by
Georges Tamer

Volume 14

The Concept of Sin in Judaism, Christianity and Islam

Edited by
Christoph Böttigheimer and Konstantin Kamp

DE GRUYTER

ISBN 978-3-11-130394-9
e-ISBN (PDF) 978-3-11-131945-2
e-ISBN (EPUB) 978-3-11-131972-8
ISSN 2513-1117

Library of Congress Control Number: 2024943409

Bibliographic information published by the Deutsche Nationalbibliothek
The Deutsche Nationalbibliothek lists this publication in the Deutsche Nationalbibliografie; detailed bibliographic data are available on the Internet at http://dnb.dnb.de.

Typesetting: Integra Software Services Pvt. Ltd.

www.degruyter.com

Preface

This volume at hand of the book series "Key Concepts in Interreligious Discourses" (KCID) documents the results of a conference which dealt with the concept of "Sin" in Judaism, Christianity and Islam and was held at the Catholic University of Eichstätt-Ingolstadt. The conference was organized by the research unit "Key Concepts in Interreligious Discourses" and took place on June 23–24, 2021.

The research unit "Key Concepts in Interreligious Discourses" was jointly run by the Friedrich-Alexander-University Erlangen-Nuremberg and the Catholic University of Eichstätt-Ingolstadt between June 2018 and June 2021. As the title already implies, the mutual project focused on interreligious discourse. However, it was not about conducting an interreligious dialogue, but rather reflection upon this dialogue, thereby facilitating a theologically well-founded interreligious dialogue. For only if every dialogue partner has a clear picture of what is discussed about, a dialogue can be conducted reasonably. It was the project's ambition to provide such clarification by examining concepts that are central for Judaism, Christianity and Islam, both historically and in terms of their interdependencies and by setting them in a relation to one another. By reflecting on central ideas and beliefs historically and comparatively, common values and origins, but also differences and contradictions between the three monotheistic religions are to be clearly elaborated. By disclosing key concepts of the three closely interconnected religions: Judaism, Christianity and Islam, a deeper mutual understanding is fostered, prejudices and misunderstandings are counteracted and thus a contribution is made to peaceful interaction based on respect and recognition.

Only through precise knowledge of the central ideas of the foreign as well as of one's own religion a well-founded, objective and constructive interreligious understanding can prevail. Conferences at which international experts from the fields of theology, religious studies and philosophy of religion intensively discussed and clarified core religious ideas from the perspective of the three religions served this purpose. Developments within religious history never proceed in isolation; rather, they interpenetrate each other and are mutually dependent. Thus, the research unit "Key Concepts in Interreligious Discourses" pursued fundamental research and aimed at an "archaeology of knowledge" with its comparative conceptual-historical investigations.

Inasmuch as world peace cannot be obtained without religious peace, the project contributed importantly to a peaceful social coexistence and thus corresponds to the obligation that has been newly assigned to the universities in recent decades, namely to engage in social concerns in addition to teaching and research. This is expressed by the term "third mission."

https://doi.org/10.1515/9783111319452-202

I wish to thank Dr. Wenzel Maximilian Widenka, who helped organize the conference, and Konstantin Kamp, who helped editing this volume. In addition to the cooperation partners of the Friedrich-Alexander-University Erlangen-Nuremberg and the de Gruyter publishing house for including this volume in the book series "Key Concepts in Interreligious Discourses," we would like to express our sincere thanks to the third-party funders, the Karpos Foundation of the Diocese of Eichstätt, the Maximilian Bickhoff Foundation and the ProFor Program of the Catholic University of Eichstätt-Ingolstadt. Without their support, neither the conference nor the volumes would have been possible.

Christoph Böttigheimer,
July 2024

Contents

Preface — V

David Bashevkin
The Concept of Sin in Judaism — 1

Christoph Böttigheimer
The Concept of Sin in Christianity — 49

Ayman Shabana
The Concept of Sin in Islam — 105

Christoph Böttigheimer / Konstantin Kamp
Epilogue — 151

List of Contributors and Editors — 169

Index of Persons — 171

Index of Subjects — 173

David Bashevkin

The Concept of Sin in Judaism

1 Introduction

1.1 Many Words for Sin

Judaism contains many different words for sin; the concept and its remedies are multivalent. Among the many words for sin in Hebrew are the biblical words *ḥeṭ*, *pesh'a*, and *'avon* and the later, more generic, rabbinic term *'averah*.[1] What does this variety of words say about the Jewish concept of sin?

1.1.1 Biblical Metaphors for Sin in Judaism

Some scholars, including Gary A. Anderson, have explored the biblical conception of sin as a burden. Anderson has focused on this element on account of the biblical term *nośa 'avon*, meaning "carry iniquity" (see Micah 7:18). The implied weight of a burden, explains Anderson, reinforces the physicality of sin, or what he terms the "thingness" of sin.[2] Joseph Lam, similarly, explains that, since much of the imagery of sin is meant to depict sin as a burden, such imagery "lends itself potentially to this portrayal of the psychological effects of conscious culpability."[3] Sin is a burden, in other words, because human beings who realize they have sinned feel guilty about it afterward.

Another common biblical image is of sin as debt. This could be a dangerous description; some have pointed to the metaphor of sin as debt to negatively depict rabbinic Judaism. The financial metaphor "seems to conjure the notion that God sits in heaven with his account books open and scrutinizes every human action with an eye toward properly recording it as either a debit or a credit."[4] This image fails to account for God's potential forgiveness of sin. For example, an important text in Judaism, Isaiah's consolation of the Jewish people (40:2), portrays sin as a debt that can be not only incurred but also, if merited, forgiven.

1 Hebrew- and Aramaic-to-English transliteration in this article generally follows the guidelines set by the US Library of Congress, with exceptions for direct quotations and (some) titles of works and proper names.

2 Anderson, Gary A., *Sin: A History*, New Haven: Yale University Press, 2010, 6.

3 Lam, Joseph, *Patterns of Sin in the Hebrew Bible*, New York: Oxford University Press, 2016, 3.

4 Anderson, *Sin*, 105.

https://doi.org/10.1515/9783111319452-001

Sin can be carried, but it also can be something else. The word *ḥeṭ* is used in Judges 20:16 to describe a stone's missing its mark.[5] While the term *nośa 'avon* emphasizes the heaviness of sin, the word *ḥeṭ* describes sin as a missed opportunity. Here sin serves as a foil for a target, likely man's own self-actualization. If self-development and actualization are the objective, sin is what occurs when that objective remains unmet.

All that being said, there is a limit to metaphors' ability to accurately depict the concept of sin in Judaism. As Lam correctly notes, "The idea of sin in biblical Hebrew is no more encapsulated by the metaphors of *sin is a burden* and *sin is an account* than the notion of *love is a journey, love is a physical force, love is madness*."[6] A metaphor is a window to understanding, but it is important not to fixate on it and, instead, to consider the words for sin from other vantage points.

1.1.2 Sin in Rabbinic Literature: Severity and Intent

Whereas the Hebrew Bible offers rich, varied imagery of sin, the Talmud gets down to the details of the definition and differing levels of severity of the Bible's three words for sin: *ḥeṭ, 'avon,* and *pesh'a.* On this point, the rabbis looked to the intent of the sinner. Their prooftext was the confession of the High Priest on Yom Kippur in Leviticus, chapter 16. This chapter reveals that the priest must confess three times on the day of Yom Kippur, but it does not give the words of the confession. The *Tann'aim,* the rabbis of the Mishnah (edited in the early third century CE), noted that, on the Day of Atonement, the High Priest confessed three times: twice on his personal sacrifice and once on the communal scapegoat (see Mishnah Yoma 6:1). The confession began with a plea: "Please God!" The remainder of the confession, however, is subject to a Tannaitic dispute. Everyone agreed to the basic text of the confession, but there was some controversy surrounding the order of three important words: *ḥeṭ, 'avon,* and *pesh'a.* According to Rabbi Meir, the confession concludes as follows: "Please, God, I have sinned [*'aviti*], I have done wrong [*pashati*], and I have rebelled [*ḥatati*] before You, I and my family. Please, God, grant atonement, please, for the sins [*la'avonot*], and for the wrongs [*velapesh'aim*], and for the rebellions [*velaḥat'aim*] that I have sinned, and done wrong, and rebelled before You, I and my family" (bYoma 35b–36b).[7]

5 See Lam, *Patterns of Sin,* 221n12, for more biblical scholarship on *ḥeṭ* as missing the mark.

6 Lam, *Patterns of Sin,* 6.

7 All translations from the Talmud are from Steinsaltz, Adin (ed. and trans.), *Koren Talmud Bavli,* William Davidson (ed.), Jerusalem: Koren, 2012, with my modifications, unless otherwise noted. This translation can be accessed online at https://www.sefaria.org/texts/Talmud.

According to Rabbi Meir, throughout the confession, the synonyms for sin are ordered *'avon*, *pesh'a*, and *ḥeṭ*. This, the Talmud points out, is a rational order, given that it is the very same order found in the Bible's thirteen attributes of God (see Exod 34:7). Other rabbis of the Mishnah disagree and insist that the order is different: first *ḥeṭ*, then *'avon*, then *pesh'a*. Their reasoning is that each of these words for sin connotes a different degree of intent. A *ḥeṭ* is a sin committed inadvertently. An *'avon*, explain the rabbis, is an intentional sin. *Pesh'a* is a sin that is not only committed deliberately but also as an act of rebellion against God. As each word for sin represents a different degree of rebellious intent, it makes sense that they should be ordered in ascending order of severity.[8]

To summarize, Rabbi Meir and the Rabbis both agree that the various words for sin indicate different levels of severity. Their argument surrounds the order of the High Priest's confession. According to Rabbi Meir, the order of the confession is based upon the order as presented in the Bible.[9] According to the Rabbis the order of the Priest's confession is based upon which sins have the most pernicious intent.

The linguistic distinctions presented by the Talmud are telling. Idolatry, adultery, and murder are singled out by the Talmud as sins that require Jews to succumb to martyrdom rather than commit any one of the three. But such sins, while certainly severe, do not factor into the Talmudic classification of the different names for sin. Rather, the names for the different sins are based upon the motivation of the sinner. An otherwise minor infraction can be classified as a *pesh'a* if the sinner committed such an act as a marked act of rebellion against God. Conversely, an egregious sin can be characterized as a *ḥeṭ* if the sin was unintentional. The severity of sin, according to the Talmud, is in the mind of the transgressor.

8 See also the commentary of *Malbim* (Meir Leibush ben Yeḥiel Mikhel Wisser, 1809–1879) on Exod 34:7. A note on rabbinic sources: I have chosen, in most cases, not to cite a particular modern edition of these sources, as editions vary, and the easiest way to find the comment is to look for the name of the commentator and the chapter and verse of the biblical verse he is discussing. I have listed those. All translations of rabbinic commentaries are mine unless otherwise noted.

9 Some later commentaries question the rationale of Rabbi Meir. See the comments of *Gevurot 'Ari* (Aryeh Leib Ginsburg), *Maharsha* (Shmuel Eidels), and *Sefat Emet* (Yehudah Aryeh Leib Alter, 1847–1905) on bYoma 36b, as well as Malbim's comment on Lev 16:21.

1.2 The Language of Sin in Rabbinic Literature: The Term *'Averah*

The Bible and later rabbinic works such as the Mishnah and Talmud do not always speak the same language. There are a host of Hebrew words frequently used in Mishnaic literature that are not mentioned anywhere in the biblical canon. Regarding sin, one word frequently used in Mishnaic literature is completely absent in the Bible: *'averah.*[10] For instance, when the Mishnah in *Pirke 'Avot* instructs its students to flee from sin (mAvot 2:2), it does not use any of the more familiar biblical terms, such as *ḥeṭ, 'avon,* or *pesh'a.* Instead, the Mishnah uses the term *'averah.* Similarly, when describing sins between people and God [*ben Adam laMakom*] and interpersonal sins [*ben Adam leḥavero*], the Mishnah uses the term *'averah.* The term *'averah* does not appear in this context anywhere in the Bible. What does this rabbinic neologism tell us about the rabbinic concept of sin?

Before we go further into our discussion of *'averah* in rabbinic literature, the term *midrash,* which will be used throughout this article, should be defined. A *midrash* (pl. *midrashim*) is a rabbinic interpretation of the Bible that appears in the Mishnah and Gemar'a (which together make up the Talmud) and in later rabbinic commentaries on Jewish sacred texts. *Midrashim* can appear individually and in collections; they are a central part of the rabbinic corpus. Some, called *midrashe 'aggadah,* aim to fill in and explain lacuna in the biblical narrative, while others address questions of Jewish law (*halakhah*) and are thus called *midrashe halakhah.* Many rabbis over the generations have written *midrashim,* and rabbis continue to do so today.

The word *'averah,* with its Hebrew root *'ayin-vet-resh,* is clearly derived from the biblical word *la'avor,* meaning "to transgress." Although we do not find the noun *'averah* in the Bible, we frequently find the term *la'avor* as a verb indicating that a sin has been committed. The absence of the word *'averah* in biblical literature may be part of a larger biblical trend that avoids abstract nouns in biblical writing. For instance, in the Bible we find the term *shokhen,* a verb denoting God's dwelling, but only in later rabbinic literature do we find the conceptualized noun *shekhinah,* meaning the presence of God. Steven Fraade has argued that many biblical verbs later emerged within Mishnaic literature as conceptualized nouns. According to Fraade, Mishnaic times marked a shift towards conceptuali-

---

10 Cf. Grossman, Meir Zvi, "Le-mashm'autam shel habiṭuyim 'averah' ve'devar 'averah bileshon hakhamim" [On the uses of the expressions 'averah and devar 'averah in the language of the sages], *Sinai* 100:1 (1987), 260–72, which notes that the term *'averah* does not appear in biblical literature. Grossman provides a comprehensive presentation of its evolving usage in rabbinic literature, specifically focusing on the sexual connotations of the word.

zation of many biblical terms, as evident by the new conjugation of many words. From the verb *la'avor* – to transgress – emerged as the conceptualized noun *'averah* – a transgression.[11] Sin, with this new word, was no longer an action; suddenly sinning had become a concept.

It is not entirely clear why the authors of Mishnaic literature felt it necessary to add another word for sin to the already robust biblical catalogue of *'avon, ḥeṭ,* and *pesh'a* – but the word *'averah* certainly has become a common term for referring to sin in rabbinic literature.[12] What additional conceptual imagery does this word convey about sin? Perhaps two new dimensions can be suggested: First, the word *'averah* adds a clear spatial dimension to the act of sin. As mentioned, the word *'averah* derives from the word *la'avor*, meaning "to cross over." The physical imagery of overstepping presupposes clear boundaries that demarcate where one is and is not permitted to trespass. Perhaps sin was conceptualized in this manner, specifically in Mishnaic literature, to underscore the clear legal borders structured within the texts of rabbinic Judaism. As the rabbinic codifiers of the Mishnah and Talmud hewed the corpus of Jewish law, legal boundaries became clearer as well. Once the parameters were codified and canonized,[13] a violation of such laws could more aptly be described as an *'averah* – a transgression.

Second, the word *'averah* relates to the word *'avar*, meaning "the past."[14] While this connection is certainly more etymologically tenuous than the example above, the conceptual linkage between sin and time is actually a much-discussed theme in rabbinic works beginning in the Middle Ages. The idea is that past experiences can inform, enlighten, and educate, but they also contain a halting force; the memories of yesterday can distract from the responsibilities of today. In *Sefer haḤinukh*, an anonymous thirteenth-century work about the Jewish commandments (*mitsvot*), the author warns that an overemphasis on past experiences can be a catalyst for a spiritually absent present. The work, written as an educational curriculum for the author's son, explains that many people living in the tenth through thirteenth centuries did not don *tefillin* (phylacteries) due to a misconception about sin; some believed that previous misdeeds precluded them from

11 Cf. Fraade, Steven D., "The Innovation of Nominalized Verbs in Mishnaic Hebrew as Marking an Innovation of Concept," in: Elitzur A. Bar-Asher Siegal / Aaron J. Koller (eds.), *Studies in Mishnaic Hebrew and Related Fields*, Jerusalem: Magnes, 2017, 129–48.

12 Cf. Grossman, "Le-Mashmuatam," 260–72.

13 On canonization as a concept in the development of Jewish law, see Halbertal, Moshe, *People of the Book*, Cambridge, MA: Harvard University Press, 1997.

14 See Stern, Sacha, *Time and Process in Ancient Judaism*, Portland, OR: Littman Library of Jewish Civilization, 2007, for an introduction to the rabbinic view of time.

performing the mitzvah of *tefillin.*[15] *Sefer haḤinukh* teaches that abstaining from *tefillin* because of other misdeeds is both an incorrect assumption about *tefillin* and a dangerous misconception about the observance of commandments in general. The author writes, "In truth, this prevents many people from observance and is a great evil" (commandment 421). Past mistakes do not preclude present spiritual actions, the author says:

> This is not how I operate with God in my home, for I know that there is no one so righteous who does good and never sins. Nonetheless, they should never be inhibited from getting involved in a *mitsṿah* in the moment that the spirit of God adorns them to do good. Who knows if perhaps they will continue on their path of goodness until death. And death comes fast. (421)

Sefer haḤinukh thus warns that ruminating about mistakes and failures can distract a person from performing *mitsṿot* in the current moment. Guilt, shame, or spiritual malaise about the past easily misdirects a person's present positive trajectory. Since dwelling on the past can discourage change, it is no wonder that the Jewish concept of repentance (*teshuvah)* focuses so prominently on the future. Of the four legal qualifications for repentance famously outlined by Maimonides (1138–1204), committing oneself to a proper future is the final step.[16] If sin is becoming mired in the past, repentance is seizing control of the future.

As discussed earlier, one of the metaphorical descriptions of sin is as a burden. Perhaps the term *'averah,* given its shared root with the term *'avar,* meaning "past," is a subtle indication that Jews should realize that our past sinful experiences must not hinder our will to repent. Sin, at its worst, warps our sense of time and burdens our ability to correct our future.

2 The Origin of Sin in the Hebrew Bible and in the Talmud

2.1 The Biblical Text: Gen 2:25–3:24

The origin of sin occupies just twenty-five verses in the Bible. Here is the basic synopsis: Following the story of creation, which includes nearly the entire first

15 See Kanarfogel, Ephraim, "Not Just Another Contemporary Jewish Problem: A Historical Discussion of Phylacteries," *Gesher* 5 (1976), 106–21, for an historical consideration of the Jewish community's lapse in donning *tefillin* in the medieval period.

16 Cf. Maimonides, Moses, *Mishneh Torah, Hilkhot teshuvah,* 2:2.

two chapters of Genesis, the Bible presents the story of Adam and Eve's sin. That sin begins in the final verse of the second chapter (Gen 2:25): "They were both naked, the man and his wife, and they were not ashamed." Enter the snake (Gen 3:1). Despite God's earlier warning that eating from the Tree of Good and Evil will surely cause death, the snake reasons to the woman that God is just trying to prevent her from becoming like God (Gen 3:2–5). She eats from the Tree and proceeds to feed her husband as well (Gen 3:6). Immediately afterwards, their "eyes are opened," and they realize they are naked, so they fashion clothes for themselves (Gen 3:7). Then, the man and woman hear the sound of God "walking through the Garden"; they hide (Gen 3:8). God calls out to them, "Where are you?" (Gen 3:9). Eventually, after some back-and-forth discussion with God, they acknowledge their sin (Gen 3:10–13), and God curses first the snake (Gen 3:14–15)[17] and then humankind. He first condemns the woman (and, by implication, her female descendants) to painful and difficult labor and childbirth (Gen 3:16) and then curses her husband (and his male descendants) with grueling, often unrewarding, work to derive edible food from the land (Gen 3:17–20). The story, and Genesis, chapter 3, concludes with the two banished from Eden (Gen 3:22–24).

2.2 Questions: How and When?

The only obvious thing about the story of the sin is, paradoxically, how perplexing it is. Clearly, there are a host of questions that immediately present themselves to the reader: First, what was Adam's sin? Knowledge of good and evil seems like a helpful thing to possess, so why did God prohibit them from gaining it? Second, aside from that, how could Adam have sinned before he ate from the Tree of Knowledge, which gave him powers of discernment? Isn't knowledge of

17 The Talmud is not intensely concerned with the snake's punishment. For Christians, however, the snake becomes associated with Satan and his role in the sin and thus demands more attention. This attention reached a new height in the writings of Martin Luther (1483–1546), who interpreted Gen 3:15 as depicting the punishment of humanity and the promise of Jesus Christ's redemption. In this verse, Luther says, "The Lord placed against the Devil the Son of God . . . Adam and Eve . . . were to comfort themselves with His judgment upon Satan, for they learned from this that the Lord is at war with Satan . . . Amid the severest threats, love came forth from [*God's*] fatherly heart" (Luther, Martin, *Luther's Commentary on Genesis*, vol. 1, *Chapters 1–21*, trans. J. Theodore Mueller, Grand Rapids, MI: Zondervan, 1958, 79). Luther's students and followers often read Gen 3 through this lens. Abraham Calov (1612–1686), the leading seventeenth-century German Lutheran theologian, even called Gen 3:14–15 the "proto-Gospel." See Jung, Volker, *Das Ganze der Heiligen Schrift: Hermeneutik und Schriftauslegung bei Abraham Calov*, Stuttgart: Calwer, 1999, 187 and 187n5.

good and evil a prerequisite for sin? These questions are of course just added to the myriad narrative riddles that appear throughout: Why did they try to hide? What was the nature of God's punishment? What is the connection between sin and nudity, if the two are, indeed, connected?

As intriguing as all of these questions are, there is another question, often overlooked, that may be even more central to understanding the nature of sin's origin: When? When did the story of Adam and Eve's sin take place? A cursory reading of the Bible would suggest that the story occurs immediately following creation. Structurally, the order of Genesis would suggest that the story of the Tree of Knowledge occurs immediately following the conclusion of God's seven days of creation. The creation story ends on Saturday with the creation of the Sabbath, so it would not be far-fetched to assume that Adam and his wife (whom he names "Eve" in Gen 3:20) ate from the Tree of Knowledge sometime after the completion of creation, perhaps on Sunday morning.

Christian chronology for the sin of Adam and Eve varies, though many Christian scholars ignore this question. Some depictions of the story have the temptation to eat from the Tree of Knowledge linger for an agonizingly long time.[18] One scholar who was very interested in the Bible's chronology, Archbishop James Ussher (1581–1656), was more specific. He dated Adam and Eve's residence in Eden to a little less than two weeks. According to Ussher's calculation, man was created on October 28 and expelled on November 10. C.S. Lewis's *Perlandra* talks about the sin's continuing for "day after agonizing day."[19]

Yet, the Jewish answer to when Adam and Eve sinned is actually quite clear. The Talmud presents the following chronology for the creation and eventual sin of Adam:

> The day is divided into twelve hours – starting with sunrise and ending with sunset. The first five hours of the day were occupied with the formation and creation of Adam. During the sixth hour he named all the animals. During the seventh hour, Eve was created. Cain and Abel were born during the eighth hour. During the ninth hour, Adam was commanded not to eat from the Tree, and during the tenth hour, they all transgressed. During the eleventh hour, they were judged, and during the twelfth hour – immediately before Shabbat – they were banished from the Garden.[20] (bSanhedrin 38b)

---

18 For differing approaches on the dating of Adam's sin, see Tennant, F.R., *The Sources of the Doctrines of the Fall and Original Sin*, Cambridge: Cambridge University Press, 1903, 151n6. Tennant was hostile to rabbinic thought, but his volume remains one of the most comprehensive works on original sin. The Book of Jubilees 3:17 says that Adam was in the Garden for seven years before sinning.

19 Jacobs, Alan, *Original Sin: A Cultural History*, New York: Harper Collins, 2008, 43.

20 For alternate versions of the events on that day, see the midrashic collections *Vayiḳr'a Rabba*, beginning of *Parashah* 29 (on *Emor*); and *Avot DeRabbi Natan* 1:8. In his Genesis commentary,

The Talmud's chronology is startling. We are used to thinking about the sin of Adam and Eve as a perversion of God's pristine creation – a post-creation act. That is how the Bible situates the story of sin. Creation is complete; sin destroys the perfect world. The Talmud's chronology tells a very different story. The story of Adam and Eve's sin was a part of the seven days of creation. Sin was an act of creation. What, however, did sin create?

2.2.1 Adam, Sin, and Free Will in Rabbinic Literature

Many rabbinic descriptions of Adam prior to his sin go to great lengths to describe the lofty state of his connection to God. One example is Nahmanides (1194–1270) on Genesis 2:9; he says that, prior to the sin, Adam naturally reflected the will of God, like all His other creations: ". . . he [Adam] did whatever was proper for him to do naturally, just as the heavens and all their hosts do – faithful workers whose work is truth, and who do not change from their prescribed course."[21] In other words, Adam, prior to sinning, was not autonomous. Rather, like the stars and moon, he innately reflected God.

The state of Adam prior to the sin, however, poses a problem. If, before sinning, he naturally followed the will of God, what possessed him to sin? In other words, how could Adam sin before he was given free will?

Herein lies the crucial importance of the question of "when." A plain reading of the Bible presents the story of Adam as happening after the creation story. Such a reading suggests that sin was a corruption of creation. However, based on the Talmud's chronology, Adam's sin occurred during creation. Sin was an act of creation. What did sin create? Adam's sense of self.

We can look back to the Bible's account of the immediate aftermath of the sin to support this viewpoint: Adam just realizes he has sinned. His eyes are open. What does he see? First, the Bible mentions that he recognizes that he and the woman are not dressed, a biblical allusion to the prominent role of sexuality in sin.

---

however, the later Jewish leader Saadia Gaon (882–942) seems to present an alternative timeline to the account in bSanhedrin. Saadia Gaon, *Perushe Rav Saadia Gaon laBereshit*, New York: Beit ha-Midrash la-Rabbanim ba-America, 1984, 296–301. See, in particular, 300n505. I am indebted to Rabbi Abraham Lieberman for pointing this out to me.

21 Translation in Yisraeli, Oded, *Temple Portals: Studies in Aggadah and Midrash in the Zohar*, trans. Liat Keren, Jerusalem: Magnes, 2016, 56. For a more robust presentation of the approach of Nahmanides to the sin of Adam, particularly the connection between his sin and the subsequent punishment of death, see Halbertal, Moshe, "Mavet, ḥeṭ, ḥoḳ, vege'ulah be-Mishnat ha-Ramban" [Death, sin, law, and redemption in the Ramban's Mishnah], *Tarbiz* 71:1–2 (2002), 133–62.

Immediately afterwards, they hear a noise: "They heard the sound of the LORD God moving about in the Garden at the breezy time of day; and the man and his wife hid from the LORD God among the trees of the garden" (Gen 3:8).[22] The Bible's description of God following Adam's sin is quite telling. God is now an Other – someone who can be avoided and evaded. The creation of self is complete. No longer does Adam look at himself as an extension of God – God is now an Other strolling through the Garden. In the space created for self, there is now room for failure, growth, shame, and anxiety. There is also free will and the capacity for choice.

The dual implications of the biblical and Talmudic chronologies of Adam's sin reflect the two sources' differing opinions on the nature of sin and free will. The biblical implication is that sin is avoidable. The Bible's introduction of sin following the creation story means that Adam's sin corrupts an otherwise pristine world. In this reading, sin is not a part of creation but a rebellion against it; a fully developed Adam commits the sin. The Talmudic reading, which is the one elaborated upon by later rabbinic commentaries, presents sin as part of creation. Here sin, self, and free will are just as much a part of the creation story as light, water, and the stars. Which reading one prefers will affect whether one believes that sin and, by extension, human beings' capacity for choice, is pre-ordained or a product of human agency. This duality – sin as a part of creation or a corruption of creation – remains a central theme throughout Jewish philosophy. Is all of creation, sin included, suffused with God, or are there limits to God's immanence? The tension between Divine immanence and Divine transcendence, and its relationship to the question of God's presence in acts of sin, which has been debated throughout Jewish history, has its root in the very origin story of sin.

2.3 Original Sin

2.3.1 The Christian Concept of Original Sin

Sin's origins were embedded in creation, but what of original sin? The Christian doctrine of original sin has a long and fascinating history on which several volumes have already been written.[23] Basing himself on the teaching of Paul (Rom 5:12–19), Augustine of Hippo (354–430) brought the doctrine to the attention of the

22 Unless otherwise noted, all biblical translations in this article are from the *JPS Hebrew-English Tanakh*, 2nd ed., Philadelphia: Jewish Publication Society, 1999, with occasional bracketed modifications.

23 E.g., Williams, N.P., *The Ideas of the Fall and of Original Sin: A Historical and Critical Study*, London: Longmans, Green and Co., 1927; Tennant, *Sources of the Doctrines of the Fall*. For a more popu-

mainstream Christian public. According to Augustine, the sin of Adam created an indelible and permanent stain on mankind that could only be removed through the sacrament of baptism.

The latter point, it turned out, created much more controversy, even within the Christian world. If baptism were needed to redeem the effects of original sin, what about infants who die without the rite? According to Augustine, such infants, with the stain of original sin still apparent, would be doomed to eternal damnation. This helpless account of human salvation was rejected by Pelagius, Augustine's contemporary and an English monk who refused to accept that man could only be redeemed through God's grace. According to Pelagianism, original sin did not remove man's capacity to live a decent and ethical life; human redemption is achieved through man's decisions and free will.[24] The early Church, however, declared Pelagius's position heretical.

2.3.2 Original Sin in (and outside of) Medieval Jewish-Christian Polemics

During the wave of Jewish-Christian polemics in the Middle Ages, original sin became a frequent target of Jewish criticism. Jewish polemicists objected to the implication that those who did not receive baptism – including Patriarchs Abraham, Isaac, and Jacob – would suffer damnation. This objection was coupled with the interpretation of Deuteronomy 24:16: "Parents shall not be put to death for children, nor children be put to death for parents: a person shall be put to death only for his own crime [or, sin]." Surely, the doctrine of original sin contradicted the Torah's assurance of no ancestral punishment.

Joel Rembaum, in his comprehensive survey of medieval Jewish arguments against the Christian doctrine of original sin, summarizes the mainstream Jewish reaction as follows:

> They contended that this concept led to a number of absurd and blasphemous conclusions regarding God and divine justice. Given the Jewish concept of the evil inclination, Jews were generally willing to admit that the effects of Adam's sin were physically transmitted to all of Adam's descendants. They vehemently denied, however, that Adam's sin generated a permanent spiritual corruption that was transmitted to the souls of all humans.[25]

---

lar presentation of the doctrine with more contemporary context, see Jacobs, *Original Sin*; and Fredriksen, Paula, *Sin: The Early History of an Idea*, Princeton: Princeton University Press, 2012.

24 Cf. Jacobs, *Original Sin*, 48–54.

25 Rembaum, Joel E., "Medieval Jewish Criticism of the Christian Doctrine of Original Sin," *AJS Review* 7/8 (1982–83), 377. For more on medieval polemics, see also Maccoby, Hyam, *Judaism on Trial*, Portland, OR: Littman Library of Jewish Civilization, 1993. For more on the rabbinic concep-

Yet, the reaction of medieval Jewish polemicists to the doctrine of original sin should not be accepted entirely at face value. Generally, polemical works are poor sources for actual Jewish doctrine. Daniel Lasker, in the introduction to his work on Jewish–Christian polemics, notes the healthy skepticism deserved by extrapolation of theological truth from polemical tracts:

> Polemical compositions were intended as polemics, a genre for which objective truth is one of the first casualties. [. . .] If one wants to know a particular author's true view on a subject, a polemical treatise is the last place one would look to determine it. When this literature is analyzed without due recognition of "polemical license," the research runs the risk of reading too much into the texts.[26]

Given this warning, it is not surprising that the vehemence with which the doctrine of original sin was opposed within polemic literature may not actually reflect its patent rejection within Jewish sources. In fact, as pointed out by Lasker, the doctrine of original sin "was not entirely foreign to Judaism," as some polemics would otherwise suggest.[27] The Talmud (bShabbat 146a) seems to acknowledge the long-term effects of Adam's sin but asserts that the collective revelation at Sinai countered its effects for the Jewish people. It writes: "Why are the idolaters polluted? Because they did not stand at Sinai. When the serpent copulated with Eve, he imposed pollution in her. The Jews who stood at Sinai – their pollution has ceased; the idolaters who did not stand at Sinai – their pollution has not ceased."

Presumably, the pollution referred to here is the lingering poison of Adam and Even's sins (and particularly Eve, who is described, as in the Christian tradition, as having sexual intercourse with the snake). Of course, the antidote in the Jewish view is not baptism but, rather, the revelation at Sinai. In fact, Rabbi Avraham Ibn David of Posquières (Ra'avad, ca. 1125–1198) uses this Talmudic passage as a prooftext to explain a difficult passage in the Passover Haggadah. In the hymn *Dayenu*, we praise God's beneficence by saying, "If He had brought us to Mount Sinai and not given us the Torah, it still would have been sufficient." The statement is puzzling: What would be gained by standing at Sinai, had we not received the Torah? Ra'avad explains, based on the aforementioned passage, that

tualization of sin, in particular the concepts of good and evil inclinations, see Katz, Steven T., "Man, Sin, and Redemption in Rabbinic Judaism," in: id. (ed.), *The Cambridge History of Judaism*, vol. 4, *The Late Roman-Rabbinic Period*, Cambridge: Cambridge University Press, 2006, 925–945.

26 Lasker, Daniel J., *Jewish Philosophical Polemics against Christianity in the Middle Ages*, 2nd ed., Portland, OR: Littman Library of Jewish Civilization, 2007, xx.

27 Lasker, *Jewish Philosophical Polemics against Christianity*, 107.

the aftereffects of Adam's "original sin" were, in fact, cleansed by our collective presence at Sinai.[28]

While Jewish tradition certainly had rejected the role of Jesus and Christian salvation in eradicating the sin in the Garden, the rabbis, nonetheless, seem to have admitted that eradication was necessary. We can say, therefore, that the contradiction between Judaism and the doctrine of original sin is smaller than many medieval Jewish polemics would suggest.[29] Rabbis continued to discuss Adam and Eve's sin in the early modern period. Among many others, Rabbi (Shlomo) Ephraim Luntschitz (1550–1619), in his famed biblical commentary *Kli Yaḳar*, and Rabbi Isaiah Horowitz, known as the Shelaḥ (ca. 1555–1630), make use of this Talmudic passage to suggest a broader notion of original sin than is presented in polemics.[30]

2.3.3 Original Sin in Lurianic Ḳabbalah

Aside from the Talmudic reference, many more mystically influenced Jewish commentators, particularly within the school of Lurianic Ḳabbalah, were quite receptive to a broader conception of the effects of original sin – one that more closely aligns with Christian conceptions.[31] Lasker explains their approach as follows:

> Certain kabbalists taught a doctrine of original sin in that Adam's transgression gave evil an active existence in the world. The entire creation became flawed by this first sin. Unlike the Christians, however, the kabbalists taught that every man had the power to overcome the state of corruption by his own efforts with divine aid . . . [not] by the sacrifice of a God-man.[32]

---

28 See *Responsa Ra'avad*, #11. See also Jacobs, Louis, *Theology in the Responsa*, Portland, OR: Littman Library of Jewish Civilization, 2005, 49–50. For a more extensive analysis of Ra'avad's approach to original sin, see Sherwin, Byron L., *Studies in Jewish Theology: Reflections in the Mirror of Tradition*, Portland, OR: Vallentine Mitchell, 2007, 240–48.

29 Scholars of Late Antiquity, the early Middle Ages, and the Judaism of those times have pointed out many similarities in Jewish and Christian theology in the early Christian period and beyond. For just one example, see Becker, Adam H. / Reed, Annette Yoshiko (eds.), *The Ways That Never Parted: Jews and Christians in Late Antiquity and the Early Middle Ages*, Tübingen: Mohr Siebeck, 2003.

30 Cf. Cooper, Alan, "A Medieval Jewish Version of Original Sin: Ephraim Luntschitz on Lev. 12," *Harvard Theological Review* 97:4 (October 2004), 445–59.

31 See Magid, Shaul, "From Theosophy to Midrash: Lurianic Exegesis and the Garden of Eden," *AJS Review* 22:1 (1997), 37–75, for a more extensive discussion of the story of Adam's sin in Lurianic Ḳabbalah.

32 Lasker, *Jewish Philosophical Polemics*, 226n19.

Lurianic Ḳabbalah is the system of Jewish mysticism developed by Rabbi Isaac Luria (1534–1572), also known as the 'Arizal, in Safed in the Land of Israel. This kabbalistic system reframed mystical practice and prayer as a cosmic redemptive process. After Luria's death, his student, Ḥayyim Vital (1543–1620), recorded and gave shape to a large collection of Luria's kabbalistic ideas. These editions of Luria's thought led to Lurianic Ḳabbalah's emergence as the most important mystical system in Jewish thought.

Using three main concepts, Lurianic Ḳabbalah describes the world's creation and subsequent degeneration, and then a practical way to restore the world's original pristine status. These concepts are: *tsimtsum* (contraction), *shevirat hakelim* (breaking of the vessels), and *tiḳḳun* (repair, restoration). Because God is Infinite (*En Sof*), in order to create space for the world, God must withdraw into Himself to make room for the creation. After this *tsimtsum*, God effects creation through a beam of light from the Infinite into the new space. At a later time, God encloses the divine light in finite "vessels," most of which shatter from the pressure, and, with this catastrophic *shevirat hakelim*, evil and disharmony emerge. The goal, and the struggle, then becomes eliminating this evil from the world, thus redeeming the cosmos and history. This can occur in *tiḳḳun*, the stage that sees the rebuilding of both the divine realm and *Adam Ḳadmon* (primordial man, suffused throughout with divine light), as well as the return of the divine sparks to their source. Human beings have an important role in *tiḳḳun;* they can effect change – up to and including restoration of the world's original harmony and even the divine name – by using certain *ḳavvanot* (mystical intentions) in their prayer and in invoking secret combinations of words.[33]

Indeed, the prominence of Adam's sin in Lurianic mysticism, particularly the notion of *tiḳḳun*, attracted many Christians to Lurianic mysticism. In her groundbreaking study on the impact of Ḳabbalah on the Scientific Revolution, Allison Coudert details the story of an entire community of Christian scholars and thinkers that became enchanted with kabbalistic thought.[34] Led by Francis Mercury van Helmot (1614–1698) and Christian Knorr von Rosenroth (1636–1689),[35] they translated kabbalistic texts into Latin, collected into the work *Kabbala denudata* (*Ḳabbalah* re-

33 Cf. Schatz-Uffenheimer, Rivka, "Isaac ben Solomon Luria," in: *Encyclopedia Britannica*, https://www.britannica.com/biography/Isaac-ben-Solomon-Luria.

34 Cf. Coudert, Allison P., *The Impact of the Ḳabbalah in the Seventeenth Century: The Life and Thought of Francis Mercury van Helmont*, Leiden: Brill, 1999.

35 Cf. Gershom Scholem, *Ḳabbalah*, Jerusalem: Keter, 1974, 416. For more on the Christian Ḳabbalah movement, see ibid., 196.

vealed; lit. "*Ḳabbalah* naked") and disseminated them to many emerging thinkers in Christian circles, most notably Gottfried Wilhelm Leibniz (1646–1716).[36] Normally, the emphasis on the vast repercussions of Adam's sin are seen as a Christian idea, but, within the esoteric world of Lurianic thought, Adam's sin and the subsequent struggle for restitution became markedly Jewish.[37] In fact, this Jewishness is what attracted Christian mystics to Ḳabbalah. Whereas Augustine's presentation of original sin, against the Pelagian objections, minimized man's ability for redemption without Christian rites of sacrament, the Lurianic reading highlighted man's singular power and responsibility to attain redemption.

In summary, Lurianic mysticism recast the narrative of original sin into a recurring contemporary notion of redemption. Yes, original sin had grave repercussions. But the magnitude of the sin was overshadowed by the capacity for redemption.

2.4 Intention and Action in Sin

Another important issue debated by the Talmud is the role of thought, in the sense of conscious intent, in sin in Judaism, i.e., whether a certain mindset is necessary for culpability for sin, and also whether a thought itself (without a corresponding action) can constitute a sin. Thought frequently carries legal consequences in certain areas of Jewish law, such as tithing, withdrawing ownership, and the nullification of *ḥamets* (leaven) right before Passover.[77]

On the one hand, the Talmud in bKiddushin 39b states quite clearly that – except for thoughts about committing idolatry – God does not punish people for their thoughts about committing sins. No conceptual idea or rationale is presented to justify the exclusion of thoughts from culpability; the Talmud instead cites verses to support its claim:

> the Holy One, Blessed be He, does not link a bad thought to an action, as it is stated: "If I had regarded iniquity in my heart, the Lord would not hear" [Ps 66:18]. But how do I realize the meaning of the verse: "Behold I will bring upon these people evil, even the fruit of their thoughts" [Jer 6:19]? In the case of an evil thought that produces fruit, i.e., that leads to an

36 Cf. Coudert, *Impact of the Ḳabbalah*, 308–29.

37 For a more detailed discussion on the effect of Lurianic mysticism on the divide between original sin in Jewish and Christian thought, see Magid, "From Theosophy to Midrash," 36–37. He summarizes his thesis as follows: ". . . Lurianic exegesis actually brings Judaism and Christianity closer together, perhaps because his mystical fraternity flourished at a time when New Christians were returning to Judaism, thinning the opacity between these two competing religions."

> action, the Holy One, Blessed be He, links it to the action and one is punished for the thought as well. If it is a thought that does not produce fruit, the Holy One, Blessed be He, does not link it to the action.

Similarly, on the same page, the Talmud derives a scriptural justification (based on Ezek 14:5) to exclude idolatry from this rule. Aside from the exception of idolatry, the Talmud seems to establish as a general rule that God does not deem thoughts without action a religious crime.

In a different tractate, however, the Talmud appears to contradict its statement in Kiddushin. Another passage, on bYoma 29a, states, "thoughts of [*hirhure*] sin are worse than the sin itself." This passage seems to indicate that thoughts are accounted when assessing sin. Even without this passage, in fact, the above Kiddushin passage that excludes thought from culpability seems to be contradicted by a host of religious prohibitions. Some commentaries consider the biblical command "and stiffen your necks no more" (Deut 10:16) to be a general prohibition, even though it apparently can be transgressed only with thought.[38] Similarly, the prohibition on coveting a neighbor's possessions (Deut 5:18), which is included in the second list of the Ten Commandments, prohibits, according to some, covetous thoughts.[39] So when is the principle from Kiddushin that excludes thoughts from religious liability operative, and when are thoughts indeed considered to be sins?

Oddly, most commentaries do not address this apparent contradiction. In his *Guide for the Perplexed* (3:8), Maimonides explains the passage in bYoma 29a as emphasizing the general elevation of the mind over the body. Since the mind is superior to the body, the thoughts of the mind also have graver repercussions than physical actions. Rabbi Yehudah Loew (1512–1609), the rabbi of Prague known as the Maharal, suggests a simple distinction in his *Ḥiddushe 'aggadot* on bKiddushin 39b. He explains that when the initial formulation of a sin requires action, such prohibitions cannot be violated with thought alone. However, thought can still be

38 See Eliezer of Metz, *Sefer Yere'im*, mitzvah 365. See also, however, Maimonides, *Sefer haMitsvot, shoresh* (foundation) 4. Maimonides does not include this in his count of the commandments. His reason, it should be noted, is not that it can be transgressed only in thought, but, rather, that it is a general prohibition that includes within it all religious violations.

39 The first presentation of the Ten Commandments, in Exodus, chapter 20, also includes a prohibition on coveting (20:14). The Hebrew there is *lo taḥmod* (do not covet). As explained by the *midrash* collection called *Mekhilta*, it is a prohibition that is only violated once an action, such as theft or even, according to some, purchase, has been carried out. The second presentation of the Ten Commandments features a different Hebrew term forbidding coveting, *velo tit'avveh*. This term invokes a prohibition that, according to many commentators, applies even to thought alone. See *Sefer haḤinukh*, commandments 38 and 416; and Maimonides, *Sefer haMitsvot*, commandment 266.

considered a sin when the thought is the action, meaning that the very definition of the particular sin includes thought. This means a prohibition such as murder, which clearly includes an action, cannot be violated by mere thought, but if thoughts, by dint of their formulation, are the subject of the prohibition, then they are sufficient to be considered a sin. Rabbi Yosef Engel (1858–1920), in his Talmudic glosses known as *Gilyone ha-Shas*, on Kiddushin, echoes the distinction of Rabbi Loew.

Therefore, we may conclude that thoughts can, in fact, be prohibited in Judaism. But the prohibition must, by definition, require thought alone. If, however, an action is needed to violate a given prohibition, then thought alone will not be considered a transgression.[40]

2.5 "Sin for a Purpose" (*'Averah lishmah*)

Finally, as we conclude our exploration of the Talmud's many discussions of sin, we consider the concept of "sin for a purpose" (*'averah lishmah*). In the fourth chapter of the Book of Judges, the Canaanite general Sisera fled the battleground after failing to attack the Jewish people at Mount Tabor. Looking for a place to hide from the Jewish soldiers who were trying to capture him, Sisera entered the tent of Yael. We don't know a great deal about Yael. She was likely not Jewish.[41] But, once alone with Sisera, Yael (according to the Talmud's interpretation) seduced him and then promptly killed him by driving the stake of her tent through his skull.

On the one hand, she actively seduced Sisera – a sin. On the other hand, she vanquished a notorious enemy of the Jewish people. Should her actions be praised or condemned? In the next chapter of Judges, she is praised by Deborah, one of the leaders of the Jewish people at the time. "Most blessed of women is Yael, wife of Hever the Kenite," says Deborah in a poetic song, "by women in the tent she will be blessed" (Judg 5:24). Based on this praise, the Talmud introduces a seemingly paradoxical concept: an *'averah lishmah*, literally translated as "a sin for a purpose":

> Rav Naḥman bar Yitshak said: Greater is a transgression committed for its own sake, than a *mitsvah* performed not for its own sake.

---

40 In his biblical commentary (Deut 29:18), Rabbenu Baḥya (1255–1340) also notes the contradiction between the Talmud in Kiddushin and the passage in Yoma. He resolves the contradiction by explaining that the Talmud in Yoma, describing the gravity of thinking about sin, only refers to someone who actually follows through with their fantasies. Rabbi Menaḥem Meiri (1249–1306) seems to have made a similar distinction.

41 See the midrash *Shimoni* #9 on Joshua.

> But didn't Rav Yehudah say that Rav said: A person should always occupy himself with Torah and *mitsyot* even not for their own sake, as it is through acts performed not for their own sake that good deeds for their own sake come about?
>
> Rather, a transgression for the sake of Heaven is equivalent to a *mitsyah* not for its own sake. The proof is as it is written: "Blessed above women shall Yael be, the wife of Hever the Kenite, above women in the tent shall she be blessed" [Judg. 5:24], and it is taught: Who are these "women in the tent?" They are Sarah, Rebeccah, Rachel, and Leah. [Yael's forbidden intercourse with Sisera for the sake of Heaven is compared to the sexual intercourse in which the Matriarchs engaged.] (bNazir 23b)

The term *'averah lishmah* is vague and may mean a number of things in Talmudic literature. It certainly connotes some sort of intention, but what type of intention is less clear. Yuval Blankovsky presents several different connotations for the word *lishmah.*[42] It may mean doing a sin for the sake of God, or perhaps for the sake of fulfilling a future commandment.

Blankovsky explains that there are three ways to understand the concept of an *'averah lishmah.*[43] One approach understands the concept as a legal principle that arbitrates when it is permissible to perform an action that has components of sin and components of *mitsyah.* According to those who subscribe to this view, the term *'averah lishmah* is much like other halakhic (Jewish legal) principles, such as the laws permitting one to violate *halakhah* in order to save a life. Most halakhic authorities seem to accept this version of the term; it does not present *'averah lishmah* as a subversion of Jewish law but, rather, as a principle working within the system of Jewish law.[44]

A second approach understands the concept of *'averah lishmah* as a referendum on the importance of intention relative to the importance of an action. In other words, *'averah lishmah* teaches that the most important component of our deeds is not the technical category of the action (sin or commandment) but, rather, our intention while performing such an action. This approach is certainly the most dangerous. As will be discussed below, if it is only proper intentions that distinguish the sinners from the righteous, one can easily drift into antinomian behavior.

---

42 Cf. Blankovsky, Yuval, *Ḥeṭ Leshem Shamayim* [Sin for the sake of Heaven], Jerusalem: Magnes, 2017.

43 Cf. Blankovsky, *Ḥeṭ Leshem Shamayim*, 6, citing Tsvi Heber, "'averahLeshem Shamayim," *Ma'aliot* 21 (5759/1999), 205–28.

44 Cf. Blankovsky, *Ḥeṭ Leshem Shamayim*, 6n33, which cites several sources that align with this view, including the comment of Maharik in *shoresh* 167, the Netziv on Gen 27:9, and Rabbi Avraham Yitzhak Kook in *Mishpat Kohen*, at 143–44.

A final approach is that *'averah lishmah* is a concept that is only to be used *ex post facto* – once a deed has already been done. According to this view, *'averah lishmah* is never to be invoked as a positive norm dictating that one should perform a sinful action. Instead, it is a principle that, in retrospect, once an action has been done, adds halakhic legitimacy to what occurred.

One's conceptual approach to *'averah lishmah* will affect that person's reading and translation of the term *lishmah*. Those who approach this concept as a legal principle, as in the first approach, would favor reading the term *'averah lishmah* as "a sin done for the sake of a commandment." The term *lishmah* there refers to another commandment that justifies transgressing a sin. This *'averah lishmah* is almost a two-step process: the initial sin and the later commandment the sin enables. Conversely, if *'averah lishmah* is really a conceptual affirmation of the power of intention – that even a sin, with the proper intention, can be holy – then it would make more sense to read the term *'averah lishmah* as "a sin for the sake of God." In this reading, the term *'averah lishmah* is not a narrow legal principle justifying sin for the sake of a particular commandment but, rather, an affirmation that, regardless of its sinful status, when coupled with the proper intention, any action can be performed for the sake of the service of God.

In the current Jewish discussion of *'averah lishmah*, this distinction between "sin for the sake of a commandment" and "sin for the sake of God" has continued to exist. Rabbi Hershel Schachter of Yeshiva University, a prominent halakhist, has interpreted *'averah lishmah* narrowly, like many other codified Jewish laws.[45] Others view the concept more broadly, as more of a philosophical idea than a legal principle, an idea that was at the heart of one of the greatest controversies and heresies in all of Jewish history: Sabbateanism, which will be treated in detail below.

2.6 A Summary of Sin in the Bible and Talmud

Expanding on the brief story of Adam's sin in the Bible, the Talmud is a rich text that looks at sin from many perspectives. It considers not only the how but, also, the "when" of the sin, which it considers to have happened at the end of, but still during, creation. The implication is that the sin was also creative, and that what it created was Adam's sense of self, which enabled his free will. Original sin in the Christian sense does not exist in the Talmud, though some recognition that the sin must be rectified does; the rabbis posit that it happened for Jews at Mount Sinai. Throughout Jewish history, some have seen an expanded role for the first

45 Cf. Schachter, Hershel, *Bi-Ikvei Ha-Tzon*, 3:14–18.

sin, particularly in Lurianic Ḳabbalah, which periodically attracted Christians for this reason. In addition, in most cases, intention is seen as necessary for sin, with the exception of idolatry and of sins that are, themselves, thoughts. Finally, there is a category of sin in the Talmud called *'averah lishmah*, which can mean either "sin for the sake of a commandment" or "sin for the sake of Heaven," depending on whether one interprets the concept as a narrow legal category or as a broad philosophy of the relationship between humankind and God.

3 From Sin to Penance: The Approach of the Rhineland Pietists (*Ḥaside Ashkenaz*) and Its Influence

3.1 The *Ḥaside Ashkenaz*, Sin, and Penance

In the Talmudic period, which lasted from the early third century CE to approximately the mid-eighth, Jewish life was centered in Israel and then in Babylonia. After the Talmud's redaction, academies devoted to its study flourished for a time in Babylonia. Starting around the year 1000, however, the center of Jewish life and scholarship began its shift to Western Europe, and particularly to what is today Germany, and then France.

In this context, beginning in Germany during the twelfth and thirteenth centuries, a pietist movement whose members became known as the *Ḥaside Ashkenaz* emerged and radically changed the Jewish approach to sin. The *Ḥaside Ashkenaz* were a group of mystical pietists who advocated a strict adherence to a notion of understanding, living by, and spreading knowledge of God's Will.[46]

The expanded notion of God's Will advocated by the *Ḥaside Ashkenaz* made for some prescriptions seemingly with little, if any, precedent in previous rabbinic writing. *Sefer Ḥasidim*, a work then attributed to Rabbi Yehudah of Regensburg (known as Rabbi Yehudah heḤasid, 1150–1217), is the most enduring text of the movement.[47]

The most notoriously unusual aspect of the *Ḥaside Ashkenaz* was their approach to sin. They, for example, had radical ideas regarding repentance. One distinctive feature of their thought was the doctrine of *teshuvah haba'ah*, repentance

46 Cf. Soloveitchik, Haym, "Three Themes in the 'Sefer Hasidim,'" *AJS Review* 1:1 (1976), esp. 315.

47 Scholars of Jewish studies have written much about *Sefer Hasidim*. In addition to the Soloveitchik article cited above (not his only article on the topic), see, e.g., Marcus, Ivan G., *Sefer Hasidim and the Ashkenazic Book in Medieval Europe*, Philadelphia: University of Pennsylvania Press, 2018.

that enables one to deny succumbing to sin even when given the opportunity. This form of repentance, based on a passage in bYoma, figures prominently in their thought. While they laud it, they caution that it cannot be arranged voluntarily, meaning that, in today's parlance, alcoholics would be prohibited from voluntary entering a bar to prove their resolve. Engineering opportunities to resist temptation was simply considered too risky, however valuable *teshuvah ha-ba'ah* might seem.[48] Given the danger of entering such situations, *Ḥaside Ashkenaz* noted, in fact, that this type of repentance was not frequently realized.[49]

Rabbi Eleazer of Worms (ca. 1165–1238), a student and then colleague of Rabbi Yehudah, wrote *Sefer haRoḳeaḥ*, which details the approach of the *Ḥaside Ashkenaz* to sin and repentance. The work advocates for what is called *teshuvat hamishka*, literally "weighed repentance," and thus gives detailed directions for the penances required for each major sin. The range of sins mentioned extends from sexual immorality to dishonesty; recommended penance proceeds from regret to fasting and even to self-mortification.

Just as the *Ḥaside Ashkenaz* expanded the notion of the Will of God, they ritualized and expanded the penance needed to atone for violating that Will. The medieval Jewish historian Haym Soloveitchik explains that Rabbi Eleazar (along with Rabbi Yehudah) believed that existing Jewish texts did not adequately express the vast Divine Will. While Rabbi Yehudah had many examples of omissions of this sort, Rabbi Eleazer focused primarily on penance.[50] If acts of penance were not specified in Jewish scripture and tradition, then they had to be delineated by him.

Scholars have noticed the parallels between the penance among the *Ḥaside Ashkenaz* and some concepts of penance in medieval Christian thought. They thus have debated whether the emphasis on fasting and self-mortification found in *Sefer haRoḳeaḥ* are a collection of disparate and elusive Jewish traditions that had long existed within rabbinic writing, or whether, by contrast, they were a product of Christian influence on Jewish atonement practices. (Some medieval monks and priests also considered the question of whether one should expose oneself to sin in

---

48 Cf. Rubin, A., "The Concept of Repentance among the Hasidey Ashkenaz," *Journal of Jewish Studies* 16 (1965), 161–76. See also Fishman, Talya, "The Penitential System of Hasidei Ashkenaz and the Problem of Cultural Boundaries," *Journal of Jewish Thought and Philosophy* 8 (1999), 207–09. There she also cites *bAvodah Zarah* 17b as another possible source for placing oneself into situations of temptation.

49 Cf. Eleazer of Worms, *Sefer haRoḳeaḥ*, 206.

50 Cf. Soloveitchik, Haym, "Re-evaluation of Eleventh-Century Ashkenaz," in: id., *Collected Essays*, vol. 2, Portland, OR: Littman Library of Jewish Civilization, 2014, 104–05.

order to resist it.[51]) Jewish historian Talya Fishman, in her study on the origins of the practices of penance in *Ḥaside Ashkenaz,* acknowledges that there is some precedent in Jewish thought for the type of penance they discuss.[52] She concludes, however, that it is unlikely that their penitential practices emerged independent of Christian influence. She proposes that the *Ḥaside Ashkenaz* both brought to the fore previously marginal Jewish practices from ancient Israel and "unconsciously appropriated the demanding penitential practices" then newly popular among "their Christian neighbors" in the Rhineland.[53]

Many later rabbinic writings on sin, as will be discussed below, eventually made a marked effort to depart from this approach to penance. Yet, for centuries, such behavior – influenced by Christians or not – had a major impact on the rabbinic approach to sin. In fact, of all the diversified interests in the orbit of the *Ḥaside Ashkenaz,* this area of their thought likely left the largest imprint on rabbinic writing, in Jewish communities in pietist and non-pietist Germany and also in France, Spain, and Safed, among others.

3.2 The Centuries-long Effect of the *Ḥaside Ashkenaz* on Jewish Approaches to Sin

Hundreds of years following the death of Rabbi Eleazer haRoḳeaḥ (sometimes called, simply, "haRoḳeaḥ," i.e., "the Roḳeaḥ"), his program of penance continued to be positively invoked. Late medieval and early modern Jews would write to their rabbis, describing their sins and asking for the penitential regimen necessary to achieve atonement. Typical examples of this sort of correspondence can be found throughout rabbinic responsa (halakhic questions sent by letter to rabbis, who then answered them and sometimes later circulated those answers, in manuscript or in print). For instance, Rabbi Yaakov ben Yehudah Weil (ca. 1385–ca. 1456), the fifteenth-century German rabbi, was asked for the proper course of penance for someone who swore falsely. Invoking the regimen of the Roḳeaḥ, he recommends that the man, Phoebus of Munich, should fast for forty days, accompanied by a biweekly flogging and fasting (following the initial forty day fast).[54] In an earlier responsum,[55] to an adulteress, Rabbi Weil concedes that the regimen of the Roḳeaḥ may be too intense for a penitent sinner to enact all at once. Rabbi Weil refers to

51 Cf. Rubin, "Concept of Repentance," 166n21.
52 Cf. Fishman, "Penitential System," 201–29.
53 Cf. Fishman, "Penitential System," 222.
54 Cf. *Teshuvot Mahari Weil* 123.
55 Cf. *Teshuvot Mahari Weil* 12.

the Roḳeaḥ program as an obligation but suggests that the requirements, including rolling around in the snow and sleeping on the floor, can be delayed until a proper confession is extracted.[56]

By the time Rabbi Weil was writing, Jewish life in Europe had changed quite a bit since the time of the *Ḥaside Ashkenaz*, and it would continue to change rapidly as the early modern period continued. Faced with expulsions from Iberia and most of Western Europe and the resulting forced migrations (and some voluntary ones spurred by growth in trade) and increased mixing of previously separate communities, early modern Jews created new communities, challenged rabbinic authority, and had increased contact with their non-Jewish neighbors.[57] It should be no surprise, then, that the early modern period also saw one of the great heresies in Jewish history, one largely distinguished by its approach to sin: Sabbateanism.

4 The False Messiah's Sin

4.1 Shabbetai Tsevi

Throughout Jewish history, there have been men who have proclaimed themselves to be the messiah, ushering in the final redemption promised in the Bible and rabbinic sources. Arguably, none have been as successful or as problematic for the Jewish community as Shabbetai Tsevi (1626–1676), a rabbi from Smyrna (now Izmir, Turkey). The Sabbatean messianic movement, which began in 1665, swept through the Ottoman Empire and fomented controversy across the rabbinic establishment. Many Jews truly believed that Tsevi was the Messiah, and that redemption was nigh. Gershom Scholem, the prolific scholar of Jewish mysticism, points to several factors that contributed to Tsevi's success.[58] Certainly, the Jewish people, reeling from the 1648–1649 Chmielnicki massacres in Ukraine that left tens of thousands of Jews dead, were looking for a savior. Tsevi also capitalized on the mystical fervor sweeping through Europe, driven primarily by the

56 For an English synopsis of the aforementioned responsa, see Jacobs, Louis, *Theology in the Responsa*, Portland, OR: Littman Library of Jewish Civilization, 2005, 101–02, which has an English synopsis of this responsum.
57 Cf. Ruderman, David, *Early Modern Jewry: A New Cultural History*, Princeton: Princeton University Press, 2010. In the introduction, Ruderman identifies "five primary components" (14) of early modern Jewish experience: mobility, communal cohesiveness, knowledge explosion, crisis of rabbinic authority, and blurring of religious identities (14–16).
58 See Scholem, Gershom, *Ḳabbalah*, Jerusalem: Keter, 1974, 259, which mentions five factors that "contributed to the overwhelming success of the messianic awakening."

mystical eschatology from the teachings of Lurianic Ḳabbalah. Peddling his own brand of mysticism through his chief proselytizer, Nathan of Gaza (1643–1680), Shabbetai Tsevi convinced laypeople and rabbinic leaders alike that his messianic revolution was authentic. The approximately year-long messianic fever in Eastern Europe (by then the center of much of Jewish life) and the Mediterranean only broke when Tsevi, arrested in 1666 by a representative of the Ottoman sultan and threatened with death, converted to Islam. For most, a messiah who had converted from Judaism was simply inconceivable, and the movement began to lose momentum. Yet, others continued to have faith in him as a redeemer, attributing his conversion to some mysterious mystical quest. Even following his death, several factions within the Jewish community – some secretly, others openly – clung to their belief in the Sabbatean movement.

4.2 Sabbateanism and Sin

One distinctive factor of particular relevance to our discussion is the Sabbatean movement's relationship to sin. Even prior to his apostasy, Tsevi had a markedly antinomian persona. Throughout his life, he performed rituals that openly flaunted his abrogation of Jewish law. While sinning, he was known to make a heretical blessing to God, "who allows the forbidden," a repurposing of the traditional blessing to God, who "frees the imprisoned," as both "the forbidden" and "the imprisoned" can be rendered as *'asurim* in Hebrew. One year, he celebrated all three of the major Jewish festivals – Passover, Shavuot, and Sukkot – in one week. Against Talmudic law, he pronounced the ineffable name of God, and he was known to eat forbidden animal fats. Eventually, once his movement reached a euphoric peak, he abolished the fast days of the seventeenth of Tammuz and the ninth of Av, both of which commemorated the destruction of the Holy Temples in Jerusalem, and replaced them with days of celebration.

Why did he do this? For Tsevi and his followers, *'averah lishmah* was a philosophy, not just a halakhic principle. They performed rituals that contravened Jewish law for the sake of some other, higher-order commandment. Sin in the Sabbatean movement confirmed a messianic age that had evolved from the allegedly temporal constraints of Jewish law. Torah itself, in Sabbatean thought, had evolved. Pre-messianic Torah and law were no longer necessary. The Sabbateans attempted to usher in a mystical antinomian age that required reorienting the Jewish people's relationship to their laws. As Scholem quotes: "*Bittulah shel*

Torah zehu kiyyumah: the violation of the Torah is now its true fulfillment."[59] In the supposed messianic age of Sabbateanism, sin was not the subversion of God's will; it was its expression.

Truth be told, even before the advent of Sabbateanism, the messianic idea in Judaism had some antinomian undertones. The Messiah is always identified as the offspring of King David, who himself was a descendant of Ruth the Moabite.[60] According to the Bible, the entire Moabite family originated from an act of incest between Lot and his daughters, who had thought that their act was necessary to preserve humanity (Gen 19:31–32). In fact, the Talmud (bNazir 23a) references the story of Lot and his daughters as a possible source for the very concept of *'averah lishmah*. The messianic idea – Lot's incestuous relationship with his daughter, which begat the Moabite roots of the Messiah – itself emerges from antinomian behavior. This connection was not lost on the Sabbatean movement. Some Sabbatean apologists pointed to the licentious origins of the messiah as a justification for Shabbetai Tsevi's antinomian behavior: "Lest no one, therefore rashly cast aspersions at the Lord's Anointed (i.e., Shabbetai Tsevi)."[61]

The history of Shabbetai Tsevi, his followers, and his successors shows that Jewish ideas about sin and redemption were no mere academic debates; they had the potential to divide communities, antagonize non-Jewish authorities, and incite apocalyptic fervor. They also, arguably, provoked lasting religious change within normative Judaism, as we will see in the next section.

5 The Hasidic Revolution: Empathy for Sinners

5.1 The Roots of Hasidism

Beginning in the eighteenth century, the rabbinic approach to sinners began to soften. A major turning point in the rabbinic approach to sin began with another pietist (Hasidic) revolution, this one led by the *Ḥasidim* of Rabbi Israel Baal Shem Tov of Poland (present-day Ukraine), also known as the BeSHT (ca. 1700–1760).

---

59 Scholem, Gershom, *The Messianic Idea in Judaism: And Other Essays on Jewish Spirituality*, New York: Schocken, 1995, 110.

60 For one traditional source on this issue, see Maimonides, *Mishneh Torah, Hilkot malakhim u-milhamotehem* [Laws of kings and their wars], chapter 11.

61 Scholem, Gershom, *Sabbatai Sevi: The Mystical Messiah*, Princeton: Princeton University Press, 1973, 813. See also Polen, Nehemia, "Dark Ladies and Redemptive Compassion: Ruth and the Messianic Lineage in Judaism," in: Peter S. Hawkins (ed.), *Scrolls of Love: Ruth and the Song of Songs*, New York: Fordham University Press, 2006, 59–74.

Scholars disagree about the roots of this Hasidism and about the Besht's precise contribution to it, but its popularity and impact are undeniable. In an age in which most Jews faced poverty and persecution, and the small rabbinic elite was increasingly detached from their troubles, the Baal Shem Tov (lit. "master of the Good Name," since he was originally an itinerant miracle worker) offered a way for the common Jewish people to connect with God – through ecstatic prayer, song, and connection with a *rebbe* (rabbi). Michael Rosen has described the revolution of the Baal Shem Tov as comprised of, and producing, a "God-intoxicated people – who felt a sense of God's energy in everything."[62]

From its inception, the Besht's Hasidic movement had to distance itself from Sabbateanism. When the Hasidic movement began, the Jewish community was still reeling from the Sabbatean movement and its later offshoot, the Frankists.[63] The rabbinic establishment could hardly be faulted for its distrust of a new sectarian movement. Much of the early opponents to Hasidim, known as *mitnagdim* (lit. "opponents"), cast the Hasidic movement as a new Sabbatean movement.[64] To be sure, some in the early Hasidic movement did take liberties with strict halakhic practice. Many Hasidim prayed past the prescribed time in Jewish law. Others prayed with an ecstatic fervor foreign to traditional synagogues.[65] In response to the many antinomian actions within the Hasidic community, Rabbi Ḥayyim of Volozhin (1749–1821), a leading rabbi of the *mitnagdim*, penned *Nefesh haḤayyim* (Soul of life), which articulated some of the primary concerns of the *mitnagdim* about Hasidism.[66] In *Nefesh haḤayyim*, Rabbi Ḥayyim emphasizes the importance of strict adherence to the details of Jewish law. Proper intention, Rabbi Ḥayyim cautions, cannot come at the expense of the proper execution of the commandments. However lofty one's intentions may be, he notes, what good is matzah eaten after the night of Passover?[67] Religious conflicts between Ḥasidim and *mitnagdim* continued for decades, with both sides at times bringing in the

62 Rosen, Michael, *The Quest for Authenticity: The Thought of Reb Simhah Bunim*, Jerusalem: Urim, 2008, 27. For some academic discussion regarding the precise contribution of the Baal Shem Tov, see ibid., 27n1.

63 On Frankism, see, e.g., Maciejko, Pawel, *Mixed Multitude: Jacob Frank and the Frankist Movement*, Philadelphia: University of Pennsylvania Press, 2011.

64 Cf. Wilensky, Mordechai, "Hasidic-Mitnaggedic Polemics in the Jewish Communities of Eastern Europe: The Hostile Phase," in: Gershon David Hundert (ed.), *Essential Papers on Hasidism: Origins to Present*, New York: New York University Press, 1991, 259–61.

65 Cf. Schochet, Elijah, *The Hasidic Movement and the Gaon of Vilna*, Northvale, NJ: Jason Aronson, 1993, 52.

66 See Magid, Shaul, "Deconstructing the Mystical: The Anti-Mystical Kabbalism in Rabbi Hayyim of Volozhin's Nefesh Ha-Hayyim," *Journal of Jewish Thought and Philosophy* 9 (2000), 21–67.

67 Cf. Ḥayyim of Volozhin, *Nefesh haḤayyim, sha'ar* 3.

(Christian) political authorities for support. In the meantime, though, Hasidism survived and thrived.

5.2 Hasidism, Sin, and Repentance: Three Views

5.2.1 Hasidism: Sin and the Common Jew

Since the *Ḥasidim* of the Baal Shem Tov, and the later sects that followed his general approach, championed the relationship that even the common man can have with God, the movement theorized a great deal about the importance of the relationship formed with God through repentance, and how such a relationship is accessible to all. Repentance is given far too voluminous a treatment in Hasidic writing to give a detailed analysis of each approach, but it is possible to give an overall outline of the central themes.

Each strand of Hasidism (Heb. *Ḥasidut*) has its own personality. This is largely due to the outsize influence on each dynastic sect of its founding *rebbe* and his descendants. So, each Hasidic sect manifests its own idiosyncratic approach to sin and sinners, reflecting the distinct intuition of its rebbe. An old adage in the Hasidic world states that the work *Noam Elimelekh* by Rabbi Elimelekh of Lizhensk (1717–1787) is for the righteous; the works of Rabbi Shneur Zalman of Liadi (1745–1812), the founder of the Chabad branch of Hasidism, are for people struggling between righteousness and sin; and the works of Rabbi Naḥman of Bratslav (1772–1810) are for the sinners. Some have added that the works of Izbica Hasidism are for Jews who embody each of these characteristics (or maybe for Jews who are not sure to which category they belong). Each of these approaches will now be considered.

5.2.2 Elimelekh of Lizhensk: The *Tsadik*

The world of Rabbi Elimelekh of Lizhensk was dominated by the *tsadik*. *Ḥasidut* emerged when the average Jew had trouble connecting to the ideal of piety. So, its leaders attempted to answer the question: How can piety and righteousness, often so detached from the masses, be accessible to a simple Jew? According to Rabbi Elimelekh, everyday people could attain holiness by connecting to the *tsadik* – a righteous leader who, in this model, is the center of the Hasidic community. And the *tsadik*, as Rabbi Louis Jacobs explains, had two jobs: "He brings man near to God and he brings down God's grace from heaven to earth."[68] As the channel for spirituality, the *tsadik* also played a central role in his community's dealings with sin and repentance. Those struggling with sin were strongly encouraged to visit the righteous, "for the Evil urge is powerless in the presence of the zaddikim."[69] A *tsadik*, who was also often a *rebbe*, tended to hold court in the town where his sect was founded; his followers made pilgrimages there, perhaps around the holidays or before a major life event.

5.2.3 Shneur Zalman of Liadi: The "Average Man"

Rabbi Shneur Zalman of Liadi had a different emphasis. His magnum opus, *Tanya*, of which the first section is called "The Book of the Average Men" (*Sefer shel benonim*), is replete with reflections for those struggling with internal conflict between attaining righteousness and thinking of sin. His audience were those who considered themselves neither saints nor sinners but people in the middle. The third chapter of *Tanya*, *Iggeret haTeshuvah* (Letter on repentance), serves as the core presentation of his philosophy of repentance. As opposed to Rabbi Elimelekh's emphasis on the *tsadik*, *Iggeret haTeshuvah* focuses on God. Sin, Rabbi Shenur Zalman explains, can have an impact on the very presence of God in this world. The act of repentance returns God's presence to this world. Hence, the word *teshuvah* is an amalgamation of the Hebrew word *shuv* (return) and the letter *he* (ה), representing God's presence. *Teshuvah* returns God's immanence to this world. On its more basic level, then, the focus of *teshuvah* is, in fact, on the repentant, who can help bring about this massive change.[70]

---

68 Jacobs, Louis, *Their Heads in Heaven: Unfamiliar Aspects of Hasidism*, Portland, OR: Vallentine Mitchell, 2005, 76. On the role of the *tsadik* in the thought of Rabbi Elimelekh of Lizhensk, see Rapoport-Albert, Ada, "God and the Zaddik as the Two Focal Points of Hasidic Worship," *History of Religions* 18:4 (May 1979), 321.

69 Rabbi Elimelekh of Lizhensk, *Noam Elimelekh* (to *Metzora*), trans. in Lamm, Norman, *The Religious Thought of Hasidism*, Hoboken, NJ: Ktav, 1999, 356–57.

70 For more on the approach to sin of Rabbi Shneur Zalman, see Mayse, Ariel Evan, "The Sacred Writ of Hasidism: Tanya and the Spiritual Vision of Rabbi Shneur Zalman of Liady," in: Stuart Halpern (ed.), *Books of the People: Revisiting Classic Works of Jewish Thought*, Jerusalem: Maggid, 2017, 109–56.

5.2.4 Naḥman of Bratslav: Struggles with Sin

Rabbi Naḥman of Bratslav spoke candidly about his own struggles with sin and belief. His biography, written by his student, Rabbi Nathan, spends an entire chapter detailing his spiritual volatility. It is likely that his personal spiritual battles informed his theological writings. Rabbi Naḥman, when it came to sin and distance from God, does not dismiss the questions of heretics; rather, he validates them. In his complex mystical structure, Rabbi Naḥman provides grounding for those who feel like the world is bereft of God's presence. Those Jews struggling with faithlessness are not grappling with mere illusion; in fact, they have stumbled upon the divine absence that remained after God's creation. Rabbi Naḥman's approach empathized with this sense of God's absence. Instead of dismissing those who felt abandoned by God, Rabbi Naḥman, in the words of Shaul Magid, "began . . . with the assumption that the heretical question [of whether God is absent from the world] must be taken seriously if it is to be overcome."[71] The rabbi's influence proved so pervasive that his sect, unlike most others, did not get a new *rebbe* when he died. There are still Bratslav *Ḥasidim*, called "Bratslavers"; every Rosh Hashanah, many make a pilgrimage to Rabbi Naḥman's grave in Uman, in what is today Ukraine.

5.3 The Alleged Heresies of the Hasidic School of Izbica

5.3.1 Izbica's Leaders

No discussion of Hasidism and sin would be complete without an exploration of one of its more radical sects, that of Izbica/Radzyn (sometimes called Izbica/Lublin after its move there). The Hasidic court of Izbica was established on Simḥat Torah, 1839, when, dramatically and mysteriously, Rabbi Mordekhai Yosef Leiner (1801–1854) left the *Ḥasidim* of Kotzk to establish his own community. Rabbi Mordekhai Yosef led the Hasidic community of Izbica until his death in 1854.

In addition to Rabbi Mordekhai Yosef, three leaders fashioned the theology of Izbica: Rabbi Yaakov Leiner (1818–1878), Rabbi Gershon Ḥenokh Leiner (1839–1891), and Rabbi Zadok ha-Kohen Rabinowitz of Lublin (1823–1900). Following the death of Rabbi Mordekhai Yosef, the court of Izbica amicably divided in two. One community remained in Izbica. It was led by Rabbi Mordekhai Yosef's son, Rabbi

71 Magid, Shaul, "The Absence of God in Rabbi Nahman of Bratzlav's 'Likku-tei MoHaRan,'" *Harvard Theological Review* 88:4 (Oct. 1995), 503.

Yaakov, and afterwards by Rabbi Yaakov's son Rabbi Gershon Ḥenokh, who moved the community to Radzyn. Rabbi Leible Eiger (1816–1888) initially led the second community, which moved to Lublin. There, following Rabbi Leible's death, it was led by Rabbi Zadok Ha-Kohen, also known as Rabbi Zadok of Lublin. Though each of the three leaders certainly had his own unique style and approach to the radical elements of Izbician theology, together they constitute the essential intellectual legacy of this Hasidic movement.

5.3.2 Izbica's Theology

Why was this school of Hasidism controversial? Starting with Rabbi Mordekhai Yosef, it repurposed the Talmudic phrase "All is in the hands of heaven, except for the fear of heaven" (bBerakhot 33a) to "All is in the hands of heaven, including the fear of heaven."[72] This raises the old problem, both in general philosophy and specifically in Hasidic thought, of determinism. The reason this seemingly deterministic formulation is so controversial is because it can be understood to pave the way toward antinomianism, the abrogation of the law. As neatly presented by Morris Fairstein: "is the person who has already attained this level of understanding still required to fulfill the obligations imposed by the commandments?"[73] Another question that might occur to a student of this thought is, if all action and thought derives from God, can sin be deemed an appropriate religious expression?[74]

Its leaders acknowledged the allure of antinomianism in Izbician thought. Several biblical and Talmudic personalities are described in this thought as mistaking the doctrine of divine immanence with the permission for (or even encouragement of) antinomian behavior. Of note are the stories of Adam and Eve, Koraḥ (Num 16), the sons of Aaron struck down before God (Lev 10), Pinḥas's killing of Zimri (Num 25), and the heresy of the Talmudic sage *Aḥer*,[75] all of which are reimagined as cautionary tales about properly negotiating between a personal spiritual intuition invested with divine significance and the antinomian tendencies

72 For example, see Gershon Ḥenokh, *Me haShilo'aḥ*, vol. 1, Jerusalem: Mishur, 1990, 27, 245. For instances of this phrase in the work of Rabbi Zadok, see his *Resise laylah*, Machon Har Bracha, 2002, 41, 50. See also his *Dover Tsedek*, Machon Har Bracha, 2007, 9.

73 Fairstein, Morris M., *All Is in the Hands of Heaven: The Teaching of Rabbi Mordechai Joseph Leiner of Izbica*, Hoboken, NJ: Ktav, 1989, 36.

74 For a contemporary scholarly analysis of Izbica Hasidism, see Hefter, Herzl, "'In God's Hands': The Religious Phenomenology of R. Mordechai Yosef of Izbica," *Tradition* 46:1 (Spring 2013), 50.

75 All of the former examples are discussed by Hefter, "In God's Hands." The story of *Aḥer* is interpreted in this context in Rabbi Zadok's *Sefer zikhronot*, Machon Har Bracha, 2002, 293:11.

that can arise from such an intuition. Each of these personalities was left to grapple with a question: if, indeed, the personal revelations I experience are also part of God's will, how should I respond when my intuition conflicts with God's will as expressed by the Torah?

Current scholars do not entirely understand why, given the radical currents of Izbician thought, the movement never became an antinomian one, especially since Rabbi Mordekhai Yosef was ostracized by much of mainstream Polish Hasidic leadership for his theology.[76] I have some thoughts about this issue. Religious life has both a floor and a ceiling. The ceiling is built upon the ideals and values to which we aspire but may never attain. The floor, however, is the framework and perspective from which we deal with failure and those still mired in sin. Much of religious life is spent vacillating between the two. The more radical deterministic elements of Izbica-Lublin can provide cushions of comfort on the floor of Judaism without altering the ceiling. Sometimes, when religious life feels closer to the floor, there may be a feeling that Godliness and spiritual meaning are unattainable. It is here that Izbician theology is most instructive, reminding us that "[w]herever a Jew may fall, he falls into the lap of God."[77] Further, Rabbi Zadok couches much of his approach to sin in the Talmudic phrase, "A person cannot stand on words of Torah until they have caused him to stumble" (bGittin 43a).[78]

This approach is possible because Judaism leaves room to apply a deterministic theology as a retrospective means of making spiritual sense of religious failure. This method is not considered, necessarily, to undermine Jewish ideals.[79] For instance, the encouragement and strategies developed for someone struggling with the halakhic observance of Shabbat (the "floor") need not become the ideal for Shabbat observance for those confident in their faith (the "ceiling"). Sin may, indeed, both be an intractable part of religious life, but the theological means by which we soften our "floor" do not have to become the theological ends with which we secure our "ceiling." The communal world of Izbica likely remained traditional because its leaders adapted this distinction in applying its radical theology. Whatever radical elements existed in the textual tradition of Izbica, they were not given

76 Cf. Magid, Shaul, *Hasidism on the Margin. Reconciliation, Antinomianism, and Messianism in Izbica/Radzin Hasidism*, Madison, WI: University of Wisconsin Press, 2003, xiii.
77 Zadok ha-Kohen Rabinowitz, *Pri tsadik*, Nasso 15, citing Rabbi Mordekhai Yosef Leiner.
78 See Rosenfeld, Jennie, "Talmudic Re-Readings: Toward a Modern Orthodox Sexual Ethic," PhD diss., City University of New York, 2008, 108–109, where Rosenfeld notes the centrality of this phrase in Rabbi Zadok's thought.
79 Cf. Wiskind-Elper, Ora, *Wisdom of the Heart: The Teachings of Rabbi Ya'akov of Izbica-Radzyn*, Philadelphia: Jewish Publication Society, 2010, 102–03.

precedence in dictating the community's overall lifestyle. In other words, Izbica was not radicalized because it simultaneously imparted traditional values that tempered the radical components of its theology. And not all (or most) Izbica *Ḥasidim*, of course, had access to these texts, not least because of their levels of education and literacy. Even so, *Me haShiloaḥ* begins with a cryptic caution: The ideas contained within, cautioned Rabbi Gershon Ḥenokh, are only published "for the sake of our intimates who understand their true value." Whatever textual radicalism existed in Izbica, there was a concomitant experiential tradition among the "intimates" that prevented communal radicalism.

Given the above discussion on Hasidic paths for the righteous, those in the middle, and the unrighteous, what about those who are a little bit of each? Such confused souls may find comfort in the world of Izbica. Even within the deterministic structure of Izbica *Ḥasidut*, each person is cautioned not to assume that his or her actions are divinely sanctioned. Instead, a continual process of self-evaluation known as *berur* is necessary in order to be assured of God's endorsement of an individual's actions.[80] Navigating this tension of continuous self-doubt in a world of determinism is certainly confusing, but Izbica Hasidism is, in many ways, intended for the confused. Izbica *Ḥasidut* provides a complex mystical decision-making system that allows certain individuals to reach total harmony between their individual prerogatives and the transcendent Divine Will. As Alan Brill says: "When the consecration of daily life in the heart reaches a state of clarified consciousness [*berur*], it is possible to perform one's actions, even sin and desire, in harmony with inner Divine will."[81]

We have seen, then, that Hasidic literature is rich with creative paths and hidden doorways through which sinners can rediscover their relationship with God. A central tenet of Hasidic thought is the passage in the Zohar, the foundational kabbalistic text, "there is nothing besides Him" [*en od milvado*].[82] Regardless of your level of righteousness (or lack thereof), there is a path in Hasidic thought that seeks to allow you to stand beside God.

---

80 Cf. Brill, Alan, *Thinking God: The Mysticism of Rabbi Zadok of Lublin*, Jersey City, NJ: Ktav, 2002, 146–68.
81 Brill, *Thinking God*, 157.
82 *Tikkunei Zohar* 122:2.

6 Jews and Sin in Modernity: Reform Judaism and the Shadow of Antinomianism

6.1 Modernity, Emancipation, and Reform

Modernity brought many changes to Western and Central Europe, and its Jews experienced them as well. In what Jewish scholars call "Emancipation," the Jews of Western and Central Europe received more rights – the relaxation of past anti-Jewish laws and taxes and, sometimes, even citizenship – and had more access to the dominant society than Jews had had in over 1500 years.[83]

Reactions to this were many. In nineteenth-century Germany, in particular, Jewish scholars familiar with both Jewish texts and the new German history, or *Wissenschaft*, embarked on an effort to infuse the Jewish view of the world with something it had lacked: a sense of history.[84] The result, *die Wissenschaft des Judentums* (lit. "the science of Judaism), led to a new appreciation of how Judaism had developed over time. It is no coincidence that, around mid-century, only a few decades after Leopold Zunz (1774–1886) introduced the concept of *Wissenschaft des Judentums*, Jewish religious reformers began to suggest unprecedented changes to Jewish ritual practice and law: prayer and sermons in the vernacular, clergy costumes and synagogue seating arrangements borrowed from Protestant churches, and, most importantly for our purposes, less strictness in following traditional Jewish law. Since Judaism had always changed with the times, they reasoned, the new world of modernity should be a catalyst for further innovations, and if these seemed dramatic, well, so were the changes that modernity had brought. But what did all of this mean for sin?

6.2 Reform Judaism: Antinomianism Renewed?

There is another view of Reform Judaism that directly addresses this question of Reform and sin. It places the movement's origins not in emancipation-era Germany but much earlier, in an era we previously discussed. According to this view, the antinomian tension lurking in the underbelly of the Jewish community did

83 Cf. Schorsh, Ismar, *From Text to Context: The Turn to History in Modern Judaism*, Hannover, NH: University Press of New England for Brandeis University Press, 1994, 9–10.
84 Cf. Schorsh, introduction to *From Text to Context*, 1–2. On Jews' previous lack of interest in the study of history, see Yerushalmi, Yosef Hayim, *Zakhor: Jewish History and Jewish Memory*, Seattle: University of Washington Press, 1996.

not disappear following the 1676 death of Shabbetai Tsevi. In fact, one could argue, that is when it truly began. Those who appreciate the ambiguity of the conceptual role of sin within Judaism – and see the thread of antinomian tension running throughout – will hardly be surprised. This view was championed, most notably, by Gershom Scholem, the first academic scholar of Ḳabbalah, who read this tension into the entire dialectics of Jewish history.[85] According to Scholem, Jewish history can be understood through the Hegelian lens of opposites' interacting – in this case, the antinomian, unstructured mystical impulse and the institutionally rigid halakhic impulse – and transforming into some higher ideal. In this approach, following the death of Shabbetai Tsevi, the antinomian impulse was transformed and once again emerged within both the Hasidic and Reform communities. As Scholem writes:

> the nihilism of the Sabbatian and Frankist movements, with its doctrine so profoundly shocking to the Jewish conception of things that the violation of the Torah could become its true fulfilment (*bittulah shel torah zehu kiyyumah*), was a dialectical outgrowth of the belief in the Messiahship of Sabbatai Sevi, and . . . this nihilism, in turn, helped pave the way for Haskalah [Jewish Enlightenment] and the reform movement of the nineteenth century, once its original religious impulse was exhausted.[86]

This view was hardly accepted by all, with many preferring the more historical, Germany-centered view. Scholem's genealogical line connecting early Reform and Sabbateanism is tentative at best, seemingly ignoring the contributions of Moses Mendelssohn (1729–1786) and other early Jewish Enlightenment thinkers.[87] Still, historical concerns notwithstanding, Scholem's view offers an attractive conceptual framework for understanding later developments in Jewish history. Sabbateanism reimagined the nature of Jewish community, considering Jewish life untethered (or perhaps differently tethered) to Jewish law. Whether or not Sabbateanism was an overt historical catalyst for Reform Judaism may be (mostly) beside the point. Sabbateanism offered a vision of Jewish life and community that did not measure its own success exclusively through the metric of fealty to the

85 See Scholem, Gershom, *The Messianic Idea*, New York: Shocken, 1971; for more on Scholem's approach to history, see Biale, David, *Gershom Scholem: Ḳabbalah and Counter-History*, 2nd ed., Cambridge, MA: Harvard University Press, 1982; and Macienjko, Pawel, "Gershom Scholem's Dialectic of Jewish History: The Case of Sabbatianism," *Journal of Modern Jewish Studies* 3:2 (2004), 207–20.
86 Scholem, *Messianic Idea*, 84.
87 For approaches contrary to Scholem's, see, e.g., Lowenstein, Steven (ed.), *The Mechanics of Change: Essays in the Social History of German Jewry*, Providence, RI: Brown University Press, 1992.

law as traditionally observed. The very nature of sin was reimagined, and the concept of Jewish life unmediated by Jewish law became a very real possibility.[88]

And it is that Sabbatean revelation that still animates much of the discourse regarding sin within the non-Orthodox Jewish community. Specifically, if Jewish law is not the exclusive barometer for Jewish identity, what, if anything, does it even mean to sin? What role, if any, does *halakhah* and Jewish practice have in Jewish life? This has been considered and debated from the very inception of the Reform movement. It has given rise to a diverse pallet of what the law and sin should mean to the contemporary non-Orthodox Jewish community, which flourishes today in the United States, Canada, the United Kingdom, and (in much smaller numbers) Israel, among other places. Other non-Orthodox Jewish communities include the Conservative movement (also founded in Germany, not long after Reform) and the Reconstructionist movement (founded in the United States in the twentieth century).

These new approaches hardly mean that talk of sin has been eradicated from these communities, but it certainly has been reconstructed outside the strict bounds of *halakhah*. Some contemporary non-Orthodox scholars consider sin through the lens of ethics and political advocacy, such as *tiḳḳun olam* (repairing the world), while others consider sin as a starting point for engagement with personal reflection and growth.[89] All of these newfound approaches, unshackled from the narrower conception of *halakhah*, seem to retain some connections to the antinomian conception of sin that Sabbateanism highlighted in Jewish history.

---

88 For more on the theological implications of Sabbateanism for subsequent Jewish life, see Goldish, Matt, "Toward a Reevaluation of the Relationship between Ḳabbalah, Sabbateanism, and Heresy," in: Daniel Frank / Matt Goldish (eds.), *Rabbinic Culture and Its Critics: Jewish Authority, Dissent and Heresy in Medieval and Early Modern Times*, 393–408, Detroit, MI: Wayne University Press, 2008.

89 For an anthology of contemporary Jewish approaches to sin, primarily in the non-Orthodox Jewish community, see Hoffman, Lawrence A. (ed.), *We Have Sinned: Sin and Confession in Judaism; Ashamnu and Al Chet*, Nashville, TN: Jewish Lights Publishing, 2012. For a more popular example of approaching sin as an opportunity for personal growth, unmediated by halakha, see Lew, Alan, *This is Real and You Are Completely Unprepared: The Days of Awe as a Journey of Transformation*, Boston: Little, Brown & Co., 2003.

7 Modern Rabbinic Correspondence: Practical Empathy in a Rapidly Changing World

7.1 Modern Rabbinic Correspondence

What of the Jews who continued to observe *halakhah* but were not Hasidic? As modernity dawned, they, too, had a path to repentance from sin. Non-Hasidic rabbinic writing is replete with correspondence from those seeking a path toward repentance. In general, rabbinic correspondences do not have the same overt mystical and theological tone found in Hasidic sources, but their approach to repentance is nonetheless quite creative.

There is something unique about rabbinic correspondence. The fact that correspondence addresses a specific individual, who him- or herself has initiated contact by writing a letter to the rabbi about a particular issue, infuses this genre of rabbinic writing with a deeply personal tone. Unlike classic rabbinic commentaries, rabbinic correspondence exists on the nexus where abstract theology meets practical communal and personal policy.

7.2 Responsa in the Age of Jewish Enlightenment: Rabbis Yeḥezkel Landau and Moshe Sofer

Rabbi Yeḥezkel Landau (1713–1793) of Prague, often referred to as the *Nodah BiYehudah* after the title of his responsa collection, was first and foremost a halakhist. His responsa remain a classic contribution to the genre and are still quoted today. One responsum of his in particular is frequently cited regarding the penance for a repentant sinner. In 1770, a future rabbi, unnamed for obvious reasons, sent Rabbi Landau an astonishing letter. The anonymous questioner had an affair with a married woman for three years. Now, he is married to this woman's daughter. His question is twofold: is he obligated to tell his father-in-law about the affair, and how should he perform *teshuvah* for it? In response to the inquiry about *teshuvah*, Rabbi Landau gives a detailed response about his view on the penance process. In general, Rabbi Landau explains, he does not answer such questions, "since I am not accustomed to responding to questions that I cannot find a source for in the Talmud and halakhic authorities."[90] Rabbi Landau is

90 Landau, Yeḥezkel, *Nodah BiYehudah, Oraḥ ḥayyim, Mahadura kama*, 35. For an English account of many of the details of Rabbi Landau's response, see Jacobs, *Theology in the Responsa*, 175–76.

quite clear that he does not look favorably upon the more detailed penance plans popularized by many associated with the *Ḥaside Ashkenaz*. While he expresses reverence for the work of Rabbi Eleazar haRoḳeaḥ, he explains that later books that detail penance "are by and large built upon logic from their stomachs without any foundation – each work just relying on the words of the other."[91] Fasting and acts of asceticism are not an essential part of repentance. Instead, "The essence of *teshuvah* is leaving the sin, confession with a broken heart, and wholehearted regret."[92] Yet, given the gravity of the sin, Rabbi Landau does not let his correspondent off easily. He details an onerous menu of fasting, Torah study, asceticism, prayer, and charity to atone for the affair. Nonetheless, he continually emphasizes the importance of distinguishing between the essential components of *teshuvah* and the ritual; the latter is ancillary. In essence, *teshuvah* is not about fasting and penance. Real repentance is a brokenhearted confession with a wholehearted commitment not to repeat the sin.

Rabbi Moshe (Schreiber) Sofer (1762–1839) of Hungary, called the *Ḥatam Sofer* after his responsa collection, lived in the generation following Rabbi Landau. Together they were the towering halakhic figures who shaped Jewish life during the upheaval caused by the Jewish Enlightenment (*Haskalah*), which they both opposed.[93] In a response to a letter requesting his views on penance, Sofer reinforces much of Rabbi Landau's position: The essence of *teshuvah* is not fasting but, rather, confession, regret, and a commitment to abandon the practice of sin.[94] Rabbi Sofer, however, adds an innovative ritual to the process of *teshuvah*: a personal day of reflection. Yom Kippur is traditionally the day on which the Jewish people collectively focus on repentance. Rabbi Sofer suggests that those who have struggled with a particular sin add an additional personal day of reflection:

> either the day on which he initially succumbed to sin, or the day on which he resolved to return to God. That day should be for him each year a day of fasting and repentance with tears and grief as well as confession and regret. This is along the lines of the verse "and my iniquities are always before me" [Ps 51:5]. This is no less reasonable that someone who had a miracle performed for him which saved him from bodily harm, for which it is proper to establish a day to remember the miracle [bBerakhot 54a]. All the more so, he should do such for a spiritual danger, when his soul was saved.[95]

---

91 Landau, *Nodah BiYehudah*, 35.

92 Landau, *Nodah BiYehudah*, 35.

93 For a comparison of the contributions of Rabbis Landau and Sofer, see Kahana, Maoz, "*Mi-Prag la-Pressburg: Ketivah Hilkhatit ba-olam mishtaneh me-ha'Node B-Yehudah 'el ha-'Hatam Sofer,' 1730–1839*" [From Prague to Pressburg: Halakhic writing in a changing world from the '*Node B-Yehudah*' to the '*Hatam Sofer*,' 1730–1839], PhD diss., Hebrew University, 2010.

94 Sofer, Moshe, *Teshuvot Ḥatam Sofer*, *Oraḥ ḥayyim*, 1:173.

95 Sofer, *Teshuvot Ḥatam Sofer*, 1:173.

Though it is unclear if this ritual was ever actually observed, and Sofer mentions an earlier source suggesting a similar idea, it is still a remarkable innovation. This practice is a reminder of the personal component of the repentance process. On Yom Kippur, the Jewish people return to God collectively, but Sofer identified a person's individual need to create a personal Yom Kippur as well, in order to truly contemplate his or her past sin and renew the commitment to repentance.

7.3 Rabbinic Correspondence in the Twentieth-Century United States: Rabbis Moshe Feinstein and Yitzḥak Hutner

7.3.1 Rabbi Moshe Feinstein

Rabbi Moshe Feinstein (1895–1986), born in Belarus, became the foremost halakhic authority in the American Orthodox world after immigrating to the United States in 1937. He made Jewish legal decisions during an exciting time: technology was flourishing, and Jews were acclimating to life in the United States. It was also a contentious time for *halakhah*. The United States, with its commitment to religious freedom, proved a fertile ground for the flourishing of multiple denominations within Judaism. As Orthodox Judaism struggled to find footing in American society, Conservative Judaism was quickly embraced as the perfect blend between the innovation of Reform Judaism and the old-world traditions of Orthodoxy. Rabbi Feinstein was sent many questions from members of the Orthodox community regarding the legitimacy of Conservative and Reform Jewish practice. His answers drew clear boundaries around the Orthodox community, separating it from the practice of other denominations. Prayer led by women, non-Orthodox divorce, and conversion were not, he ruled, legitimate practices according to Jewish law.

His magnum opus of responsa, *Iggerot Moshe*, spans eight volumes and represents nearly three-quarters of a century of letters. At the end of the sixth volume are four responsa in answer to questions posed by people dealing with serious sin. As opposed to most of Rabbi Feinstein's responsa, which concern practical questions of *halakhah*, these letters deal with the process of repentance and give advice to the repentant. It is worth noting that some Jews in the late-twentieth century United States who struggled with behaviors far outside of the bounds of normative halakhic practice still felt compelled (and comfortable) to address the leading Jewish legal scholar of their time. All of the questions are dated between 1975 and 1977; in order of publication, they deal with homosexuality, masturbation, an affair, and extramarital sex. Atypically for this collection, all are published anonymously. Rabbi Feinstein's approach could be characterized as practical empathy; he commiserates with the pain of the questioner while affirming traditional halakhic standards. For example, the third letter responds to a woman who engaged in an inappropriate relationship with her boss while serving as his secretary. She turned to Rabbi Feinstein several years after the incident for advice on how to repent properly. His response ends with a tender note of optimistic encouragement: "Furthermore, you need to understand that, God forbid, you should not be depressed. Rather, you should rejoice that you have merited repentance and a marriage to a scholar. And on Yom Kippur God will grant you complete forgiveness."[96] For someone who had not repented, the author of the letter on homosexuality, Rabbi Feinstein did not condone his actions. As he indicated, the letter-writer was not really asking a question about Jewish law, as the Bible and Talmud clearly forbid homosexual relations. But in this case, too, he expressed concern about depression and how the questioner might be consoled in his sorrow.

Like Rabbis Landau and Sofer, Rabbi Feinstein tempered the rather ominous and onerous process of repentance developed by the *Ḥaside Ashkenaz.* He saw that, as the Hasidim of the Baal Shem Tov and later required encouragement, those who wrote to him about *halakhah* needed empathy as well as a more streamlined process of repentance grounded firmly in traditional Jewish texts.

7.3.2 Rabbi Yitzḥak Hutner

Rabbinic responsa is probably the most well-known form of rabbinic correspondence, but there is another category: *iggerot,* personal correspondence, which even more plainly capture the practical advice rabbis offered people who struggled with religious crisis or failure.[97] In general, responsa are primarily concerned with halakhic questions, while *iggerot* mostly address personal and communal issues. (Rabbi Moshe Feinstein's responsa, as discussed above, are called *Iggerot Moshe,* though nearly all of them are halakhic responsa rather than rabbinic correspondence in the style of *iggerot.* A notable exception is the correspondence referred to in the previous section, which bears the style of rabbinic correspondence more than of Jewish legal correspondence.)

96 See Feinstein, Moshe, *Iggrot Moshe, Orah hayyim,* vol. 4 #117. See also responsa 115–16, 118.
97 For a discussion of the unique candor found in correspondence, see Shapiro, Marc B., "Scholars and Friends: Rabbi Jehiel Jacob Weinberg and Professor Samuel Atlas," *Torah U-Madda Journal* 7 (1997), 105–21.

This section will focus on one rabbi whose personal correspondence dealt extensively with religious crisis and failure: Rabbi Yitzḥak Hutner (1906–1980). While he published on a wide range of topics, he never published formal halakhic responsa. The only correspondence we have from him are his *iggerot*, personal letters, released in a work called *Paḥad Yitzḥak*. These letters show that he developed a radical empathy toward those dealing with sin, religious failure, and crisis. Rabbi Hutner, who became the leader of Yeshivat Chaim Berlin in Brooklyn two years after he moved to the United States in 1934, spent his youth studying in traditional Eastern European Talmudic academies (*yeshivot*), such as Yeshivat Knesset Yisrael, also known as the Slabodka Yeshivah. A story circulates that, one morning, when the head of the *yeshivah* asked where his study partner (*ḥevruta*) was, Hutner explained that he was studying with his *yetser har'a* – his inclination to do evil. When asked why he didn't study with his inclination to do good [*yetser haṭov*], Hunter replied, "I can always count on my *yetser har'a* to show up on time for morning studies. The *yetser ṭov* is not as reliable."[98] This story captures both Rabbi Hutner's wit and much of his approach to sin and failure. He thought it was preferable to have his evil inclination as a study partner than to learn Torah with his more angelic nature. This was because the latter was bland; challenging the former produced the friction that could propel someone to greatness.

Throughout his letters, Rabbi Hutner returns to a single theme: greatness that emerges from challenge. He explains that you can only detect the strength of a person's grasp when you try to remove the object from that person's hand. He writes: "It is entirely possible to study with diligence in yeshivah and, nonetheless, based on that, you still cannot evince the person's relationship with Torah."[99] Since a relationship is only proven after it is challenged, Rabbi Hutner often reminds his students that his ideas may resonate only after they have departed from his presence. Cleverly marshaling the verse in Psalms (34:12), "Come, my sons, listen to me," Rabbi Hutner explains that a remote relationship often establishes the imperative for attentiveness.[100] Intimacy is forged through absence. In addition to absence from the walls of the *yeshivah*, spiritual voids are also invested with the presence of spiritual meaning. In an oft-cited letter (no. 94), Rabbi Hutner offers this analogy to someone whose non-Torah-study accomplishments feel like a hypocritical duality in an otherwise spiritual existence: "Someone who rents a room in one house to live a residential life and another room in a hotel to live a transient life is certainly

98 Oral transmission to the author from one of Rabbi Hutner's students.
99 Hutner, Yitzhak, *Paḥad Yitzḥak: Iggerot Uketavim*, Brooklyn, NY: Gur Aryeh Institute for Advanced Jewish Scholarship, 1998, letter 112.
100 Cf. Hutner, *Paḥad Yitzḥak*, letter 155.

someone who lives a double life. But someone who has a home with more than one room has a broad life, not a double life."[101]

At a time when some segments of the Orthodox world were struggling with the question of how much time to devote to traditional Talmud study and how much to more worldly pursuits, such as careers, Rabbi Hutner advocated for a broad life, and he modeled it. He also understood that, in the pursuit of breadth, some students may fall short. It was in the possibilities and realities of failure, in fact, that Rabbi Hutner's letters were most innovative. He writes that people may not know which tests are which, but, certainly, in the course of life, people will confront failures that are simply inevitable.[102] The true test, according to Rabbi Hutner, is not one's ability to avoid sin but, rather, whether and how one develops an appropriate evaluation of and reaction to the occurrence of sin. Such assessment should not happen, writes Rabbi Hutner, during times of self-doubt and insecurity. Just as Jewish law prohibits judgment during the nighttime, our self-assessment should not occur during times of personal darkness.[103] Failure, when properly assessed and integrated, can be a fertile ground for personal and spiritual development.

Rabbi Hutner's consoling approach to sin and failure is likely the most enduring legacy of his *iggerot*. Current American and Israeli students at yeshivot and women's seminaries, who may have never heard of Rabbi Hutner or seriously studied his writings, have likely read portions of his one hundred and twenty-eighth letter – his fundamental treatise on sin and failure. The letter, which begins by lamenting the hagiographic nature of rabbinic biographies, reminds a student that greatness does not emerge from the serenity of our good inclinations but, rather, from our struggles with our baser tendencies. The verse in Proverbs (24:16), "Seven times the righteous man falls and gets up," has been perennially misunderstood, Rabbi Hutner argues. It is not despite the fall that the righteous stand up; it is because of the fall that the righteous are able to stand confidently. Greatness does not emerge despite sin and failure; it is a product of sin of failure.

If the medium is the message, then the message of these missives is the integration of theological profundities into personal correspondence. Throughout the collection of Rabbi Hutner's letters, none of the recipients' names are listed. Listing those names would certainly have increased the letters' historical value, but their absence likely increases the feeling of contemporary relevance they convey.

101 Hutner, *Paḥad Yitzḥak*, letter 94.
102 Cf. Hutner, *Paḥad Yitzḥak*, letter 9.
103 Cf. Hutner, *Paḥad Yitzḥak*, letter 96.

The names are missing because the modern reader is intended to be their enduring addressee.

8 Contemporary Jewish Ideas about Sin

8.1 Hasidic Ideas, Non-Hasidic Jewish Communities

From the founding of Hasidism until the postwar period, there was some, but not much, cross-pollination between Hasidic and non-Hasidic thought within Orthodoxy. (Both Hasidic and non-Hasidic Orthodox Jews are often referred to as *Ḥaredim*, literally "those who tremble" [before God].) Almost all of this occurred at the most advanced levels of rabbinic discourse. Now, however, more radical conceptions of sin and repentance, as presented by Hasidic thinkers such as Rabbi Mordekhai Yosef Leiner and Rabbi Zadok of Lublin, have moved into the center of contemporary *Ḥaredi* Jewish thought and life. Through central figures in the *Ḥaredi yeshivah* world, such as Rabbi Hutner, Rabbi Eliyahu Dessler (1892–1953), and Rabbi Gedalia Schorr (1910–1979), these more radical formulations of sin and failure are now considered mainstream within many contemporary Orthodox non-Hasidic communities.

8.2 The Weinberger/Shafran Exchange: A Case Study in Contemporary Jewish Discourse about Sin

More recently, Rabbi Moshe Weinberger (b. 1957), a leading Hasidic rabbi and educator in Woodmere, New York, has brought Hasidic thought into the more modern Orthodox community since 1992. His ideas, and the subsequent criticism they have engendered, offer insight into the continued relevance of this revolutionary school of Hasidic thought.[104]

In May 2018, *Mishpacha Magazine*, a popular weekly in the American Orthodox community, published a cover story entitled, "Meeting the Baal Shem Tov in

104 For more on the integration of Hasidic ideas into non-Hasidic Orthodox communities, see Zuckier, Shlomo (ed.), *Contemporary Uses and Forms of Hasidut*, New York: Yeshiva University Press, 2022.

the 21st Century."[105] The article featured some of the leading figures who teach Hasidic ideas within non-Hasidic communities, including Rabbi Weinberger. In a subsequent issue of the magazine, Rabbi Noach Shafran, a high school educator at Yeshivat Ner Israel in Baltimore, took issue with the article's characterization of the implications of Hasidic thought on Orthodox observance. Rabbi Shafran wrote:

> I'm also concerned by some disturbing explanations of Torah quoted in the article. For example, the *mishnah* [teaching] of "*Da ma l'maalah mimcha*" [sic; know what is above you] doesn't just mean that Hashem [God] is watching all the good things we do. It means exactly what it says. He is above us, watching everything we do, say, and think. Not because He's out to give us tickets for every infraction, but because He loves us and cares for us as a parent loves a child, and what we do to ourselves makes a difference to Him.
>
> Is it possible that this widespread movement sweeping the world, as described in the article, may be distorting the truth by disguising sugarcoated feelings toward Hashem as genuine *aliyah* [advancement] in Torah and *yiras Shamayim* [fear of Heaven]? Real growth must be difficult, and yes, the many professionals who yearn to return to their Gemaras [Talmud] at night or in the morning or both, remain connected to Hashem and His Torah all day because of that yearning.
>
> It's easy to say that a person has a relationship with Hashem wherever he is, regardless of what he is doing, but it's not true. Many of us break that connection through destructive habits and the like, and sugarcoating them doesn't make them any less destructive. "Feeling spiritual" may be better than feeling bad about yourself, as quoted in the article, but are we to be content with feeling spiritual?[106]

This concern echoes earlier critiques of Hasidic thought, namely that the emphasis on the spiritual and immutable connection to God, rather than rigorous observance of Jewish law, can lead to antinomian tendencies. It is both a theological and pedagogical concern. If we teach *yeshivah* students that God loves them no matter what, what will motivate them to avoid sin? Rabbi Shafran argues that educational institutions should, instead, be primarily tethered to traditional Talmudic education that more easily, in his view, translates into the rigorous and intricate relationship with *halakhah* that Judaism demands.

In the same issue, Rabbi Weinberger responds to Rabbi Shafran. Rabbi Weinberger emphasizes that the traditional approach to education in *yeshivah* is insufficient and needs to be complemented with Hasidic ideas. He writes:

---

105 Ginsburg, Rachel, "Meeting the Baal Shem Tov in the 21st Century," *Mishpacha*, May 16, 2018.
106 Shafran, Noach / Weinberger, Moshe, "Counterpoint: Meeting the Baal Shem Tov in the 21st Century, Revisited," *Mishpacha*, May 30, 2018.

> Rabbi Shafran asks, "Is it possible that the widespread movement may be distorting the truth by disguising sugarcoated feelings toward Hashem as genuine *aliyah* in Torah and *yiras Shamayim*?" Of course it is possible. It's also possible that thousands of younger and older men are convinced that there is more to the ultimate purpose of a Jew and are not satisfied by *shlugging* up [rebutting] their chavrusa or clocking in for the *daf yomi* [lit., "daily page," a reference to the common *yeshivah* practice of studying one folio page of Talmud per day].

Interestingly, in a class that was first available online but later removed, entitled "Hashem's Unbreakable Love for Every Jew," Rabbi Weinberger directed his critique less to Rabbi Shafran's pedagogical points about the aim of *yeshivah* study and more to the other rabbi's theological idea that our relationship with God can be broken through sin. Couched in many Hasidic sources, including Rabbi Zadok of Lublin, Rabbi Weinberger's talk rejected the notion that, in the words of Rabbi Shafran, "Many of us break that connection [to God] through destructive habits."

This dialogue between Rabbi Weinberger and Rabbi Shafran is an important example of the enduring debate on the role of sin within the contemporary Jewish community. Where this dialogue took place also merits emphasis. *Mishpacha Magazine* is a popular Jewish weekly that many Orthodox Jews read in their homes, often on the Sabbath. Today, the dialogue about the role sin plays in Jewish life is much less elite than the rabbinically-led conversation on sin that occurred during the rise of Sabbateanism and *Ḥasidut* hundreds of years ago. Sin is not just an issue with which rabbis contend. As a result, contemporary dialogue about the theological and pedagogical importance of sin is unfolding in more popular forums that better reflect the common Jewish experience.

9 Conclusion: Some Themes in Judaism's Conception of Sin

This survey of nearly two millennia of Jewish ideas about sin reviews a number of themes that recur with some regularity, including: firm grounding but not always consistent messages in traditional Jewish sources, particularly the Hebrew Bible and Talmud; as a result, multivalence, from a series of words for sin to multiple paths to repentance; debate over the relevance of intent in sin; the importance of historical context, from medieval Christian ideas about penance to messianic fervor in early modern Eastern Europe and the Mediterranean to American religious freedom granted to Jews in the twentieth and twenty-first centuries, in shaping Jewish conceptions of sin; tension between *halakhah* and antinomianism, often coming to the fore in times of great change for Jews; the role of rabbis and their thought in determining Jewish ideas about sin; and the common Jew's desire to connect to God and therefore to have an accessible path to repentance. Despite the continued great change that Jews face today – or, perhaps, because of them – if history is any indication, these themes will likely continue to recur as Judaism faces its present, and its future.

Bibliography

Anderson, Gary A., *Sin: A History*, New Haven: Yale University Press, 2010.

Becker, Adam H. / Reed, Annette Yoshiko (eds.), *The Ways That Never Parted: Jews and Christians in Late Antiquity and the Early Middle Ages*, Tübingen: Mohr Siebeck, 2003.

Biale, David, *Gershom Scholem: Ḳabbalah and Counter-History*, 2nd ed., Cambridge, MA: Harvard University Press, 1982.

Blankovsky, Yuval, *Ḥeṭ Leshem Shamayim* [Sin for the sake of Heaven], Jerusalem: Magnes, 2017.

Brill, Alan, *Thinking God: The Mysticism of Rabbi Zadok of Lublin*, Jersey City, NJ: Ktav, 2002.

Cooper, Alan, "A Medieval Jewish Version of Original Sin: Ephraim Luntschitz on Lev. 12," *Harvard Theological Review* 97:4 (October 2004), 445–59.

Coudert, Allison P., *The Impact of the Ḳabbalah in the Seventeenth Century: The Life and Thought of Francis Mercury van Helmont*, Leiden: Brill, 1999.

Faierstein, Morris M., *All Is in the Hands of Heaven: The Teaching of Rabbi Mordechai Joseph Leiner of Izbica*, Hoboken, NJ: Ktav, 1989.

Fishman, Talya, "The Penitential System of Hasidei Ashkenaz and the Problem of Cultural Boundaries," *Journal of Jewish Thought and Philosophy* 8 (1999), 201–29.

Fraade, Steven D., "The Innovation of Nominalized Verbs in Mishnaic Hebrew as Marking an Innovation of Concept," in: Elitzur A. Bar-Asher Siegal / Aaron J. Koller (eds.), *Studies in Mishnaic Hebrew and Related Fields*, Jerusalem: Magnes, 2017, 129–48.

Fredriksen, Paula, *Sin: The Early History of an Idea*, Princeton: Princeton University Press, 2012.

Ginsburg, Rachel, "Meeting the Baal Shem Tov in the 21st Century," *Mishpacha*, May 16, 2018.

Goldish, Matt, "Toward a Reevaluation of the Relationship between Ḳabbalah, Sabbateanism, and Heresy," in: Daniel Frank / Matt Goldish (eds.), *Rabbinic Culture and Its Critics: Jewish Authority, Dissent and Heresy in Medieval and Early Modern Times*, Detroit, MI: Wayne University Press, 2008, 393–408.

Grossman, Meir Zvi, "Le-mashm'autam shel habiṭuyim 'averah' ve'devar 'averah bileshon hakhamim" [On the uses of the expressions 'averah and devar 'averah in the language of the sages], *Sinai* 100:1 (1987), 260–72.

Halbertal, Moshe, "Mavet, ḥeṭ, ḥoḳ, vege'ulah be-Mishnat ha-Ramban" [Death, sin, law, and redemption in the Ramban's Mishnah], *Tarbiz* 71:1–2 (2002), 133–62.

Halbertal, Moshe, *People of the Book*, Cambridge, MA: Harvard University Press, 1997.

Hefter, Herzl, "'In God's Hands': The Religious Phenomenology of R. Mordechai Yosef of Izbica," *Tradition* 46:1 (Spring 2013), 43–65.

Hoffman, Lawrence A. (ed.), *We Have Sinned: Sin and Confession in Judaism; Ashamnu and Al Chet*, Nashville, TN: Jewish Lights Publishing, 2012.

Jacobs, Louis, *Their Heads in Heaven: Unfamiliar Aspects of Hasidism*, Portland, OR: Vallentine Mitchell, 2005.

Jacobs, Louis, *Theology in the Responsa*, Portland, OR: Littman Library of Jewish Civilization, 2005.
Jacobs, Alan, *Original Sin: A Cultural History*, New York: Harper Collins, 2008.
Kahana, Maoz, *"Mi-Prag la-Pressburg: Ketivah Hilkhatit ba-olam mishtaneh me-ha'Node B-Yehudah 'el ha-'Hatam Sofer,' 1730–1839"* [From Prague to Pressburg: Halakhic writing in a changing world from the 'Node B-Yehudah' to the 'Hatam Sofer,' 1730–1839], PhD diss., Hebrew University, 2010.
Kanarfogel, Ephraim, "Not Just Another Contemporary Jewish Problem: A Historical Discussion of Phylacteries," *Gesher* 5 (1976), 106–21.
Katz, Steven T., "Man, Sin, and Redemption in Rabbinic Judaism," in: id. (ed.), *The Cambridge History of Judaism*, vol. 4, *The Late Roman-Rabbinic Period*, Cambridge: Cambridge University Press, 2006, 925–45.
Lam, Joseph, *Patterns of Sin in the Hebrew Bible*, New York: Oxford University Press, 2016.
Lamm, Norman, *The Religious Thought of Hasidism*, Hoboken, NJ: Ktav, 1999.
Lasker, Daniel J., *Jewish Philosophical Polemics against Christianity in the Middle Ages*, 2nd ed., Portland, OR: Littman Library of Jewish Civilization, 2007.
Lew, Alan, *This is Real and You Are Completely Unprepared: The Days of Awe as a Journey of Transformation*, Boston: Little, Brown & Co., 2003.
Lowenstein, Steven (ed.), *The Mechanics of Change: Essays in the Social History of German Jewry*, Providence, RI: Brown University Press, 1992.
Maciejko, Pawel, "Gershom Scholem's Dialectic of Jewish History: The Case of Sabbatianism," *Journal of Modern Jewish Studies* 3:2 (2004), 207–20.
Maciejko, Pawel, *Mixed Multitude: Jacob Frank and the Frankist Movement*, Philadelphia: University of Pennsylvania Press, 2011.
Magid, Shaul, *From Metaphysics to Midrash: Myth, History, and the Interpretation of Scripture in Lurianic Kabbala*. Bloomington, IN: Indiana University Press, 2008.
Magid, Shaul, "From Theosophy to Midrash: Lurianic Exegesis and the Garden of Eden," *AJS Review* 22:1 (1997), 37–75.
Magid, Shaul, *Hasidism on the Margin: Reconciliation, Antinomianism, and Messianism in Izbica/Radzin Hasidism*, Madison: University of Wisconsin Press, 2003.
Magid, Shaul, "'A Thread of Blue': Rabbi Gershon Henoch Leiner of Radzyń and his Search for Continuity in Response to Modernity," *Polin* 11 (1998), 31–52.
Magid, Shaul, "Through the Void: The Absence of God in R. Nahman of Bratzlav's 'Likkutei MoHaRan'," *The Harvard Theological Review* 88:4 (Oct. 1995), 495–519.
Marcus, Ivan G., *Sefer Hasidim and the Ashkenazic Book in Medieval Europe*, Philadelphia: University of Pennsylvania Press, 2018.
Mayse, Ariel Evan, "The Sacred Writ of Hasidism: Tanya and the Spiritual Vision of Rabbi Shneur Zalman of Liady," in: Stuart Halpern (ed.), *Books of the People: Revisiting Classic Works of Jewish Thought*, Jerusalem: Maggid, 2017, 109–56.
Polen, Nehemia, "Dark Ladies and Redemptive Compassion: Ruth and the Messianic Lineage in Judaism," in: Peter S. Hawkins (ed.), *Scrolls of Love: Ruth and the Song of Songs*, New York: Fordham University Press, 2006, 59–74.
Rapoport-Albert, Ada, "God and the Zaddik as the Two Focal Points of Hasidic Worship," *History of Religions* 18:4 (May 1979), 296–325.
Rembaum, Joel E., "Medieval Jewish Criticism of the Christian Doctrine of Original Sin," *AJS Review* 7/8 (1982–83), 353–82.
Rosen, Michael, *The Quest for Authenticity: The Thought of Reb Simhah Bunim*, Jerusalem: Urim, 2008.
Rosenfeld, Jennie, "Talmudic Re-Readings: Toward a Modern Orthodox Sexual Ethic," PhD diss., City University of New York, 2008.

Rubin, A., "The Concept of Repentance among the Hasidey Ashkenaz," *Journal of Jewish Studies* 16 (1965), 161–76.
Ruderman, David, *Early Modern Jewry: A New Cultural History*, Princeton: Princeton University Press, 2010.
Schochet, Elijah, *The Hasidic Movement and the Gaon of Vilna*, Northvale, NJ: Jason Aronson, 1993.
Scholem, Gershom, *Ḳabbalah*, Jerusalem: Keter, 1974.
Scholem, Gershom, *The Messianic Idea in Judaism: And Other Essays on Jewish Spirituality*, New York: Schocken, 1995.
Scholem, Gershom, *Sabbatai Sevi: The Mystical Messiah*, Princeton: Princeton University Press, 1973.
Schorsh, Ismar, *From Text to Context: The Turn to History in Modern Judaism*, Hannover, NH: University Press of New England for Brandeis University Press, 1994.
Shafran, Noach / Weinberger, Moshe, "Counterpoint: Meeting the Baal Shem Tov in the 21st Century, Revisited," *Mishpacha*, May 30, 2018.
Shapiro, Marc B., "Scholars and Friends: Rabbi Jehiel Jacob Weinberg and Professor Samuel Atlas," *Torah U-Madda Journal* 7 (1997), 105–21.
Sherwin, Byron L., *Studies in Jewish Theology: Reflections in the Mirror of Tradition*, Portland, OR: Vallentine Mitchell, 2007.
Soloveitchik, Haym, "Re-evaluation of Eleventh-Century Ashkenaz," in: id., *Collected Essays*, vol. 2, Portland, OR: Littman Library of Jewish Civilization, 2014, 3–216.
Soloveitchik, Haym, "Three Themes in the 'Sefer Hasidim,'" *AJS Review* 1:1 (1976), 311–57.
Stern, Sacha, *Time and Process in Ancient Judaism*, Portland, OR: Littman Library of Jewish Civilization, 2007.
Tennant, F.R., *The Sources of the Doctrines of the Fall and Original Sin*, Cambridge: Cambridge University Press, 1903.
Wilensky, Mordechai, "Hasidic-Mitnaggedic Polemics in the Jewish Communities of Eastern Europe: The Hostile Phase," in: Gershon David Hundert (ed.), *Essential Papers on Hasidism: Origins to Present*, New York: New York University Press, 1991, 244–71.
Williams, N.P., *The Ideas of the Fall and of Original Sin: A Historical and Critical Study*, London: Longmans, Green and Co., 1927.
Wiskind-Elper, Ora, *Wisdom of the Heart: The Teachings of Rabbi Ya'akov of Izbica-Radzyn*, Philadelphia: Jewish Publication Society, 2010.
Yerushalmi, Yosef Hayim, *Zakhor: Jewish History and Jewish Memory*, Seattle: University of Washington Press, 1996.
Yisraeli, Oded, *Temple Portals: Studies in Aggadah and Midrash in the Zohar*, trans. Liat Keren, Jerusalem: Magnes, 2016.
Zuckier, Shlomo (ed.), *Contemporary Uses and Forms of Hasidut*, New York: Yeshiva University Press, 2022.

Suggestions for Further Reading

Bashevkin, David, *B'Rogez Rachem Tizkor*, Brooklyn 2015.
Bashevkin, David, "Jewish Thought: A Process, Not a Text," *Tradition* 52:4 (Fall 2020), 5–14.
Bashevkin, David, *Sin•a•gogue: Sin and Failure in Jewish Thought*, Boston, MA: Cherry Orchard Press, 2019.

Kurtz, Ernest / Ketcham, Katherine, *The Spirituality of Imperfection: Storytelling and the Search for Meaning*, New York, NY: Bantam Books, 1992.

Lambert, David A., *How Repentance Became Biblical: Judaism, Christianity, and the Interpretation of Scripture*, Oxford: Oxford University Press, 2016.

Rosensweig, Michael, *Mimini Mikhael: Essays on Yom Kippur and Teshuva*, Jerusalem: Maggid Press, 2023.

Christoph Böttigheimer

The Concept of Sin in Christianity

1 Introduction

The concept of sin is pivotal for the Christian religion, which considers itself a religion of salvation. For when referring to redemption, salvation, or deliverance, the question that immediately arises is "from what?". As fundamental as it is for the Christian religion to speak of sin, it is equally as difficult to conceive of an appropriate and overall comprehensible Christian theological understanding of sin, because the Christian discourse on sin and guilt is, these days, increasingly met with criticism and incomprehension. It is considered outdated and old-fashioned. Guilt, in particular, is not seldom suppressed, repudiated, and reduced to that which can be legally proven, and which can no longer be denied. Even "sophisticated speech" presents difficulties in its usage of the word "sin," as was discovered by the philosopher, Josef Pieper (1904–1997), in the 1970s:

> Why is it that we seem to find it difficult, if not downright impossible, to speak in impartial, matter-of-fact tones of sin? Upon reflection, it would seem rather odd to speak of sin using inflections no different from those we use when we are talking about the tangible things of everyday life. But odder yet is that, even when we are giving verbal expression to the specific content of our inner life – when the conversation turns to such topics as conscience, or justice, or death – the word "sin" rarely crops up. Obviously there is something about the topic that keeps us from invoking the word "sin" without exposing ourselves to the raised eyebrow or perhaps even to rhetorical "assault." Could this remarkable irritation in the word have something to do with the reality that this deceptively simple morpheme means and names?[1]

From where does this loss of plausibility, to which the Christian discourse on sin and guilt feels subjected today, stem? The causes are complex: The modern human sciences partly raised doubts about man's capacity for guilt. They traced back guilt to other causes preceding his freedom by analyzing the social conditions of human acts of freedom as well as by pointing to the fact of human entanglement in evil. Thus, individual accountability faded and the traditional discourse on sin and guilt was discredited as being naïve and indiscriminate. In addition to the objective side of sin, the contentual side was, thus, also called into question. Finally, the traditional understanding of sin is shaken by an increasingly strong pervasive assess-

---

1 Pieper, Josef, *The Concept of Sin*, trans. Edward T. Oakes, South Bend, IN: St Augustine's Press, 2001, 1–2.

https://doi.org/10.1515/9783111319452-002

ment of the degree of validity and obligation of objective norms. All this leads to a massive change in the rhetoric concerning sin: "What used to be a sin is, today, an embarrassment."[2]

The modern man's awareness of failure and guilt has not completely gone astray, he is very much aware of the various forms of inhumanity that exist; however, this fact contributes very little to a theology of sin. For the modern man no longer understands an incurrence of guilt towards himself, his fellow men, and the environment as having incurred guilt before and towards a transcendental reality. However, sin is more than a norm violation, it is based in the denial of the divine claim, in the defiance against God, and the negation of human dependency on God. The estrangement from God (*aversio a Deo*) leads to a disregard and infringement of divine commandments and, thus, to culpably committed acts. According to faith-based understanding, every guilt has a character of sin. Hence, the concept of sin is a religious concept; with the affirmation of the existence of God, it presupposes the knowledge that human life is owed to God. This presupposition, which is predominantly shared by other monotheistic religions – Judaism and Islam – today, is becoming, as previously implied, increasingly more fragile. When God is denied, then one's own culpable failure cannot be identified as sin. In other words: every discourse about sin is always also a discourse about God. "In and of itself, sin is not an issue, because it only comes into view *as sin* in relation to faith."[3]

Moreover, another reason for the present difficulty regarding an appropriate theology of sin lies in the Christian moral values of the modern era. The moralization of the concept of sin led to a crooked, and sometimes false, understanding of sin. A juridical view, which focused solely on the individual act, provoked a completely superficial understanding of sin and, consequently, an unyielding rigorism. In addition to this, such a superficial concept of sin was met with much critique by the European Enlightenment, which placed an additional burden on the traditional Christian discourse on sin and guilt. "Let's rid the world of the notion of *sin* – and let's soon send the notion of *punishment* that follows packing along behind it!"[4] Such was Friedrich Nietzsche's (1844–1900) programmatic battle cry against Christianity as a moral religion; similarly, he writes, "The extent to

2 Wellershoff, Dieter, *Der Himmel ist kein Ort*, Cologne: Kiepenheuer & Witsch, 2009, 248.

3 Dalferth, Ingolf U., *Sünde. Die Entdeckung der Menschlichkeit*, Leipzig: Evangelische Verlagsanstalt, 2020, 77.

4 Nietzsche, Friedrich, *Dawn. Thoughts on the Presumptions of Morality*, trans. Brittain Smith, The Complete Works of Friedrich Nietzsche 5, Stanford, CA: Stanford University Press, 2011, 147.

which I am supposed to be 'sinful' has escaped me utterly."[5] Unfortunately, preaching and theology were, in many ways, shaped by a one-sided concentration on the legal aspect, which resulted in a distorted understanding of sin. Furthermore, the fixation on sin was not uncommonly misused for moral disciplining and for the fomentation of a fear of God. Among others, Tilmann Moser (1938–2024) demonstrated this in his much-debated indictment, "Gottesvergiftung" ("Poisoned by God"), published in 1976.[6] In light of the manifold problems with the concept, the discourse on sin, today, is struggling and Pope John Paul II is perhaps correct in writing: "One must rediscover the sense for sin."[7]

Against this backdrop, how can the Christian concept of sin be expressed in such a way that it becomes comprehensible and, for the purpose of a religious interpretation of the basic human experiences, is appreciated as existentially enlightening and helpful? How can the Christian discourse on sin, once again, gain everyday practical relevance? Instead of pleading for an overcoming of the concept of sin,[8] one must assume its indispensability and be on the lookout for a theological revision, which must remain committed to the Word of God. In this context, it is of importance that there be a distinction specifically between the "treasure" of the Faith and its "earthen vessels,"[9] that is, between the substance and the form of biblical accounts, or as Pope John XXIII (1881–1963) formulated it during the initiation of the Second Vatican Council on October 11, 1962, between the "substance of the ancient doctrine of faith" and "the way in which it is presented."[10] In other words, God's Word is not unyielding but dynamic, and it must be expressed in a contemporary way if it is to remain alive.

Asking for the essence of the biblical accounts of the Faith and trying to understand this essence in a reflexive-speculative manner is a fundamental task of systematic theology. In the following, the biblical concept of sin will first be examined and its indispensable content will be determined. Then, a contemporary concept of sin will be developed, which, at the same time, takes into account developments in the history of theology and the Church.

---

5 Nietzsche, Friedrich, "Ecce homo," in: id., *The Case of Wagner. Twilight of the Idols. The Antichrist. Ecce Homo. Dionysius Dithyrambs. Nietzsche Contra Wagner*, trans. Adrian Del Caro et al., The Complete Works of Friedrich Nietzsche 9, Stanford, CA: Stanford University Press, 2011, 230.

6 Moser, Tilmann, *Gottesvergiftung*, Frankfurt a. M.: Suhrkamp, 1976.

7 John Paul II, *Bull of Indiction of the Jubilee for the 1950th anniversary of the Redemption* Aperite Portas Redemptori *(January 6, 1983)*, no. 8.

8 Cf. Huizing, Klaas, *Schluss mit Sünde! Warum wir eine neue Reformation brauchen*, Hamburg: Kreuz, 2017.

9 2 Cor 4:7. All quotations from the Bible are taken from the New American Standard Bible 1995.

10 John XXIII, "Opening Speech to the Council," in: Walter M. Abbott / Joseph Gallagher (eds.), *The Documents of Vatican II*, London et al.: Geoffrey Chapman, 1967, 715.

2 The Doctrine of Sin

2.1 The Biblical Concept of Sin

2.1.1 The Old Testament Concept of Sin

The subject of sin, with its many terms and semantic fields, is right at the center of the biblical message.[11] The reality of a behavior that contradicts the divine will is addressed already in the first few pages of the Old Testament and runs through the entire biblical covenant and salvation history like a golden thread. And yet, a standardized term (*terminus technicus*) is foreign to the Old Testament. Instead, one can find four Hebrew root words that are pivotal for the concept of "sin": חטא (to go wrong, to transgress a commandment of God); רשׁע (to be wicked, to act wickedly); עוה (to bend, to twist the way of God) und פשׁע (to rebel, to transgress). These main terms indicate a violation of an order of life and community, behind which is the will of the God of the covenant, who wants to know that mankind's decisions are directed towards him.[12] "The concept of the violation of norms, which dominates these terms, refers to the experience of an overall order of life that defines life as a whole and which is recognized as an unconditional authority."[13] Any offense against the law or rather the moral-religious order represents a rebellion against God, who is the author of the law. Since from God's point of view, the Old Testament's main terms within the semantic field of sin qualify as legal, ethically-social, or cultic transgressions, they also include the unintentionally and unconsciously committed act, irrespective of the subjective perception of guilt.

A characteristic of the Old Testament concept of sin is, furthermore, a tight link between sin and calamity: the behavior that qualifies as a sin, together with its consequences, forms a unity.[14] Sinful acts and their consequences are so tightly intertwined "that their order can, essentially, be reversed: from punishment one can infer guilt and sin."[15] The reason for this connection between deeds and con-

11 Cf. Berkenkopf, Christian, *Sünde als ethisches Dispositiv. Über die biblische Grundlegung des Sündenbegriffs*, Paderborn et al: Ferdinand Schöningh, 2013, 20–56.

12 Cf. Num 14:11; Deut 28:15–44.

13 Eichrodt, Walter, "Sünde im AT," in: Herbert Haag (ed.), *Bibel-Lexikon*, Zurich et al.: Benziger, ^{3}1982, 1664.

14 Cf. Gen 15:16; Josh 7:24–25; 2 Sam 24:17; 1 Kgs 17:18; Isa 30:12–13; Jer 32:18; Hos 5:5; Ps 31:11; Lam 5:7; Prov 10:3; 11:31.

15 Vrienzen, Theodorus Christian, "Sünde und Schuld im AT," in: *RGG*, vol. 6, Tübingen: Mohr, ^{3}1986, 482.

sequences ("Tun-Ergehen-Zusammenhang") lies with God himself. His judgment or punishment is to keep the individual imprisoned in the sphere of sin brought about by the evil act itself. However, even in the Old Testament there exists an objection to the connection between deeds and consequences in terms of a generational liability:[16] "The person who sins will die. The son will not bear the punishment for the father's iniquity, nor will the father bear the punishment for the son's iniquity; the righteousness of the righteous will be upon himself, and the wickedness of the wicked will be upon himself."[17]

The sinful act not only affects the individual offender, but also has a bearing on his fellow man. It results in social consequences, which can even have repercussions for generations to come. As a result, the aspect of community plays a central role in the Old Testament concept of sin.[18] However, the individual person does not simply merge into the community of the people of Israel, for every single individual co-influences and co-determines the fate of the community. Hence, the Old Testament not only recognizes the mutual obligation, but also the obligation of the individual person,[19] upon which the New Testament places an even greater emphasis.

Sin is more than a mere wrong deed that can be seen as an isolated act. As a violation of the moral-religious order of life, it is tantamount to a breach of the covenant. Every sinful act is, therefore, of collective relevance. It impairs communion with God, with fellow human beings and with the environment, or as Christian Berkenkopf (b. 1982) describes it,

> Sin, whether it be a transgression, a crime, or a perversion, in every case, has consequences for the entire community, for sin effectuates a disruption in the cosmic order created by God and is, thus, a transgression against the holiness of God himself. Thus, if a single human being sins, the results are no different than if many human beings sin. Even the act of one individual causes consequences for the entire community, much like a contamination.[20]

Considering this, it is understandable why the Old Testament reasoning fixates more on the objective facts than on the inner participation of the offender. "*In the Old Testament, one cannot speak of a broken personal relationship between the sinner and God as the actual and deciding consequence of the evil act, even less so*

16 Cf. Exod 20:5.

17 Ezek 18:20; cf. Job 9:22; Eccl 7:15; 9:1–2.

18 Cf. Gen 9:25–27; 2 Kgs 24:3–4; 1 Sam 2:33–34; 2 Sam 12:13–14; Exod 20:5; 34:7; Lev 26:39–40; Deut 5:9; Neh 9:2.

19 Cf. Ezek 18:3–4.

20 Berkenkopf, *Sünde als ethisches Dispositiv*, 53.

of what later Christian theology will ultimately call a 'permanent state of sin' (reatus culpae)."[21]

While the sinful act and its consequences were given much emphasis during Israel's early years,[22] the Prophets counter the danger of a formalization and an externalization of sin by increasingly connecting it with the hearts of mankind. Sin becomes a personal process[23] in which each individual is guilty before God. Because everyone is responsible for him- or herself, the Prophets reject clan liability, or rather a collective guilt.[24] The more sin is placed into the heart, or rather the center of a person, the more clearly it is understood as an inner rejection of the divine love revealed in the covenant. It is grounded in a rebelliousness against God and expresses itself in self-centeredness, inhumanity, and an orientation towards self-made values and goods. In this personal sense, the Old Testament can allegorically also speak of adultery or betrayal, prostitution, etc. rather than of sin.

In the narrative of the Fall of Man,[25] the nature and condition of mankind, which ensue from a relationship with God affected by sin, are broached. In doing so, sin is depicted as an overall human phenomenon[26] and three fundamental traits are illustrated: it springs from the freedom of man, expresses itself in the desire to be like God, and manifests itself amidst social interconnections. "Herein lies, if at all, the Old Testament root of the major hypothesis regarding the Christian-theological interpretation of sin: namely that this term, ultimately, does not signify individual human acts, but rather mankind's existence and condition before God."[27]

2.1.2 The New Testament Concept of Sin

In his message of the Kingdom of God,[28] Jesus focuses on God's boundless compassion. Nevertheless, the testimonials of the Synoptic Gospels leave no doubt about the fact that he, similar to John the Baptist, was convinced of Israel's sinfulness and

---

21 Pesch, Otto Hermann, *Frei sein aus Gnade. Theologische Anthropologie*, Freiburg i.Br.: Herder, 1983, 120.

22 Cf. Gen 20:9; Num 22:34; 1 Sam 14:1–15.

23 Cf. Jer 3:17; 6:7; 9:25; Ez 36:26 and others.

24 Cf. Ezek 18.

25 Cf. Gen 3.

26 Cf. Gen 6:5; Ps 51:11–12.

27 Pesch, *Frei sein aus Gnade*, 119.

28 Cf. Böttigheimer, Christoph, *Die Reich-Gottes-Botschaft Jesu. Verlorene Mitte christlichen Glaubens*, Freiburg i.Br.: Herder, 2020.

need to repent.[29] However, while the Baptist's sermon appears to be a merciless and threatening message of the Last Judgment,[30] God's offer of mercy is pivotal for Jesus. To be sure, Jesus also views Israel as a single collective of calamities; however, he does not associate with it the threat of God's wrath, but rather he proclaims God's eschatological election. In doing so, he apodictically promises the Salvation of the approaching Kingdom of God, while mentioning God's wrath only conditionally. Sinners are invited to entrust themselves to God's forthcoming, unconditionally forgiving mercy and to respond to the divine offer of mercy with an affirmation of faith.

Just as the Old Testament, the New Testament,[31] likewise, does not deal with the sinful act as such, but rather with the triumph over sin. The goal is not the humiliation, the exposure, or even the condemnation of the sinner, but rather his salvation. Instead of condemning him, Jesus invites him into the Kingdom of God. He calls for his repentance[32] and because of the approaching reign and forthcoming Love of God, he offers him the opportunity of an unconditional new beginning.[33] Thus, Jesus proves himself to be Lord over sin; as one who breaks the spell of evil once and for all and who frees mankind from the bondage of sin. With that, the whole human being, in his psychosomatic unity, comes into view. This becomes clear, amongst other things, through the great number of healing accounts, which frequently contain words of forgiveness.[34] It concerns the sinner in all of his existence, his wholeness, and his being healed. If, however, Jesus' holistic offer of healing is refused in the form of a denial of faith, what follows is death, instead of the forgiveness of sins: "For the wages of sin is death, but the free gift of God is eternal life in Christ Jesus our Lord."[35]

The New Testament's concept of sin, to a great extent, is in agreement with that of the Old Testament; however, the personal dimension, as it was emphasized by the prophets, undergoes a stronger accentuation. It becomes even clearer that sin, since it is contrasted less with the law than with God's offer of salvation in Jesus Christ, is to be referred directly to God. Insofar as God, through his incarnate son, becomes a fellow man to mankind, sin, ultimately, is directed not only against God, but, just as it was in the Old Testament, against all others, indeed, ultimately against the entirety of creation. It infringes on the Commandment of

29 Cf. Mark 1:14–15; Luke 13:2–5; 15:4–9.17–32; Matt 20:28; 26:28; John 8:7.
30 Cf. Matt 3:7–12 par Luke 3:7–9.16–17.
31 Cf. Berkenkopf, *Sünde als ethisches Dispositiv*, 57–81.
32 Cf. Mark 1:15; 2:17.
33 Cf. John 8:3–11; Luke 15:11–31.
34 Cf. Mark 2:1–12 par; 5:24–35 par; 10:46–52 par.
35 Rom 6:23.

God's Love, Love of One's Neighbor and of Oneself.[36] In light of the divine offer of love, which is revealed in his mission, Jesus ties the salvific gift of reconciliation to mankind's willingness to reconcile,[37] whereby the social aspect of sin is, again, underlined and mankind's relationship with God is placed in the context of humanity. It also includes the responsibility of others toward the sinner, specifically the duty to rebuke.[38]

Furthermore, Jesus radicalizes sin, that is, he internalizes it, in order to sharpen "the conscience in view of the present hour of salvation, in view of the gift of God, and the afflictions of mankind"[39] and to win over mankind to God's unconditional forgiveness.[40] The tendency towards internalization[41] is also reflected in Jesus' perfecting of the law: He demands far less its external observance than the internal attitude that must precede it. "For from within, out of the heart of men, proceed the evil thoughts, fornications, thefts, murders, adulteries, deeds of coveting and wickedness, as well as deceit, sensuality, envy, slander, pride and foolishness. All these evil things proceed from within and defile the man."[42] With Jesus, sin doesn't so much become the focal point in terms of an evil act, but rather in terms of an inner turning away from God; what is more important is the subjective side, the wanting to be like God, letting oneself be seduced by or rather the admittance of evil. By focusing on the human heart rather than the outward fulfillment of the law, Jesus reveals the full depths of human sin.

An internalization of sin and the associated demand for an inner attitude that corresponds to God's offer of salvation permeates the entire New Testament, especially the Pauline and Johannine writings. Against this background, one can justifiably speak of a biblical-personal understanding of sin. This means that man is not only responsible for an act carried out, but already for his attitude. "You have heard that it was said, 'You shall not commit adultery'; but I say to you that everyone who looks at a woman with lust for her has already committed adultery with her in his heart."[43] In the strong emphasis on introspection as the place and source of sin, the focus is primarily on the individual along with their inner need, which is why Jesus decidedly rejects the Old Testament's connection between

36 Cf. Luke 15:21.
37 Cf. Matt 6:12.14–15.
38 Cf. Matt 18:15–17; cf. Gal 2:11–14.
39 Häring, Bernhard, *Frei in Christus. Moraltheologie für die Praxis des christlichen Lebens*, vol. 1, Freiburg i.Br.: Herder, 1989, 369.
40 Cf. Luke 15:11–32.
41 Cf. Matt 5:21–32.
42 Mark 7:21–23.
43 Matt 5:27–28.

deeds and consequences ("Tun-Ergehen-Zusammenhang"): "And His disciples asked Him, 'Rabbi, who sinned, this man or his parents, that he would be born blind?' Jesus answered, 'It was neither that this man sinned, nor his parents [. . .].'"[44]

Like the Old Testament, the New Testament also understands sin to be a transgression against the divine commandment or rather as a disregard for the divine will, which includes its omission: "Therefore, to one who knows the right thing to do and does not do it, to him it is sin."[45] At the same time, it reinforces the element of free will, which is intimately connected to the inner part of the person, to their heart. Jesus consciously confronts the free decision, the human heart with God, because both virtue and sin originate from the center of the person. With the free decision of man comes his responsibility.[46] This is particularly emphasized by John, who primarily speaks of sin in the singular, and "is even exacerbated by the emphasis on the decisive nature of Christ's mission (John 8:24; 15:22)."[47]

Concerning the Pauline concept of sin, while, on the one hand, it is similar to that of the Old Testament, it, on the other hand, exhibits significant differences. There is a fundamental agreement insofar as the Pauline concept of sin is also characterized by an active component: sin consists in the active violation of the divine commandments or the law. However, the word "law" already addresses the discrepancy with Old Testament thinking. According to Paul, the law comes from God and as such is good. As a matter of fact, however, it can never be completely fulfilled by man, which is why it can only become a means of salvation if man becomes aware of his powerlessness and his sinfulness through the law and, thus, recognizes and understands the righteousness of God revealed in the Gospel.[48] Thus, the "law, holy in itself" proves "itself a helper, encroached upon by sin ([Rom] 7:9–13)."[49] So, while both times it is the law that convicts people of their sins, in the Old Testament it stands for God's common will, while in Paul it becomes the unveiling verdict of God. "The purpose of emphasizing the aporia of the law in Romans and Galatians is to defend the 'sinful Gentiles' as

44 John 9:2–3, cf. Luke 13:4–5.
45 Jas 4:17.
46 Cf. Matt 15:19.
47 Scheffczyk, Leo, "Sünde," in: Heinrich Fries (ed.), *Handbuch theologischer Grundbegriffe*, vol. 2, Munich: Kösel, 1963, 600.
48 Cf. Rom 7:7–25.
49 Vögtle, Anton, "Sünde im NT," in: *Lexikon für Theologie und Kirche*, vol. 9, Freiburg i. Br.: Herder, [2]1964, 1176.

equal members of the new people of God in Christ."[50] A similar continuity with a simultaneous discrepancy can also be observed with regard to the connection between deeds and consequences ("Tun-Ergehen-Zusammenhang"). Although here as there it is God Himself who holds man captive in the sphere of evil caused by the evil deed, in the Old Testament, however, this sphere of doom is understood primarily as the repercussion of sin upon the sinner himself. In contrast, Paul links this sphere of evil primarily to the fact that all human beings "fall short of the glory of God,"[51] thus explaining the insurmountable nature of sin.

2.2 The Concept of Sin at Different Stages in the History of Theology

2.2.1 The Early Church

The penitential practice of the Early Church expresses the conviction that sin, together with its social consequences, must be banished from the Christian community. Either the excommunication penance or the church penance serves this purpose, which makes necessary a differentiated evaluation of the sins. If the former was punished with expulsion from the church, the latter took place within the church. While capital or mortal sins (*peccatum mortale*) are subject to a canonical, public, and one-time penance, daily or venial sins (*peccatum veniale*) are subject to private penance. In this way, the concept of sin develops further in the context of the Church's practice of penance – more precisely: it follows it. The consequence of this is a tendency towards a more objective, factual understanding of sin.

2.2.2 The Middle Ages

Just as the Early Church's penitential system, the medieval theology of sin essentially concerns itself with making practicable answers and assistance available to the ecclesiastical discipline. This is necessary in particular due to the fact that the penitential practice of the $6^{th}/7^{th}$ century, through the influence of Iro-Scottish monasticism, further developed towards an auricular confession, which could be

50 Stendahl, Krister, "Sünde und Schuld im NT," in: *Religion in Geschichte und Gegenwart*, vol. 6, Tübingen: Mohr, [3]1986, 486.
51 Rom 3:23.

repeated multiple times. Mortal or rather grave sins are subject to auricular confession and due to the repeatability of the confession, these were increasingly broadened. However, the theological criterion for distinguishing between mortal and venial sins is disputed throughout early and high scholasticism. Leading the way is Thomas Aquinas (1225–1274), who does not determine the two categories of sin through the object of the sinful act, but with the help of the subjective orientation, i.e., in view of the inner disorder associated with the sin:[52] While the disorder of grave sins extends to the ultimate goal itself, in the sense of an absolute decision against God, the disorder of venial sins concerns the right use of creaturely things, which should ultimately serve as a means of strengthening one's relationship with God.[53] In this context, Aquinas connects the four cardinal virtues (prudence, justice, fortitude, temperance)[54] with the ongoing discourse on mortal sins and vices and, following Gregory the Great (c. 540–604), names seven mortal sins: *superbia, avaritia, luxuria, invidia, gula, ira, acedia* (pride, greed, lust, envy, gluttony, anger, and sloth).[55] Against the biblical view of sin, which associates it with a quasi-personal, calamitous power that mesmerizes and destroys man, Thomas Aquinas, following Augustine (354–430), understands sin, above all, as a reality in man himself. It springs directly from man's will: "[S]in is nothing else than a bad human act. Now that an act is a human act is due to its being voluntary."[56] With this, the tendency to demythologize or anthropologize the understanding of sin, which can already be seen in the New Testament, finds a continuation and deepening in Aquinas. However, the close connection between sin and punishment is not broken through the internalization of sin; man remains imprisoned in the bondage of sin, but behind all this, there is no longer any external alien power, but man himself. If, according to Aquinas, sin is to be understood as man's turning away from God, as a rejection of divine love, then through sin, man is bent back towards himself, he makes himself a substitute god and, because he remains alone with himself, his own servant. Thus, Aquinas himself writes that the punishment of sin appears as an inner-human affair: God leaves man alone with his false spirit.[57] Against this background, it is understandable why Aquinas views hatred of God and pride as the greatest forms of sin. Since

52 Cf. Thomas Aquinas, *ST* I–II, q. 81, a. 1.

53 Cf. Thomas Aquinas, *ST* I–II, q. 88–89.

54 Cf. Thomas Aquinas, *ST* I–II, q. 64.

55 Cf. Thomas Aquinas, *ST* II–II q. 84.

56 Thomas Aquinas, *ST* I–II, q. 71, a. 6. All translations of the *Summa Theologiae* are taken from Thomas Aquinas, *Summa Theologica*, trans. Fathers of the English Dominican Province, 3 vols., New York et al.: Benziger Brothers, 1947.

57 Cf. Thomas Aquinas, *ST* I–II, q. 87, a. 1.

man cannot reverse his estrangement from God[58] himself, he is fundamentally dependent on divine mercy. Redemption through God is, thus, focused on deliverance from sin.

The different perspectives of sin are evident: While the Bible thinks in more mythological terms and understands sin as an extra-human power, powerless in relation to God, the concept of sin in the Middle Ages experiences an anthropocentric turn, so to speak: It is only the sinful man who is seen in opposition to God. The tendency towards a personalization of sin, which can already be observed in Paul, thus, finds its implementation in medieval theology.

2.2.3 The Modern Era

Aquinas' approach, in which the differentiation of sins is based not on the action but on the attitude, is superseded in the late scholastic period by a resurgence of the objective understanding of sin. The view of the nature of sin and the overall moral context loses importance. The focus is on the individual case (*causa*), which is assessed using general moral principles. Liberation from a fruitless casuistry, i.e., from a juridical and rigid doctrine of sin, in modern times, is brought about, amongst others, by the so-called Catholic Tübingen School. Using the biblical basis as a starting point, the Catholic Tübingen School specifically asks about the nature of sin and about the guilt of man as the acting subject responsible to his conscience. In addition, reflection on conscience, in modern times, leads to a stronger internalization of sin. The regained biblical-personal understanding of sin is eventually reflected in the Second Vatican Council: "Examining his heart, man finds that he has inclinations toward evil too, and is engulfed by manifold ills which cannot come from his good Creator."[59] Therefore, sin is not so much about individual transgressions, but more so about the relationship with God. The Catechism of the Catholic Church also follows this line: as "an offence against reason, truth and right conscience" and as a "failure in genuine love for God and neighbour,"[60] sin essentially marks the denial of man's dependence on God. The differentiation between venial sin and mortal sin depends on the degree of destruction of the love relationship with God: "*Mortal sin* destroys charity in the

58 Cf. Thomas Aquinas, *ST* I–II, q. 72, a. 4; q. 77, a. 8.

59 *GS* 13. All translations of texts of the Second Vatican Council are taken from Abbott, Walter M. / Gallagher, Joseph (eds.), *The Documents of Vatican II*, London et al.: Geoffrey Chapman, 1967.

60 *Catechism of the Catholic Church*, London: Burns & Oates, 1999, no. 1849. Abbreviated as *CCC* in the following.

heart of man by a grave violation of God's law [. . .]. *Venial sin* allows charity to subsist, even though it offends and wounds it."[61]

3 The Doctrine of Original Sin

3.1 Biblical Foundations

3.1.1 The Old Testament

The Old Testament concept of sin can hardly be seen as a precursor of the doctrine of original sin. At best, the narrative of the Fall of Man in Genesis 3 can be considered significant. This is an etiology, i.e., it speaks of "what never was and always is"; it is revealed "what everyone knows and yet does not know."[62] The human situation of perdition, for which mankind is held responsible, is discussed in a way that is generally understandable. The broken relationship with God is traced back to the sin of Adam. What is striking, however, is that the Old Testament does not make any reference to the narrative of the Fall of Man in connection with a general fall of man into sin. According to Genesis 3, the crossing[63] of a boundary set for man,[64] as well as the respective desire to be like God leads to a profound defect in the relationship between God and man. As a result of eating from the Tree of the Knowledge of Good and Evil,[65] the original harmoniousness is lost, and with it the sanctifying grace of God. Thenceforth, social reality is characterized by distrust and fatal violence, and the dichotomy of human existence is reflected in the knowledge of good and evil. By failing to recognize his own creatureliness, the self-empowered and God-defying human being must realize that he lacks the potential for his own perfection. Evil, as the downside of good, is not only inevitably associated with the good that he has produced himself; in fact, this evil exerts such an irresistible attraction upon him that a disposition to evil develops within him.

The Old Testament contains tentative indications that Adam's sin and the loss of original grace associated with it would not remain without consequences for

61 *CCC*, no. 1855.

62 Zenger, Erich, "Zum biblischen Hintergrund der christlichen Erbsündentheologie," in: Siegfried Wiedenhofer (ed.), *Erbsünde – was ist das?*, Regensburg: Pustet, 1999, 25.

63 Cf. Gen 3:14–19.

64 Cf. Gen 2:17.

65 Cf. Gen 3:5.

his descendants. For example, Genesis 5:3 states that Adam begot "a son like himself, in his image" and "gave him the name Set." He, therefore, was not conceived in the likeness of God,[66] but in the likeness of the fallen creature. Accordingly, the psalmist confesses, "Behold, I was brought forth in iniquity, / And in sin my mother conceived me."[67] Only Paul explicitly concludes that "through the one man's disobedience the many were made sinners."[68]

3.1.2 Paul

It is Paul who reflects upon the fate of sin in terms of its universality and, thus, its radical nature and he is the first to develop a theological doctrine of sin. In doing so, he differentiates between sin in the singular, the fundamental sin (ἁμαρτία), and sins in the plural, i.e., those transgressions that arise from the center of man, the "flesh" (παράπτωμα). It is the individual sins and their consequences that lead Paul to recognize a universal sinful fate; the individual sins ultimately arise from a fundamental sin, they arise from disobedience, man's turning away from God.

In his Letter to the Romans, Paul starts with the assumption of universal salvation through Jesus Christ and, from there, speaks of the universality of sin.[69] In the course of his Adam-Christ typology,[70] he sharpens the Christian concept of sin towards a general need for redemption, although the idea of original sin as such is still foreign to him. It is only later that attempts are made to make it clear why all human beings – with the exception of Mary[71] – are in need of divine redemption from the moment of birth.

Paul himself speaks neither of any kind of inheritance nor of man's being guilty from birth. Nevertheless, for him, sin is a disastrous characteristic of man's

---

66 Cf. Gen 1:27.
67 Ps 51:5.
68 Rom 5:19.
69 Cf. Rom 3:23; 5:12.
70 Cf. Rom 5:12–21.
71 According to the statement of faith that Pope Pius IX (1792–1878) elevated to the rank of infallible dogma on December 8, 1854, the Virgin and Mother of God Mary was conceived without original sin: "the Most Blessed Virgin Mary, at the first instant of her conception, by the singular grace and privilege of almighty God and in view of the merits of Jesus Christ, the Savior of the human race, was preserved immune from all stain of original sin" (Denzinger, Heinrich, *Compendium of Creeds, Definitions, and Declarations on Matters of Faith and Morals*, Peter Hünermann / Robert Fastiggi / Anne Englund Nash (eds.), San Francisco: Ignatius Press, 2012, no. 2803 [abbreviated as DH in the following]).

nature; "all have sinned and fall short of the glory of God."[72] Sin is consequently an expression of enmity towards God. As a lack of acknowledgment of dependence on God, it is "far less a single lawless or unlawful act, but rather the fundamental ingratitude towards and conflict with God, in which man, mysteriously, always finds himself, into which he has hopelessly fallen in spite of his longing for God (Rom 7:5–24) and which then, through his individual and concrete decisions, goes against God (cf. 1:24–31; Gal 5:19ff; Eph 2:1ff)."[73]

With this, Paul personalizes sin: He speaks of sin in terms of a fate under which, from the beginning, Jews and Gentiles alike dwell,[74] in the sense of a quasi-personal power that has an effect on and in people. "[. . .] the willing is present in me, but the doing of the good is not. For the good that I want, I do not do, but I practice the very evil that I do not want. But if I am doing the very thing I do not want, I am no longer the one doing it, but sin which dwells in me."[75] Thus, the consequence of the Fall is a being sold to a false desire that seduces one into a culpable self-reversal and allows the weakness of man to come to light.

Man does not first make himself a sinner, rather all men are sinners,[76] they are enslaved[77] to their own passions. This supra-personal destiny, which severely restricts the will of the individual but in no way excuses the individual, cannot be broken and overcome through obedience to the law, but only through obedience to faith, through faith in Jesus Christ. They are "justified as a gift by His grace through the redemption which is in Christ Jesus."[78] Paul, thus, understands sin as well as grace as a situation in which man lives.[79] In order to open people's hearts to the grace of God, which leads to life, and which is greater than all evil, Paul radicalizes sin and mercilessly uncovers the abyss of human guilt. Ultimately, all individual sins lead back to a fundamental sin, to man's self-assertion before God: instead of being dependent solely on the grace of God, man would like to safeguard his life through what he has created himself.

Paul speaks of sin primarily in terms of a fate that Jews and Gentiles alike face from the beginning. However, he sees the reason for this not in any kind of theory of original sin, but in the universality of Jesus Christ's act of redemption.

---

72 Rom 3:23; cf. 5:12.

73 Limbeck, Meinrad, "Sünde im NT," in: Herbert Haag (ed.), *Bibel-Lexikon*, Zurich et al.: Benziger, ^{3}1982, 1673.

74 Cf. Rom 5:12; 7:19–20.

75 Rom 7:18–20.

76 Cf. Rom 5:21; 6:17.23; 7:14.

77 Cf. Rom 6:12–14.

78 Rom 3:24.

79 Cf. Rom 5:12–21.

From the universal significance of Christ's salvation, he infers the universal significance of Adam's damnation. Although Paul's considerations in the Letter to the Romans are anything but insignificant for the later doctrine of original sin, it, nevertheless, must be stated that Paul, as already noted, develops neither a doctrine of original sin nor any kind of transference theory. He understands sin as well as grace as a constellation that determines every human being. What Paul thinks in terms of mythology is, at this point, only later reduced to an anthropological concept.

> The text [Rom 5:12–21] – in simplified terms – merely says: Sin is as old as mankind. Paul reflects not on the 'how' but on the fact concerning the 'that' (of death and sin). There exists, therefore, a solidarity of mankind in sin. But an original sin of the individual as guilt before God cannot be derived from this. Guilt exists only as personal sin.[80]

According to Paul, every human being sins and, like salvation in Christ, sin is universal.

3.2 Historical Development

3.2.1 Augustine

The actual authority on the doctrine of original sin (*peccatum originale*) is Augustine. For him, even more than for Paul, the so-called narrative of the Fall of Man in Genesis 3 plays an important role. His original sin construct, which has profoundly shaped Western theology to this day, is based upon it. Unlike the Western Church, the Eastern Church did not develop a doctrine of original sin; the idea of the perpetuation of Adam's sin is foreign to her. Nevertheless, she also assumes that Adam's fall from grace was not without consequences, since the punishments for Adam's sin are passed on to all people, especially corruption of the body and the doom of death as well as the depravity of nature. In this respect, according to the teachings of the Eastern Church, all people are in need of divine redemption.

Augustine assumes that divine grace is completely undeserved and inaccessible and, inversely, emphasizes the total corruption of mankind and man's inability to obtain his salvation on his own. More specifically, an inevitable disposition to sin passes from Adam to all human beings. Behind this is a statement by Paul,

80 Sand, Alexander, "Sünde, Gesetz und Tod. Zum Menschenbild des Paulus," in: Nobert Lohfink et al., *Zum Problem der Erbsünde. Theologische und philosophische Versuche*, Essen: Ludgerus, 1981, 85.

which Augustine, however, misinterprets, since he reads Romans 5:12 according to the Ambrosiaster – he did not know the original Greek text – as follows: "Per unum hominem peccatum intravit in mundum, et per peccatum mors; et ita in omnes homines pertransiit, in quo omnes peccaverunt (Rom V,12)."[81] Augustine adds "peccatum" as a subject for "pertransiit" and, on the other hand, understands the "in quo" relatively, related to "per unum hominem": "Through one man sin entered the world and through sin death, and thus it has passed to all men, in whom all have sinned."[82] According to the original Greek text, however, "mors" would have belonged to "pertransiit" as a subject, and the "in quo" (ἐφ' ᾧ) – on this point modern-day exegetes largely agree – should have been understood causally (because, therefore because) instead of relatively. "Therefore, just as through one man sin entered into the world, and death through sin, and so death spread to all men, because all sinned" (Rom 5:12).

According to his interpretation, Augustine concludes that *in* Adam all humans have sinned, since all human beings were already present in Adam or rather all of humanity was represented by Adam.[83] Augustine can explain the transfer of Adam's original sin to all human beings only by means of procreation, such that the original sin must appear as a natural fate. According to the principle of procreation, the life of all future offspring is already contained in Adam, and, thus, all of humanity has fallen in and with Adam. "[. . .] [T]he sin of that one [Adam] is the death of all, and all perished in that one [. . .] [T]his was not said on account of the choice of each individual, but on account of the origin of the seed from which all were going to come. In accord with this origin all were in that one man, and all these who were still nothing in themselves were that one man."[84] The sin of Adam, thus, becomes a "natural sin" that now stands for the fall of every human being. Every human being is born in Adam's sin, he inherits it with his nature. This determination is the real guilt of every human being, since everyone sinned in Adam himself. Human existence, thus, appears corrupt in its entirety and incapable of salvation; it is inextricably entangled in guilt and sin. For Augustine, the depravity of man is, at the same time, the justification for the practice of infant baptism. It is necessary for salvation because Adam's original sin is imputed as guilt to every human being from birth.

---

81 Augustine, *In Johannis Evangelium tractatus* XLIX,11 (PL 35,1752).

82 Augustine, *Tractates on the Gospel of John, 28–54*, trans. John W. Rettig, Fathers of the Church: A New Translation, Washington, D.C.: The Catholic University of America Press, 1993, 249.

83 Cf. Augustine., *De pecc. mer.* IX,10 (PL 44,115).

84 Augustine, *Op. Imp.* IV,104 (PL 45,1400f.). English translation from: id., *Answer to the Pelagians, III: Unfinished Work in Answer to Julian*, trans. Roland J. Teske, The Works of Saint Augustine I/25, Hyde Park, NY: New City Press, 1999, 466.

Although all human beings sinned in Adam and every human being is corrupted as a result of Adam's sin, Augustine still wants to see human freedom and, thus, human responsibility preserved. Original sin possesses a real character of guilt and sin, in which man, as a punishment, is found guilty; however, it is not a personal sin. Strictly speaking, however, original sin, as a natural determination, cannot be the result of human abuse of freedom and, thus, cannot be ascribed to human responsibility. Although man does not become a sinner in a personal sense as a result of original sin, he is, nevertheless, guilty before God and this from birth. The obvious contradiction – guilt without personal involvement – could not be resolved even for Augustine and the antinomy between freedom and bondage is now coming to a head in the context of the modern, enlightened understanding of freedom. In light of the idea of autonomy, the doctrine of original sin appears paradoxical to the greatest extent; in terms of the analysis of freedom, it can no longer be maintained today.

Nevertheless, Augustine's original sin construct, to this day, forms the basis of both Catholic and Protestant hamartiology and soteriology. According to Catholic teaching,

> the overwhelming misery which oppresses men and their inclination towards evil and death cannot be understood apart from their connection with Adam's sin and the fact that he has transmitted to us a sin with which we are all born afflicted, a sin which is the "death of the soul" (cf. Council of Trent: DS 1512). Because of this certainty of faith, the Church baptizes for the remission of sins even tiny infants who have not committed personal sin (cf. Council of Trent: DS 1514).[85]

3.2.2 The Reception of Augustine's Doctrine of *peccatum originale*

The Augustinian doctrine of *peccatum originale* has never been formally defined by the Church. At the Synod of Carthage (418), which emphasized the existence of original sin and the need for grace,[86] there is merely mention of something pertaining to original sin, which passes from Adam's sin to the descendants,[87] and which makes infant baptism necessary. This necessity is emphasized by the doctrine of *limbus puerorum*: children who die unbaptized neither perish nor do they attain salvation, but rather they find themselves in an intermediate state.[88]

85 *CCC*, no. 403.

86 Cf. DH 222–30.

87 Cf. DH 223.

88 Cf. DH 224. On April 20, 2007, Pope Benedict XVI (1927–2022) approved the statement of the International Theological Commission according to which the doctrine of the *limbus puerorum* is

The Synod does not speak of hereditary guilt, but only of the general nature of sin and of an inherited punishment. Moreover, the resolutions of Carthage cannot be understood as universal Church teaching, since their recognition is questionable. On the one hand, essential parts of Pope Zosimus' (d. 418) letter of reply, his circular letter called "Epistula Tractoria,"[89] were lost, and on the other hand, the resolutions were hardly adopted as they were not made unanimously.[90]

In the West, where a systematic treatment of Augustine's doctrine of the *peccatum originale* was attempted, original sin was, ultimately, formally established. In terms of content, however, compromises were made, especially with regard to the quality of the guilt and the way it was conveyed. For the state of original sin was regarded as sin only in an analogous sense and was defined in the absence of supernatural justice or in the absence of the perfect order of human nature. The Catechism of the Catholic Church expresses this as follows: Original sin "is a sin 'contracted' and not 'committed' – a state and not an act,"[91] it is a sin "only in an analogical sense."[92] With this, the original depth of the Augustinian concept of sin was gradually lost; original sin became a 'pre-personal guilt', a mere 'analogous sin'. This tendency can be observed up until very recently, since "original sin is now mostly interpreted by excluding or concealing its core principle [one's own guilt before God because of Adam's sin]."[93] The reason lies in the difficulties associated with Augustine's theory of original sin. On the one hand, it makes Adam's sin a natural determination, while on the other hand, it ascribes a character of guilt and sin to the *peccatum originale*. Furthermore, in terms of the beginning and the unity of mankind, Augustine assumes what is today an untenable idea, namely monogenism. Last but not least, Augustine's naturalized concept of sin conflicts with the New Testament concept of salvation. According to Augustine, the consequences of sin continue to exist in spite of the redemption given through Jesus Christ. Because salvation does not embrace nature as a whole, there exists a dualism between nature and supernatural salvation.

---

to be classified as no longer meaningful; it is an older theological opinion that is no longer supported by the Church's Magisterium.

89 Cf. DH 231.

90 Piet Fransen (1913–1983) is convinced that today there are serious doubts "that this papal approval [Epistula Tractoria] suffices for an 'ex cathedra definition' of each of these anathematisms, both because of the content of the papal statement and because of the testimonies of Augustine and Prosper of Aquitaine" (Fransen, Piet, "Karthago, Synode v. 418," in: *Lexikon für Theologie und Kirche*, vol. 6, Freiburg i.Br.: Herder, ²1961, 4).

91 *CCC*, no. 404.

92 *CCC*, no. 404.

93 Häring, Hermann, *Die Macht des Bösen. Das Erbe Augustins*, Zurich et al.: Benziger / Mohn, 1979, 264.

Like the Synod of Carthage, that of Orange (529), which also dealt with the topics of original sin and grace,[94] was not uncontroversial, which is why its writings were never given the status of dogma – in the strict sense, they do not represent a dogmatic doctrinal decision. This was due to the fact that the doctrinal recognition given two years later by Pope Boniface II (d. 532) did not refer to the canons, which, in any case, fell into oblivion from the 10th to the 16th century and regained importance only after the Council of Trent.[95] Nevertheless, the canons of this provincial synod exerted a significant influence insofar as they confirmed Augustine's doctrine of original sin[96] and, thus, enabled it to achieve a certain historical impact, even if, as mentioned, they were no longer known after a short time. Nevertheless, it is ultimately due to the authority of these writings from the Synod of Orange that the doctrine of original sin was adopted into Western theology as common knowledge.[97]

The texts of the Synod of Orange present the Old Testament and Pauline concept of sin in a pointed form, as they are influenced by Augustine and his disputes with Pelagius (350/360–418/420). In addition, the reasoning is inverted: While Paul, based on the individual sins and their consequences, comes to the realization of a universal sinful fate, the writings of the Synod of Orange immediately begin with the latter and only subsequently consider individual sins. In this way, a universal fate of sin becomes explicit content of Church teaching. Behind man's radical need for redemption, which is derived from the universality of Jesus Christ's work of salvation, there can only be a universal sinfulness of human beings, which is propagated, if not through, then at least with birth.

> *If on Augustine's anthropological premises, one wants to hold to the Pauline inference from the universality and effusiveness of Christ's grace to the universality of transgression from "Adam," then the conception of a sin that comes to us through physical filiation of Adam is inescapable, in spite of all the consequential problems,* which, of course, were by no means overlooked at that time either, but were not considered too high a price to pay for the unabridged testimony to Christ.[98]

Accordingly, all human beings are affected by Adam's sin from birth; it takes hold of body and soul. Adam's guilt has passed to all his descendants.[99] Consequently, man's freedom is so limited that he himself is incapable of attaining

94 Cf. DH 371–97.

95 Cf. Fransen, Piet, "Die sog. II. Synode von Orange," in: *Lexikon für Theologie und Kirche*, vol. 7, Freiburg i.Br.: Herder, [2]1962, 1189.

96 Cf. DH 372.

97 Cf. Pesch, *Frei sein aus Gnade*, 131.

98 Pesch, *Frei sein aus Gnade*, 132.

99 Cf. DH 372, 385.

eternal salvation.[100] It is only through the grace of God that man can believe in God, receive God's salvation in faith and, with God's help, do good.[101] Even the good that the justified can do is, therefore, the sole result of God's grace,[102] as is the omission of evil.[103]

In Paul's terms, death and bondage were expressions of man's existence under sin as well as the law; whereas in the writings of the Synod of Orange, it is the bondage of the human will through which man's perdition is more strongly related to his inner being. While death and bondage could indicate that the consequences of Adam's sin relate solely to man's body, the reference to man's bondage unequivocally predicates that Adam's sin affects man to the innermost core and that he is, therefore, no longer capable of acting in a significantly salvific manner. This conception is continued in scholasticism.

While, according to Augustine's teaching, the burden of original sin on man is shown primarily in his covetousness, Thomas Aquinas ascribes original sin to the soul of man and not just to his capacity.[104] It manifests itself where the soul appears as a whole,[105] in the moral existence of every human being,[106] since everyone is descended from Adam; "all men born of Adam may be considered as one man, inasmuch as they have one common nature, which they receive from their first parents."[107] Human nature is, therefore, corrupted by original sin; all of them have rejected divine love from the beginning, which is fundamentally expressed in hatred of God and pride.

Aquinas' concept of original sin, while showing unmistakable parallels with the Augustinian tradition and the Council of Orange's texts, goes beyond these. On the one hand, Aquinas only recognizes the formal nature of original sin in concupiscence, while for him its material nature consists in man's turning away from original righteousness.[108] On the other hand, he specifically connects the transmission of original sin with the male sperm.[109] Since, according to the metaphysical law, matter and form mutually limit each other, the sinful flesh immediately infects the later infused soul, so that it is immediately drawn into apostasy from God.

100 Cf. DH 378, 383.
101 Cf. DH 373–78, 385–86, 396–97.
102 Cf. DH 389–93.
103 Cf. DH 379–80, 388.
104 Cf. Thomas Aquinas, *ST* I–II, q. 82, a. 3 ad 3.
105 Cf. Thomas Aquinas, *ST* I–II, q. 81, a. 1.
106 Cf. Thomas Aquinas, *ST* I–II, q. 82, a. 3.
107 Thomas Aquinas, *ST* I–II, q. 81, a. 1.
108 Cf. Thomas Aquinas, *ST* I–II, q. 82, a. 3.
109 Cf. Thomas Aquinas, *ST* I–II, q. 81, a. 2 ad 3 and 4.

Aquinas describes the human reality created by sin as a depraved nature,[110] and its essence is essentially the same as that of original sin. The term depraved nature emphasizes man's inability to voluntarily suppress his sinful state, but this does not mean that the essential determinations of humanity are lost; man, in spite of sin, does not cease to be man.[111]

> *The corruption of nature [. . .] becomes effective in the dimension of behavior, i.e., the point at which man sets goals and should align them with God as the ultimate goal. In view of this final goal, which is the significance of the doctrine of the corrupt nature, man is totally powerless*: he has no possibility of attaining the "theological virtues" of faith, hope, and love that are necessary for salvation.[112]

Because of sin, mankind is capable, at most, of ethically irrelevant things in which their responsibility is expressed.

3.2.3 Denominational Differences in the Concept of Original Sin

The Council of Trent wanted, once and for all, to establish the truth of original and hereditary sin, while omitting scholastic terminology and distinguishing it from the Lutheran view of concupiscence. During the Reformation, both the meaning of original sin and the assessment of concupiscence, which persists after baptism, were theologically controversial. Although both shared the view that the universality of Jesus Christ's work of salvation is based on the doctrine of original sin, Catholic theology was convinced that human nature was not completely corrupt due to original sin, while the reformers believed this was a reduction of sin. They focused primarily on fundamental sin and the nature of sin in general before turning to individual acts of sin. In every act of sin, the completely distinct state of being a sinner comes into play, the evil deeds of man point to his false relationship with God, to his being a sinner, because he is fundamentally wrong.

110 Cf. Thomas Aquinas, *ST* I–II, q. 85, a. 1 and 2. On the one hand, Aquinas follows the Augustinian tradition, but on the other hand, he goes beyond it by reflecting on sin and the corruption of nature against the background of the distinction between body and soul, thus unfolding the inner structures and conditions of sin and the corruption of sin. In this way, Aquinas reflects on sin more in terms of its ontological meaning rather than in terms of its effects on the relationship with God.

111 Cf. Thomas Aquinas, *ST* I–II, q. 85, a. 2.

112 Pesch, *Frei sein aus Gnade*, 143.

Because, according to the Reformation, "free will is nothing"[113] and the sinner can neither keep the divine commandments[114] nor participate in his salvation,[115] his enslaved free will can only be overwhelmed by the omnipotence of divine grace in sheer immediacy.[116] This means that a relation to justification can be thought of only as "mere passive" (purely passive). The Formula of Concord even formulated in polemical exaggeration that men "can do absolutely nothing toward their own conversion and are in this case much worse than a stone or a block of wood. For they resist the Word and will of God until God awakens them from the death of sin and enlightens and renews them."[117]

According to Martin Luther (1497–1560), resistance against God remains alive in the justified person, and concupiscence remains sin.[118] For him, however, concupiscence does not just express the desires of the human senses, but rather the fundamental sin of the person: in it the unbelief of man is expressed, the self-aggrandizement of the human spirit towards God. Sin seized the core of man himself in the form of concupiscence; it defines the essence of the human person as a living contradiction to God. Yet in spite of the sinful concupiscence the baptized is justified in the sight of God; he is 'simul iustus et peccator': sinner, because in the eyes of man, concupiscence persists and he is a sinner, justified, because concupiscence is no longer counted by God and God's salvation is bestowed upon man as a pure gift. Justification, then, changes one's being a sinner, but only in the

---

113 Luther, Martin, *De servo arbitrio* (WA 18, 722,13); cf. id., "Heidelberg Disputation," in: id., *Career of the Reformer: I*, Luther's Works 31, Harold J. Grimm (ed.), Philadelphia: Muhlenberg Press, 1957, 40: "Free will, after the fall, exists in name only, and as long as it does what it is able to do, it commits a moral sin" (= WA 1, 354,5–6).

114 Cf. Luther, Martin, *On the Freedom of a Christian. With Related Texts*, trans./ed. Tryntje Helfferich, Indianapolis / Cambridge: Hackett Publishing Company, 2013, 21: "[. . .] you hear your God speak to you, explaining how all of your life and works are nothing to God, but must, along with all that is within you, eternally perish" (= WA 7, 22,26–28).

115 Cf. Luther, *De servo arbitrio* (WA 18, 634,21–25); cf. id., "Disputation Against Scholastic Theology," in: id., *Career of the Reformer: I*, Luther's Works 31, Harold J. Grimm (ed.), Philadelphia: Muhlenberg Press, 1957, 10: "Man is by nature unable to want God to be God. Indeed, he himself wants to be God, and does not want God to be God" (= WA 1, 225,1–2).

116 Cf. Luther, *On the Freedom of a Christian*, 24: "As is the nature of the word, so too will be the nature of the soul, just as iron glows red like fire from a union with fire" (= WA 7, 24,33–35).

117 *Formula of Concord*, Solid Declaration II, 59 (*The Book of Concord. The Confessions of the Evangelical Lutheran Church*, trans. Charles Arand et al., Robert Kolb / Timothy J. Wengert (eds.), Minneapolis: Fortress Press, 2000, 555); cf. *Formula of Concord*, Solid Declaration II, 89 (*The Book of Concord*, 561). Luther does not answer the question regarding the status of those who want to believe, but cannot, in this concept of radically conditioned freedom and the overwhelming Word of God.

118 Cf. *Formula of Concord*, Epitome I, 11–12 (*The Book of Concord*, 489).

eyes of God; it is done out of pure grace and is and will remain entirely undeserved. Moreover, the Holy Spirit, through baptism, begins the work of sanctification in the justified sinner. This ensures that only the work of God brings about the salvation of man.

When the reformers spoke of original sin altering the entire core of the person and, thus, man's relationship with God, Catholic theologians viewed this as a threat to the humanity of mankind. Therefore, Trent did not assume the complete depravity of the sinner, but recognized the good in him and taught the interaction of the will with grace in preparation of justification, without, however, clarifying this fact in detail. "If anyone says that the sinner is justified by faith alone in the sense that nothing else is required by way of cooperation in order to obtain the grace of justification and that it is not at all necessary that he should be prepared and disposed by the movement of his will, let him be anathema."[119] Furthermore, the Council expressly emphasized the inner renewal of man through the reception of divine grace.[120] Hence, as result of the justification of man, nothing sinful remains in him and, consequently, concupiscence is not really sin. As a hereditary evil, concupiscence continues to exist in the sense that man must continuously fight against it. Concupiscence "cannot harm those who do not consent but manfully resist it by the grace of Jesus Christ."[121] In this way, Trent wished to preserve man's accountability. Justification is not merely a declaration of righteousness, but truly makes man righteous; it obliterates original sin and turns the sinner into a redeemed person who is actively claimed by the received grace of justification.[122] Through baptism, that which possesses "sin in the true and proper sense" is taken away.[123] Indeed concupiscence continues after baptism, but without being "sin in the true and proper sense," rather it "comes from sin" and "inclines to sin."[124] Thus, baptism obliterates all sin, so that concupiscence remains as a mere punishment and an object of struggle, not, however, as a sin. It is only a sin when temptation is consented to.

Trent viewed the doctrine of original sin in the context of justification, as well. Particular attention was given to the remission of original sin; both the effect of

119 DH 1559.

120 Cf. DH 1561: "If anyone says that men are justified either by the imputation of Christ's justice alone or by the remission of sins alone, excluding grace and charity that is poured into their hearts by the Holy Spirit and inheres in them, or also that the grace that justifies us is only the favor of God, let him be anathema."

121 DH 1515.

122 Cf. DH 1568–71.

123 DH 1515.

124 DH 1515.

baptism and of concupiscence, which remains after baptism, were to be outlined in a positive manner. The Council Fathers largely followed the statements of the Synods of Carthage and Orange, which were influenced by Augustinian theology. However, a definition of the essence and concept of the *peccatum originale* was avoided, since the theological standpoints of the Council Fathers diverged too greatly on this point. The Council Fathers agreed only on the fact that the *peccatum originale* had a sinful character and that it was of Adamic origin. Statements about the original state and its supernatural nature were avoided, save the fact that Adam's state prior to his sin was a state of "holiness and justice."[125] Through the Fall of Adam man lost his true freedom; he could no longer, undividedly and by his own efforts, turn to God. Although he had retained his freedom of will, through it, he could no longer regain salvation and original innocence, as a result of his "captivity in the power of [. . .] the devil."[126] Original sin affects the body and soul (*corpus et anima*) of man, which are consequently exposed to corruption. Turning away from God would be tantamount to being dead,[127] because man, who has turned away from true life, is enslaved to the dominion of what is contrary to God.

The Council of Trent, in believing that Adam's sin was "transmitted by propagation, not by imitation,"[128] thereby, in reference to Augustine, wished to express the absolute necessity for salvation of all of humanity: Adam's sin lives in "all men, proper to each."[129] However, there are no further statements in the Council text that explain exactly what the term "propagatio" (reproduction) is meant to express. This was an attempt to avoid controversy between the different schools of thought. Therefore, nothing more than a physical effectiveness of Adam's sin in the broadest sense can be abstracted from the document. The teaching of Pelagius (d. 418), who established the efficacy of Adam's sin in a moral process, is excluded. The harsh tension between the alleged guilt and how it comes about is not resolved at the Council. Ultimately, the Council of Trent "in this matter [. . .] did not go back in the slightest behind the fundamental statement of tradition," for according to the Council of Trent's decree on original sin, there is no doubt about the fact that "all of humanity [. . .] is corrupted from within and has turned away from God and, [. . .] by virtue of its remaining freedom of choice, as well, no longer has the ability to

125 DH 1511.
126 DH 1511.
127 Cf. DH 1512.
128 DH 1513
129 DH 1513.

help itself out of it. Trent not only does not imply a *careful* return to Pelagian and semi-Pelagian viewpoints, but rather it implies *no return at all.*"[130]

3.2.4 Ecumenical Rapprochements

From what has been presented so far, it is clear that the Catholic-Protestant controversy in the theology of sin is based on different emphases: While Protestant theology takes evil or substantial sin radically seriously and regards human nature as corrupt and human freedom as enslaved, Catholic theology attempts to protect the responsibility and humanity of mankind. Opposite each other are, on the Catholic side, a more actualistic, point-like perspective and, on the Protestant side, a more existentialist perspective. Ultimately, the question of the corruption of sin leads to the question of human freedom and the possibilities that remain to mankind. While Lutheran theology attests to man's complete inability in relation to God, Catholics are concerned with man's responsibility and would like to avoid an overly pessimistic view of mankind for pastoral reasons. Ultimately, both sides find it difficult to give a clear answer to the question of the relationship between original sin and freedom:

> The Catholic tradition holds to freedom of the will for the sake of the – undisputed – responsibility before God and the world, although it continues to emphasize dependence on God as its source. The Lutheran tradition denies freedom in favor of God's sole efficacy and the assurance of salvation, while still holding to human responsibility. Both views pay a conceptual price for this paradox, the Catholic one by ultimately being unable to rationalize freedom, the Lutheran by ultimately being unable to rationalize responsibility (including God's non-responsibility for sin).[131]

In 1999, the Catholic Church and the Lutheran World Federation were able to sign a "Joint Declaration on the Doctrine of Justification," however, the different accentuations could not be entirely overcome. In connection with the Reformation formula "iustus et peccator," the "Joint Declaration" concedes that man remains dependent on God's grace even when he is justified. However, while for Lutherans the baptized person is fully justified and yet at the same time a true sinner, the Catholic side particularly emphasizes the effectiveness of the grace of baptism or rather the inner re-creation of the wicked. "When Catholics emphasize the renewal of the interior person through the reception of grace imparted as a gift to

---

130 Pesch, *Frei sein aus Gnade*, 151.
131 Pesch, Otto Hermann, "Rechtfertigung, Ökumenischer Dialog," in: Wolfgang Thönissen et al. (eds.), *Lexikon der Ökumene und Konfessionskunde*, Freiburg i. Br.: Herder, 2007, 1133–34.

the believer, they wish to insist that God's forgiving grace always brings with it a gift of new life, which in the Holy Spirit becomes effective in active love."[132] The Catholic side concedes that even in the justified person there is still an inclination that is contrary to God's will and that, in this respect, he is constantly threatened by the power of sin.[133]

As far as man's freedom is concerned, it is jointly stated that it is "no freedom in relation to salvation."[134] The Lutheran side then makes it clear that "human beings are incapable of cooperating in their salvation, because as sinners they actively oppose God and his saving action"; "a person can only receive (mere passive) justification."[135] Conversely, Catholics emphasize that when they speak of a free human participation in the process of justification, every human action is always "an effect of grace, not as an action arising from innate human abilities."[136] Together, both acknowledge that the grace of God renews man without having to be dependent on the *cooperatio* "on the life-renewing effects of grace in human beings."[137]

As was shown at the beginning, the Christian concept of sin, which was a key concept during the scholastic period and was, therefore, at the center of the Catholic-Protestant controversy, is losing more and more of its power of conviction in the present time. This can only be counteracted by avoiding a moralization of the concept of sin and, with that, a respective negative image of man. Therefore, it must not be forgotten that the message of justification is more important than sin; the salvation promised by God is more important than redemption. "*Christianity, if it does not define man primarily as a doer, but, above all, as a recipient of good, has a positive, not a negative image of man.* The point of referencing sin is not to reveal what man cannot do, but on the contrary, to remind him of what God enables him to do."[138]

---

132 Lutheran World Federation / Catholic Church, *Joint Declaration on the Doctrine of Justification*, no. 24. Available online under the following link: https://www.lutheranworld.org/sites/default/files/Joint%20Declaration%20on%20the%20Doctrine%20of%20Justification.pdf (September 25, 2023).
133 Cf. Lutheran World Federation / Catholic Church, *Joint Declaration on the Doctrine of Justification*, no. 30.
134 Lutheran World Federation / Catholic Church, *Joint Declaration on the Doctrine of Justification*, no. 19.
135 Lutheran World Federation / Catholic Church, *Joint Declaration on the Doctrine of Justification*, no. 21.
136 Lutheran World Federation / Catholic Church, *Joint Declaration on the Doctrine of Justification*, no. 20.
137 Lutheran World Federation / Catholic Church, *Joint Declaration on the Doctrine of Justification*, no. 23.
138 Dalferth, *Sünde*, 109.

When asking about an actualization and reformulation of the traditional doctrine of sin, the first thing to start with is Jesus' message of salvation concerning the kingdom of God. From there, a light is cast onto the present human being with all his longings and hopes, fears and needs. Instead, however, the Christian religion is far too often understood more as a religion of redemption rather than as a religion of salvation and, consequently, a negative foil is first developed so that, against this background, the salvation and the redemption of the sinful human being can be presented in bright colors. By contrast, already in the Old Testament, the narrative of Adam's Fall is preceded by the narrative of the Creation Story and the original paradisiacal state.

3.3 Recent Approaches

In recent times, the doctrine of original sin has suffered an obvious loss of plausibility, which was caused, amongst other things, by the theory of evolution, the modern idea of freedom, historical awareness, and historical-critical exegesis. In order to restore the significance of the doctrine of original sin, various attempts have been made in Protestant and Catholic theology to reformulate it, however, thus far, they have only partially succeeded in resolving the contradictions that arise on the basis of the principle of accountability.

3.3.1 Historical-Empirical Approach

The historical-empirical approach is based on the option of monogenism and assumes the generative unity of mankind. Adam plays a universal role within the history of salvation; his action determines the entire history of mankind within the framework of the biological procreative context. Original sin is predominantly thought of as a natural determination, due to which every human being is guilty even before making personal decisions. Leo Scheffczyk (1920–2005),[139] for

139 Cf. Scheffczyk, Leo, "Das Dogma von der Erbsünde. Biblische Grundlagen – Geschichtliche Entwicklung – Bedeutung für die Gegenwart," in: Rudolf Schnackenburg (ed.), *Die Macht des Bösen und der Glaube der Kirche*, Düsseldorf: Patmos, 1979, 107–19; id., "Die Erbschuld zwischen Naturalismus und Existentialismus. Zur Frage nach der Anpassung des Erbsündendogmas an das moderne Denken," *Münchener Theologische Zeitschrift* 15 (1964), 17–57; id., "Adams Sündenfall. Die Erbschuld als Problem gläubigen Denkens heute," *Wort und Wahrheit* 20 (1965), 761–76; id., "Versuche zur Neuaussprache der Erbschuld-Wahrheit," *Münchener Theologische Zeitschrift* 17 (1966), 253–60.

example, sees no other way of making the universality of the fate of sin plausible than to insist on a fateful Adamic sin. For similar reasons, Karl Rahner (1904–1984) also advocates relating original sin back to the beginning, to 'humanitas originans', although he ultimately does not decide whether this primeval population, as bearers of original sin, is to be thought of as mono- or polygenetic. For Rahner, "the universality and the inescapability of this co-determination by guilt is inconceivable if it were not present at the very beginning of mankind's history of freedom."[140]

3.3.2 Evolutionist- and Biological-Empirical Approach

The evolutionist- and biological-empirical approach is found mainly in Catholic theology and attempts to create a synthesis between the evolutionary worldview and the theology of sin. According to evolutionist thinking, there can be no historical origin. In the view of Pierre Teilhard de Chardin (1881–1955), man's coming into being, in itself, does not equal guilt. This does not change until the encounter with the creative will revealed through Jesus Christ, that is, when mankind decides against the objective of creation predetermined by God.[141] For the Protestant theologian, Friedrich Daniel Ernst Schleiermacher (1768–1834), original sin manifests itself in the fact that every human being, at a new stage of development, is inhibited by their previous stage of development, namely due to sensual-natural determinations, for which Schleiermacher uses the biblical term "flesh." Original sin, then, affects the "advantage gained by the flesh during the prior time [from the beginning of the activity of the spirit]."[142] In this way, Schleiermacher anchors sin within the basic state of human existence and, at the same time, takes up the concept of the social power of sin when he defines original sin as "the corporate act and the corporate guilt of the human race."[143]

The notion that man is in development not only dominates the evolutionist-empirical interpretation of original sin, but also the biological-empirical one. For example, the behavioral researcher, Wolfgang Wickler (1931–2024), understands

140 Rahner, Karl, *Foundations of Christian Faith. An Introduction to the Idea of Christianity*, trans. William V. Dych, New York: Crossroad, 1982, 111.

141 Cf. Teilhard de Chardin, Pierre, "Note on Some Possible Historical Representations of Original Sin," in: id., *Christianity and Evolution*, trans. René Hague, New York: Harcourt Brace Jovanovich, 1971, 45–55.

142 Schleiermacher, Friedrich, *The Christian Faith*, H. R. MacKintosh / J. S. Stewart (eds.), vol. 1, New York / Evanston: Harper & Row, 1963, 274 (§ 67,2).

143 Schleiermacher, *The Christian Faith*, 285 (§ 71).

the human being primarily as a being that always falls short of the task of developing into its ideal state.[144] "[T]he original sin is a difference between the prototype of man and the real man. Of course, this difference persists only through procreation, but it says nothing about how many progenitors it goes back to."[145] Because Wickler understands original sin as a condition of biological deficiency, it, ultimately, does not fall within the area of human responsibility, but within the sphere of human duty. Redemption, therefore, means God's help with a task that, in itself, overwhelms man. "From this point of view, the so-called original sin appears to me less as a burden or a sin: I assert that original sin is a task!"[146]

3.3.3 Existential-Transempirical Approach

Another line of interpretation explains original sin to mean either the sum of one's personal sins or the personal depth of one's actual sins. The latter, in particular, applies to the evangelical approaches of Emil Brunner (1889–1966), Paul Althaus (1888–1966), and Wilfried Joest (1914–1995). This existential view of original sin abandons the history of Adam or rather the historicity of original sin as a means of historical reasoning for the overall lapse of guilt. Adam represents the human being par excellence, who does what Adam did.[147] In sin, the entirety of man's false existence is expressed. Man can no longer empirically ascertain when, where, and why the deed that brought about this reversal began. For, because of the totality of sin, he no longer succeeds in placing himself outside of his sin. Because the decisions of his will are predetermined by the past, man is not free. Through each of his deeds, he expresses what he essentially is, namely a sinner, and conversely, he discovers his false existence amidst his sinful deeds. The term "original state" is also interpreted in a personalistic way, it describes the right relationship between the creature and its creator, which, in the case of the sinner, is amiss, although personalistic interpretations vary greatly in this regard.

144 Cf. Wickler, Wolfgang, "Biologische Deutung der Erbsünde," in: Rudolf Schnackenburg (ed.), *Die Macht des Bösen und der Glaube der Kirche*, Düsseldorf: Patmos, 1979, 98–106.

145 Wickler, "Biologische Deutung der Erbsünde," 101.

146 Wickler, "Biologische Deutung der Erbsünde," 106.

147 Cf. Brunner, Emil, *Man in Revolt. A Christian Anthropology*, trans. Olive Wyon, Philadelphia: The Westminster Press, 1939; id., *Dogmatics*, vol. 2: *The Christian Doctrine of Creation and Redemption*, trans. Olive Wyon, Philadelphia: The Westminster Press, 1952; Althaus, Paul, *Die christliche Wahrheit. Lehrbuch der Dogmatik*, 2 vols., Gütersloh: Mohn, 1947/48; id., "Zur Lehre von der Sünde," in: id., *Theologische Aufsätze*, Gütersloh: Bertelsmann, 1929, 51–73; Joest, Wilfried, *Dogmatik*, vol. 1: *Die Wirklichkeit Gottes*, Göttingen: Vandenhoeck & Ruprecht, 1984; vol. 2: *Der Weg Gottes mit den Menschen*, Göttingen: Vandenhoeck & Ruprecht, 1986.

While for Althaus, for example, the original state describes the original, uncorrupted relationship between God and man, for Brunner the term "original state" expresses the invocation of man through God's Word, which calls upon him to make a decision and which, thereby, makes him a person, a responsible and responsive human being. As far as the unity of mankind in sin is concerned, its reasoning does not prove itself difficult in terms of personalistic thought; humanity is one under God's word and judgment. What God claims about the individual, he claims about everyone, and vice versa. The unity of all human beings in sin is, thus, derived from the culpable, responsible act of each individual. Althaus even speaks of a human will that goes beyond the individual will and in which humanity stands united before God. According to Brunner, mankind, because of its you-relatedness, forms a single community of fate and decision-making, in which sin becomes a solidary entity. The contradiction to the common origin finds expression in the midst of human sin.

3.3.4 Sociologic-Empirical Approach

The most frequently adopted attempt at interpreting original sin explains it as a universal condition of mercilessness, which is due to a disposition of guilt, and which co-determines the substance of human freedom before all individual accountability. Sin is viewed primarily within its social background, so that the reason for the universality of guilt is sought in the social interconnectedness. The contributions of Albrecht Ritschl (1822–1889), Piet Schoonenberg (1911–1999), and Karl-Heinz Weger (1932–1998) are particularly worth mentioning here.

The Protestant theologian, Ritschl,[148] in a sociological way, tries to make sense of what the doctrine of original sin claims. Everyone is born into an environment corrupted by the sins of others and is influenced by the sins of others to sin themselves. Thus, the "reproduction" of sin is interpreted in a social-psychological sense. Not only does sinning create a self-induced tendency (habitus) to sin, but human beings are also able to unite in common evil (principles, structures, etc.), whereby sin is increased to a nigh irresistible power of temptation. Ritschl describes this interrelation of sin as the "kingdom of sin," which he sets against the kingdom of God. "The social nexus, which explained the universality of sin, took the place of the old Traducian causal nexus."[149]

---

148 Cf. Ritschl, Albrecht, *Die christliche Lehre von der Rechtfertigung und Versöhnung*, 3 vols., Bonn: Adolph Marcus, ^{2}1882–1883, esp. vol. 3, 310–63.

149 Kinder, Ernst, "Sünde und Schuld, dogmengeschichtlich," in: *Religion in Geschichte und Gegenwart*, vol. 6, Tübingen: Mohr, ^{3}1986, 493.

Like Ritschl, the Catholic theologian, Schoonenberg, also uses the human condition as a starting point, that is the "influence that one free person exerts onto another, precisely because he is a free person, with respect to this freedom, indeed, by invoking this freedom."[150] Man always renders his free decision in a given situation, and with every decision he makes, he creates a new situation that further limits his options. At the same time, every free act also creates a new situation for other human beings. "Thus, in the domain of our natural activities concrete freedom is always a bound and limited freedom, and the fact of being bound and limited results not from a decrease or impairment of free will itself, but from the situation in which we stand or which we ourselves bring about."[151] Although man's free will is not affected by sin, he is put into such a position in which he is no longer capable of genuine love. In Schoonenberg's eyes, being in a sinful situation constitutes the "sin of the world," the "original sin."[152]

Karl-Heinz Weger, amongst others, also took up the attempt to link original sin with the situational conditionality of human freedom.[153] Existential-analytical observations showed him that human freedom is always determined by an intercommunicative being-with a personal environment. Through this historical being-with, the grace of God is to come upon man; it is to be imparted in a categorial-historical manner. Due to human guilt, however, the "sanctifying and categorically imparted grace of God"[154] has been absent since the beginning of history, so that the prepersonally determined lack of grace inwardly defines man's freedom and, in a manner analogous to personal guilt, makes him guilty before God.

Man ratifies the reality of perdition, which lies before him, in the sin for which he is personally responsible: sin is not initially caused by man's personal sin, but already exists as an inner determination of man, wherever sin exists. By this means, Weger also tried to justify the infant's need for redemption.[155] The

150 Schoonenberg, Piet, "Der Mensch in der Sünde," in: Johannes Löhrer / Magnus Feiner (eds.), *Mysterium salutis. Grundriß heilsgeschichtlicher Dogmatik*, vol. 2: *Die Heilsgeschichte vor Christus*, Einsiedeln et al.: Benziger, 1967, 890.

151 Schoonenberg, Piet, *Man and Sin. A Theological View*, trans. Joseph Donceel, Notre Dame, IN: University of Notre Dame Press, 1965, 76.

152 Schoonenberg, *Man and Sin*, 177–91.

153 Cf. Weger, Karl-Heinz, "Zur Diskussion um die Erbsünde," *Herder Korrespondenz* 21 (1967), 76–88; id., "Erbsündentheologie heute. Situation, Probleme, Aufgaben," *Stimmen der Zeit* 181 (1968), 289–302; id., *Theologie der Erbsünde. Mit einem Exkurs Erbsünde und Monogenismus von Karl Rahner*, Quaestiones disputatae 44, Freiburg i.Br.: Herder, 1970; id., *Erbsünde heute*, Munich: Don Bosco, 1972.

154 Weger, *Theologie der Erbsünde*, 158.

155 Cf. Weger, *Theologie der Erbsünde*, 174: "If one does not regard this reality of disaster constituted by the sinful situation of man as a statically unchanging reality, but if one grants it an

Magisterium of the Catholic Church also concedes that man is situated in a reality of perdition by using terms such as "social sin"[156] or "structures of sin."[157] "Sins give rise to social situations and institutions that are contrary to the divine goodness. 'Structures of sin' are the expression and effect of personal sins. They lead their victims to do evil in their turn. In an analogous sense, they constitute a 'social sin'."[158]

3.3.5 Depth Psychological Approach

Eugen Drewermann (b. 1940) introduced a further interpretive direction into the discussion on original sin. With the help of psychoanalytic findings, especially with regard to neurosis, he attempted to interpret the doctrine of original sin in an existentialist manner.[159] For Drewermann, neurosis is a sin because, as a pathological attempt to come to terms with one's own fear of existence, it is an aberration of an existence without God. "Before God, it is not necessary for man, in his fear, to dizzily circle around himself, only to stare into his own hole and fall into it."[160] Drewermann, however, can speak of being guilty of fear, only if "theologically, an existence, which is infinitely different from the human subsistence, is assumed, which, as an infinite consciousness, in the absolute sense, is its own existence, and from which the factual contingency of all finite beings experiences its reason and justification."[161]

Fear is an opportunity to meet God. "This is the step of *faith*: that I can discover myself, my contingent, unnecessary, superfluous existence, as created, affirmed,

---

inner differentiation in such a way that it can itself grow, possesses a beginning and a completion, then this pre-personal sinfulness of man must also include the unbaptized child, because the newborn child also already belongs to human history and history is always an inner and prepersonal determination of every human being, even if this historical determination of newborns – and thus original sin – can only be the very first stage of a development and a borderline case of human sinfulness."

156 John Paul II, *Apostolic Exhortation* Reconciliatio et paenitentia (December 2, 1984), no. 16.

157 John Paul II, *Encyclical* Sollicitudo rei socialis (December 30, 1987), no 36.

158 *CCC*, no. 1869.

159 Cf. Drewermann, Eugen, *Strukturen des Bösen. Die jahwistische Urgeschichte in exegetischer, psychoanalytischer und philosophischer Sicht*, 3 vols., Paderborn: Schöningh, ^{2}1979/80; id., *Psychoanalyse und Moraltheologie*, vol. 1: *Angst und Schuld*, Mainz: Matthias-Grünewald-Verlag, ^{2}1983, id., "Sünde, Schuld," in: Peter Eicher (ed.), *Neues Handbuch theologischer Grundbegriffe*, vol. 4, Munich: Kösel, 1985, 148–55.

160 Drewermann, *Strukturen des Bösen*, vol. 3, 545.

161 Drewermann, "Sünde, Schuld," 153.

willed, and justified by the infinite and that this discovery makes it possible to accept myself, to give up fleeing from myself (or towards myself) and to affirm myself."[162] The Christian doctrine of original sin diagnoses "that people are *ill* without the closeness of God";[163] it characterizes the mode of existence which man, through faith, recognizes as being sinful, because in it he is completely taken over by his senseless attempts to save himself in the wake of fear. "Original sin" can, thus, be used as a title for the monstrosity of the way of life into which man inevitably falls should he not believe "that there is a God who wills my existence over the abyss of fear and nothingness."[164] Faith opens up a more original freedom and possibility of existence for man, which unmasks the necessity of evil as only an apparent one and, with that, exposes the guiltiness for the loss of said original freedom.

> Thus, we arrive at a kind of existential sequence of experiences of man's self-perception, in which faith precedes the knowledge of the despair of human existence in sin, but the reality that faith discovers always precedes sin, so that sin, in faith, must appear as a *fall from grace* – not in the sense of a historical, but rather of an intrinsic falling away from human freedom.[165]

3.3.6 Transcendental-Historical Approach

Other approaches to reformulating the Church's doctrine of original sin try to resolve the tension between the traditional doctrine of original sin and scientific objections by interpreting the fall of a pre-existent Adam either meta-historically or transcendentally, in order to avoid all spatio-temporal questions, thereby denying the historicity of the fall.[166] The Fall of Man, thus, becomes the boundary of this historical world. "In the context of the constitutional process of human freedom, both inherited sin and original sin are reflected as a transcendental-historical event of freedom"[167] so that original sin appears as a contradiction in the original essence of freedom itself. If one imagines the *peccatum originale* in terms of transcendental history, it will appear as a real definition of freedom in the sense of a transcendental refusal. It consists in a "corruptio libertatis," in a depravity of that transcendental freedom by which human existence is determined from the very

162 Drewermann, *Strukturen des Bösen*, vol. 3, 546.
163 Drewermann, *Strukturen des Bösen*, vol. 3, 546.
164 Drewermann, *Strukturen des Bösen*, vol. 3, 553.
165 Drewermann, *Strukturen des Bösen*, vol. 3, 551.
166 Cf. Hoping, Helmut, *Freiheit im Widerspruch. Eine Untersuchung zur Erbsündenlehre im Ausgang von Immanuel Kant*, Innsbruck: Tyrolia, 1990.
167 Hoping, *Freiheit im Widerspruch*, 13.

beginning. The core problem of the dogma of original sin should be solved with a transcendental-historical concept of *peccatum originale*: to conceptualize together universality, its character of guilt, and the decision of freedom.

4 Eschatology and Sin

4.1 The Judgment and Consummation of the World

4.1.1 Sin and Atonement

According to Christian understanding, sin not only plays a role at the beginning of creation and throughout salvation and redemption history, but also at the consummation of the world, of man, and of history. Human sinfulness is of great importance especially in connection with the eschatological concept of judgment.

The Parousia of the Son of Man is connected with the revelation of the Kingdom of God, which is preceded by the Resurrection of the Dead and the Last Judgment.[168] All testimonies of faith in the New Testament and in the Early Church are related to the Coming of the Kingdom of God. The expectation of the Kingdom of God to come, as an eternal being-with-God and as a perfect community, in which there will be neither a fall nor sin, correlates with the focus on the "now time shot through with splinters of messianic time."[169] The coming Christ will celebrate the divine final judgment as an event of joy and comfort.[170] The Book of Revelation says this of the Last Judgment:

> And I saw the dead, the great and the small, standing before the throne, and books were opened; and another book was opened, which is the book of life; and the dead were judged from the things which were written in the books, according to their deeds. And the sea gave up the dead which were in it, and death and Hades gave up the dead which were in them; and they were judged, every one of them according to their deeds.[171]

According to this, all people will be subjected to a universal judgment and will be judged by Christ, the "first fruits of those who are asleep,"[172] according to their

---

168 Cf. Matt 16:28; Matt 26:29; Mark 14:25; Luke 22:16–18.

169 Benjamin, Walter, "On the Concept of History," in: id., *Selected Writings*, vol. 4: *1938–1940*, trans. Edmund Jephcott et al., Howard Eiland / Michael W. Jennings (eds.), Cambridge, MA / London: Harvard University Press, 2003, 397.

170 Cf. Matt 25:31–46; 1 Cor 15:24–26; Rev 20:11–15.

171 Rev 20:12–13.

172 1 Cor 15:20.

sins or their faith. After passing the Last Judgment, those who, according to their works[173] – namely due to their faith in Jesus Christ[174] – are noted in the "Book of Life,"[175] will receive a share in the Parousia.

The expectation of Christ's Parousia is tied to the soteriological hope for all people that, thanks to divine grace, sin, both conscious and unconscious, obvious and hidden, will be atoned for and the victims will receive their due, so that the true peace of Christ may reign.[176] "The absence of a judgment day would be the horrific expression of divine indifference: the Creator's indifference towards his own creation and especially towards the human beings he created. But nothing would humiliate man more than this, to be indifferent to God."[177] There is no question that in the history of Christianity this Christian hope was often used as a threat, more specifically, God's judgment was instrumentalized.

4.1.2 The End of Earthly Time

According to the conception of the New Testament, chronological time ends with the Coming of the Kingdom of God, i.e., the old eon,[178] and the new, eternal eon begins, a new creation.[179] For not only the sinful human being, but also the earthly, fallen creation is in need of redemption. Chaotic powers are at work within this creation, which in the biological and cosmic evolution unleash illness, suffering, and death and which man cannot escape. Often enough, man finds himself a victim of physical evil. But with the return of Christ, the existent old world,[180] which has been distorted by the powers of chaos hostile to God, will be freed and perfected. Then "all rule and all authority and power"[181] will be abolished and "at the name of Jesus every knee will bow, of those who are in heaven and on earth and under the earth."[182]

173 Cf. Rev 20:12–13; John 5:29; 2 Cor 5:10.
174 Cf. John 6:29; 3:16; 11:25; 1 John 5:12.
175 Cf. Ps 69:29; Isa 4:3; Dan 12:1; Mal 3:16; Luke 10:20; Phil 4:3; Heb 12:23; Rev 3:5; 13:8; 17:8; 20:12.15; 21:27.
176 Cf. Eph 2:14.
177 Jüngel, Eberhard, "Evangelischer Glaube und die Frage nach dem ewigen Leben," in: *Das Wesen des Christentums in seiner evangelischen Gestalt. Eine Vortragsreihe im Berliner Dom*, Neukirchen: Neukirchener, 2000, 125.
178 Cf. Matt 5:18; 12:32; 13:39–40.49; 24:3; 28:20.
179 Cf. Matt 12:32; Mark 10:30; Luke 18:30; 20:34–35; Rev 10:6.
180 Cf. Rev 21:1; Job 26:13; Jes 51:9; Ps 74:13–14.
181 1 Cor 15:24.
182 Phil 2:10.

According to biblical testimony, the whole of creation "suffers the pains of childbirth"[183] and awaits its deliverance, although man's need for redemption is attributed to his abuse of freedom. According to Paul, the "wages of sin is death"[184] and "through one man sin entered into the world,"[185] namely Adam, which, to affirm the general need for redemption, was repeated at the Second Synod of Orange.[186] By falling behind his creation mandate, through self-destructive selfishness and arrogance,[187] man not only distorted himself, but also the non-human creation.[188] Whether such theological speculations are indeed plausible remains to be seen at this point – in nature, prior to human existence, did not everything eat everything else? If, however, everything was, in fact, disfigured by human sin, then the Christian hope of salvation, naturally, must also relate to everything; that the "whole creation (πᾶσα κτίσις) [. . .], that is, not only the human world, and not merely the animal and vegetable worlds, but also the whole inorganic world; not merely our solar system, but also the galactic systems which exist outside our own and which are all subject to the same scheme of this world, this whole creation will be 'liberated.'"[189] With this in mind, the Joint Declaration of the Council of the Protestant Church in Germany and the German Bishops' Conference, *Taking responsibility for creation*, plainly and simply states: "The goal of God's ways is not only the renewal of mankind, but also the renewal of all creation."[190]

Just as Paul brought "sin" and "death" together, connecting theological and biological elements in order to express the need for the redemption of everything, it is absolutely impossible, with regard to the future redemption, to abstract from nature. What the biblical texts say about the end of time and the new creation cannot be thought of without reference to the cosmos and, thus, to physical time. The future of the unredeemed cosmos is, therefore, not a purely scientific question, it is also a question of theology. With regard to creation theology, man is so closely associated with the world that his healing is utterly unimaginable without

---

183 Rom 8:22.
184 Rom 6:23.
185 Rom 5:12.
186 Cf. DH 372.
187 Cf. Gen 3:1–24.
188 Cf. Gen 3:17–24; Rom 1:18–32; 7:14–24.
189 Heim, Karl, *The World: Its Creation and Consummation. The End of the Present Age and The Future of the World in The Light of the Resurrection*, trans. Robert Smith, Philadelphia: Muhlenberg Press, 1962, 116.
190 Kirchenamt der Evangelischen Kirche in Deutschland / Sekretariat der Deutschen Bischofskonferenz (eds.), *Verantwortung wahrnehmen für die Schöpfung. Gemeinsame Erklärung des Rates der Evangelischen Kirche in Deutschland und der Deutschen Bischofskonferenz*, Gütersloh: Mohn, ^{2}1985, no. 61.

the healing of the cosmos.[191] For Paul, too, it is clear: "the form of this world is passing away."[192] Consequently, the eschatological consummation also affects the non-human, earthly-material creation. "It was created for the indwelling of its Creator, and is hence unfinished as long as it has not yet become God's home country."[193] Because God's will to save must be applied to everything he has created, the Kingdom of God can only become reality as a perfect and unadulterated community with God, when both the human entanglement with evil and the history of suffering in nature come to an end, when the entire world joins in the praise of God and, thus, all adversity, ugliness, and abyss come to an end. This is the end of all worldly time,[194] for the present, sinful world cannot look upon or grasp the glory of him who is to come. Becoming new presupposes the passing of all that is transitory, or to use the words of Paul: the perishable must put on the imperishable, and the mortal must put on immortality.[195]

If the universal judgment is also referred to as the "Last Judgment," this can certainly be understood in a chronological sense: With the advent of God comes the absolute future, which no longer allows for a linear, inner-worldly future. This is the end of the dominion of human sin, of all temporality, impermanence, and changeability. However, the re-creating coming of God implies not only discontinuity – "Behold, I am making all things new"[196] – but also continuity. For becoming new means attuning to God's will to save: "The ability to 'approve' of an existence, which is given through one's creatureliness, is the actual reason why creation, as a whole, and all individual creatures are also capable of perfection, 'capable of eternity' in their own way."[197] The old creation is not obliterated, but transformed and transfigured, which must not be seen as an evolutionary process or an absolute break that excludes any continuity. The earthly, sinful world is transformed, it takes the form of an eternal, sinless fellowship with God. The "space for God" becomes "God as space."[198]

---

191 Cf. Finkenzeller, Josef, "Eschatologie," in: Wolfgang Beinert (ed.), *Glaubenszugänge. Lehrbuch der Katholischen Dogmatik*, vol. 3, Paderborn: Schöningh, 1995, 615.

192 1 Cor 7:31.

193 Moltmann, Jürgen, *The Coming of God. Christian Eschatology*, trans. Margaret Kohl, Minneapolis: Fortress Press, 1996, 283.

194 Cf. Kehl, Medard, "Neue Hoffnung für den Kosmos. Über das Heraustreten der Erde aus dem Schatten des Menschen," *Salzburger theologische Zeitschrift* 1 (1997), 20.

195 Cf. 1 Cor 15:53–54.

196 Rev 21:5.

197 Kehl, "Neue Hoffnung für den Kosmos," 19–20.

198 Gruber, Margareta, "Das Himmlische Jerusalem. Architektur gewordene Hoffnung für die Menschheit," *Stimmen der Zeit* 239 (2021), 927.

4.2 The Doctrine of Purgatory

4.2.1 Patristics

Sin not only plays a role in the Last Judgment, but also in the judgment of the individual or particular judgment, which, according to Catholic and Orthodox teaching, takes place immediately after death and determines the postmortem fate of the soul – the resurrection of the body only takes place with the Last Judgment.[199] The doctrine of the particular judgment is closely related to the doctrine of purgatory, according to which the individual soul undergoes purification after death.

The doctrine of postmortem purification cannot be biblically substantiated directly, but there are echoes of it in both the Old and the New Testament. For example, in 2 Macc 12:32–46, a prayer for the dead, who had become unfaithful in their faith, is attested. The motif of the parable of the prison, in which the debt is atoned for, can also be interpreted in the sense of an intermediate state.[200] The motif of fire is nourished, above all, by Paul's hope that man can be saved "through fire" in the divine judgment.[201] Finally, in the New Testament, God is often referred to as light and evil as darkness.[202] Since there can be no fellowship between light and darkness,[203] Church fathers such as Tertullian (c. 160–220) and Cyprian (c. 200/210–258) already asked themselves the question of what happens to those human beings who are not completely cleansed, i.e., those who die in sin.[204] Although there is still no uniform, systematic answer in the Early Church, the idea that the deceased would not immediately be granted the beatific vision of God, rather only with the general resurrection at the Last Judgment, was widespread. In addition, the self-evident practice of offering and praying for the deceased refers to the early Christian belief in purgatory.[205] The assumption of a purgatory is also reflected in the writings of the Church Fathers. Among them was Origen (185–253/254) who, following Clement of Alexandria (c. 150–215) and with the help of an allegorical interpretation of 1 Cor 3:10–15, was one of the first to develop a kind of doctrine of purgatory: All those who had accepted the Gospel

---

199 Cf. *CCC*, no. 997.
200 Cf. Matt 5:25–26.
201 1 Cor 3:15.
202 Cf. John 1:4–8; 2 Cor 4:6; 1 Tim 6:16; Jas 1:17; 1 John 1:5, 7 a.o.
203 Cf. 2 Cor 6:14; Eph 5:8–10.
204 Cf. Merkt, Andreas, *Das Fegefeuer. Entstehung und Funktion einer Idee*, Darmstadt: Wissenschaftliche Buchgesellschaft, 2005, 33–51.
205 Cf. Merkt, *Das Fegefeuer*, 53–64.

in faith would build upon this foundation in different ways (gold, silver, precious stones, wood, hay, or straw) and would ultimately have to undergo a testing, judging, and purifying fire, which acts as divine power in the human soul. The length of time depends on the severity of the sins until, finally, all are saved.[206]

Origen's views were received in various ways by the Eastern Church Fathers: some accepted them without reservation (Gregory of Nyssa [c. 335/340–after 394], Maximus Confessor [c. 580–662]), while others rejected his teaching of a universal salvation, not, however, the idea of a purifying function of the fire of judgment (Gregory of Nazianzus [c. 329–390]); still others (Cyril of Jerusalem [313–386], Chrysostom [344/349–407]) identified the fire of judgment with the fire of hell without assuming a further fire of purification[207] – a doctrinal position which the Eastern Church upholds to this day; the Western doctrine of purgatory is foreign to her. The union negotiations between the Western and Eastern churches at the Second Council of Lyon (1274)[208] and at the Council of Ferrara-Florence (1439)[209] were unsuccessful in the controversy surrounding the doctrine of purgatory.

4.2.2 Magisterial Development

There are various reasons why the Western tradition developed a doctrine of purgatory. On the one hand, the Church's practice of intercessory prayer and soon also the celebration of the Eucharist for the deceased suggested that they must be in an imperfect, tormented state due to the temporal punishment for their sin, and on the other hand, visions were handed down, which tell of souls in a terrible fire.[210] Pope Benedict XII's (1285–1342) doctrine, according to which "the souls of those who [. . .] have incurred no stain of sin" would be "received immediately into heaven,"[211] while "the souls of those who die in mortal sin" would "go down immediately to hell,"[212] resulted in the necessary presumption of a third place between heaven and hell for all other souls. The Catholic Church, to this day, believes this: "Each man receives his eternal retribution in his immortal soul at the

206 Cf. Gnilka, Joachim, *Ist 1 Kor 3,10–15 ein Schriftzeugnis für das Fegfeuer?*, Düsseldorf: Triltsch, 1955, 20–25.
207 Cf. Gnilka, *Ist 1 Kor 3,10–15 ein Schriftzeugnis für das Fegfeuer?*, 25–43.
208 Cf. DH 856–58.
209 Cf. DH 1304–06.
210 Cf. among others Gregory the Great, *Dialogorum* IV,39 (PL 77, 396–97); Bede the Venerable, *Historia Ecclesiastica* IV,12 (PL 95, 250).
211 DH 857.
212 DH 858.

very moment of his death, in a particular judgement that refers his life to Christ: either entrance into the blessedness of heaven – through a purification or immediately – or immediate and everlasting damnation."[213] Accordingly, for those who have died in the state of justifying grace, a process of purification follows immediately after death, in which the temporal punitive consequences are purified, before the purified soul rises together with its transfigured body to the unveiled beatific vision at the Last Judgment.[214] In the background there is a distinction between the guilt of and the punishment for one's sins, which goes back to early Scholasticism. While the guilt of sin and the eternal punishment for sin are redeemed through the Sacrament of Penance, this does not apply to the temporal punishment. Penance for this must be performed either in life or in purgatory.

The doctrine of purgatory was rejected by Martin Luther, but even more so by the reformers, Zwingli (1484–1531), Calvin (1509–1564), and Melanchthon (1497–1560). Luther increasingly regarded it as unbiblical, contrary to the doctrine of justification and as a gateway for misapplication, in the sense of promoting righteousness of works. In the *Smalcald Articles* he writes: "Purgatory, therefore, with all its pomp, requiem Masses, and transactions, is to be regarded as an apparition of the devil. For it, too, is against the chief article that Christ alone (and not human works) is to help souls."[215] Instead of assuming an intermediate state, the certainty of being with God, with Christ, even in death, is crucial. The deceased sleeps only in body, but in and through death he is blissfully connected to Christ. For the same reason, the sacrifice of the Mass for the dead is also rejected.[216] In contrast, the Council of Trent (1545–1563) consciously adhered to the doctrine of purgatory and taught that the sacrifice of the Mass should be offered as atonement for the dead.[217] However, in the sermons, the "more difficult and subtle questions" should "be excluded."[218]

---

213 *CCC*, no. 1022.

214 Cf. DH 1000, 1066–67.

215 *Smalcald Articles*, Second Part, Art. 2 (*The Book of Concord*, 303).

216 Cf. *Augsburg Confession* 24 (*The Book of Concord*, 68–73;) *Apology of the Augsburg Confession* 24 (*The Book of Concord*, 274–77).

217 Cf. DH 1743; 1753.

218 DH 1820.

4.2.3 Systematic-Theological Thoughts

The *purificatio* takes place in the encounter with God. "*Purgatory is God himself* in the wrath of his grace";[219] "God himself, our meeting with him, is our purgatorial fire."[220] Man dies into God and recognizes his sinfulness in the light of divine love; he becomes aware of it in comparison with his positive basic form, which has reached finality in death. That is why repentance begins to burn in him like a 'fire', which cleanses and frees him from all sinful resistance and prepares him for union with God. "'Bathing in the truth of divine love', in the face of one's partial denial and inadequacy, becomes the 'painfully burning suffering' of repentance into which the soul voluntarily immerses itself in order to melt and become free."[221]

Thus, postmortem purification must be understood as a process of completion in the human being, which embraces him to the full depth of his existence and where, with the help of the fire of divine love, the overall reality of the justified human being is painfully integrated into his fundamental yes to God through suffering of perfection. However, the assertion of this fundamental decision must not be misunderstood as having been deepened in the process of purification or integration, since it has already been finalized in death. In the same way, the eradication of temporal punishment is, ultimately, not the work of human achievement, but rather an act of divine grace, which God performs in the justified under suffering and shameful pain:

> Where he [the human being] – figuratively speaking – in his earthly life, was not enough of a vessel for the fullness of divine life, there *God prepares* the vessel for *himself*, there he "burns out" with the fire of his love. [. . .] "Purgatory" means [. . .] that in the personal encounter of the deceased with God the fire of divine love prepares for the reception of eternal life. [. . .] God reaches mankind with his grace and love, even where their openness was only a poor, miserable, barely successful matter for him.[222]

But then, this encounter becomes "deeply shameful, painful and, therefore, cathartic."[223]

---

219 Küng, Hans, *Eternal Life? Life After Death as a Medical, Philosophical, and Theological Problem*, trans. Edward Quinn, New York et al: Doubleday, 1985, 139.

220 Boros, Ladislaus, *The Mystery of Death*, trans. Gregory Bainbridge, New York: Herder and Herder, 1965, 135.

221 Beck, Heinrich, *Reinkarnation oder Auferstehung. Ein Widerspruch?*, Innsbruck: Resch, 1988, 41.

222 Greshake, Gisbert, *Tod – und dann? Ende – Reinkarnation – Auferstehung. Der Streit der Hoffnungen*, Freiburg i.Br.: Herder, 1988, 84.

223 Greshake, Gisbert, *Stärker als der Tod. Zukunft – Tod – Auferstehung – Himmel – Hölle – Fegefeuer*, Mainz: Matthias-Grünewald-Verlag, [11]1991, 92–93.

4.3 Indulgence

4.3.1 The Development of the Indulgence System

In the Early Church, the unique penitential process ended with the sacramental re-admission into the Church. Previously, in the case of grave sins, an act of penance had to be made, which indicated the willingness to repent and an inner conversion. The power to redeem sins was attributed to them, without, however, calling into question the fact that God alone forgives sins. With the advent of the sacramental private or auricular confession (6th to 10th centuries), which could be repeated several times, acts of penance and the Sacrament of Penance diverged in terms of time and subject matter: the acts of penance now followed absolution, which is why they were no longer believed to have the power to redeem sins. In addition, over time, penance in the form of deeds became less important in favor of penance in the form of prayer and, eventually, in favor of monetary penalties, which further weakened the inner connection between sacramental reconciliation and a renewed way of life.

While after the introduction of private confession, the Church's prayer of intercession was initially understood as a purely spiritual support for the penitent, from the 11th/12th century on, it was also applied to the authoritative and legal remission or indulgence of temporal punishments for sin, which are inherent to sin.

> An indulgence is the remission before God of temporal punishment for sins whose guilt is already forgiven, which a properly disposed member of the Christian faithful gains under certain and defined conditions by the assistance of the Church which as minister of redemption dispenses and applies authoritatively the treasury of the satisfactions of Christ and the saints.[224]

In the 11th century, a so-called plenary indulgence granted the remission of all temporal punishments for sin, and since the 13th century, living persons, who were themselves in a state of grace, could also give the indulgence to the deceased who died in justifying grace and who were then subjected to the purification process of purgatory.[225] The indulgence for the deceased was interpreted as a vicarious atonement.[226]

---

224 *CIC*, can. 992.

225 Cf. DH 1405–07; 1448.

226 Cf. Thomas Aquinas, *ST* III, Suppl., q.71, a.10.

What gives the Church authority to legally enact temporal punishments and canonical penalties for sin? This question was first answered in the 13th century by Pope Clement VI (1291–1352) using the image of the Church treasury: Jesus Christ, through his vicarious, salvific suffering, rendered once and for all, i.e., complete reparation, for all trespasses and eternal punishments of sin. This inexhaustible treasure of grace, together with the merits of the saints, was handed over to the papal power of the keys.[227] From it the Church bestows the remission of temporal punishments upon its penitent sinners, and because of Christ's abundant reparations there are sufficient amends for the remitted penance. Since the early Middle Ages, the authoritative-official remission of punishment pertained to works of piety (pilgrimages, prayers, good deeds, monetary donations, etc.), which the Church itself sets as a condition for the granting of indulgences. Due to the fact that they were, in part, of great economic importance, they often served as a gateway for profiteering and greed. This was all the more the case as of the 14th century, when indulgences became detached from the Sacrament of Penance, resulting in the acts of penance losing their gracious nature and, subsequently, becoming part of a legal and fiscal system.

> The spiritual intercession of the confessor, the granting of an alleviating subsidy (subsidium) for penance or redemption (redemptio), and the promise of a remission of punishment (absolutio) to the active penitent, were replaced by the general, legal dispensation (dispensatio) of graces to every penitent-minded, fed from the infinite fund of spiritual merit maintained by the Church.[228]

4.3.2 Reformatory Critique

If the reformers already identified an offense against the uniqueness and inimitability of Jesus Christ's mediatorship in the intercessory invocation of the saints,[229] then they certainly recognized a violation of the sole causation of divine grace in the teaching of Christ's and the saints' treasury of grace. They also questioned the biblical compatibility of the doctrine of indulgences. Added to that were the abuses of the late medieval practice of indulgences.

> The increase in indulgences, but especially their use as a source of money to finance church projects of all kinds, the gross exaggerations of untrained collectors of indulgences [. . .]

227 Cf. DH 1025–27.
228 Benrath, Gustav Adolf, "Ablaß," in: *Theologische Realenzyklopädie*, vol. 1, Berlin / New York: De Gruyter, 1993, 349.
229 Cf. *Augsburg Confession* 21 (*The Book of Concord*, 58–59).

> who sometimes ran their business professionally and for a share of the proceeds [. . .], the fraud regarding invented or falsified certificates of authority, the embezzlement, shifting and misappropriation of the collected funds, the rival participation in the profits, not only of different ecclesiastical but also secular authorities, the occasional leasing of the indulgence business to lay people in exchange for an advance payment of a lump sum [. . .] and much more contributed to the well-known secularization of the Western Church.[230]

With his theses[231] (1517), Martin Luther demanded a theological clarification of the question of indulgences. Without completely rejecting the system of indulgences,[232] he fundamentally questioned the Church's claim to be able to dispose of God's grace.[233] The Church can merely mitigate and reduce[234] the canonical penalties it has itself imposed. Other than that, it can only assist the sinner through intercession.[235] Instead of sedulously acquiring indulgences, the reformer called upon the believers to desire the Gospel and to active love, i.e., to live by the spirit of forgiveness and reconciliation. Anyone who believes in the love and mercy of God and, thereby, allows themselves to be reconciled with God receives divine grace for the forgiveness of sins, for conversion and for renewal. Moreover, since the reformers transformed the Sacrament of Penance into a lifelong return to baptism, indulgences lost their theological place. "When our Lord and Master Jesus Christ said, 'Repent' [Matt. 4:17], he willed the entire life of believers to be one of repentance."[236]

The reformers rightly criticized the mechanization of the mediation of salvation and the pope's arbitrary, calculating power to dispose of divine salvation. They also denounced penance, which could easily be understood as self-righteousness and self-redemption, as a magical ritual of personal merit, as a listing of good, salutary works. This criticism had been raised again and again since the early Scholastic period, namely the criticism of the legal effects of the Church's intercessory prayer and of the sometimes plenary remission of penalties for sin. According to

---

230 Benrath, "Ablaß," 351.

231 Cf. Luther, Martin, "Ninety-Five Theses or Disputation on the Power and Efficacy of Indulgences," in: id., *Career of the Reformer: I*, Luther's Works 31, Harold J. Grimm (ed.), Philadelphia: Muhlenberg Press, 1957, 25–33 (= WA 1, 233–38).

232 Cf. theses 47, 48, 71.

233 Cf. theses 8–13, 20. The "treasures of the church, out of which the pope distributes indulgences" (thesis 56) are not "the merits of Christ and the saints, for, even without the pope, the latter always work grace for the inner man, and the cross, death, and hell for the outer man" (thesis 58).

234 Cf. theses 5, 20.

235 Cf. thesis 28: „[W]hen the church intercedes, the result is in the hands of God alone."

236 Thesis 1.

Reformation theology, a distinction must be made between God-given justification and the subsequent sanctification that is still necessary.

Luther himself summed up the tension between the singularity of justification and the process of appropriating divine grace as "iustus et peccator." He was convinced that the gift of justification requires a renewal of life in the spirit of the Gospel and that this inner conversion should be demonstrated in 'good works' as 'fruits of repentance'. However, human works of penance should not be viewed separately from the act of penance and should not be understood as a devotion to or a piety of works, nor is the Church able to dispense from the renewal of life or to remit parts of the punishments for sin, but it can, nevertheless, help to overcome them.

Although the Council of Trent combated the abuses that took place in the practice of indulgences, in particular fiscalism, i.e., the sale of indulgences, it, nevertheless, reaffirmed the authority given by Christ to grant indulgences.[237] However, no further information on the theology of indulgences was given. In his Apostolic Letter, "Quamplenum" (1567), Pope Pius V (1504–1572) even punished the sale of indulgences with the penalty of excommunication. Finally, in 1967, Pope Paul VI (1897–1978) took upon himself the reform of the indulgence system in his Apostolic Constitution, "Indulgentiarum doctrina."[238] An indulgence must be understood as an intercessory prayer by the Church, although it makes "use of its power as minister of the Redemption of Christ" and, thus, "by an authoritative intervention dispenses to the faithful suitably disposed the treasury of satisfaction which Christ and the saints won for the remission of temporal punishment" (ID no. 8). Thereby, the punishments for sin would be redeemed, which, as the inner consequences of sin, would self-destructively intervene in the temporal, spiritual life (ID no. 2). The penitent would be encouraged to begin a renewed life in Christ and would be reintegrated into the overall system of the loving fellowship of God and man. It is expressly pointed out that the acquisition of indulgences is not a matter of a purely superficial repetition of formulas and actions, nor is it about the mere fulfilling of requirements, but about the Christian life and a growing in faith. In addition, the pope abolished the daily tally of remitted punishments for sins.

Pope John Paul II also strived to renew the indulgence tradition[239] and emphasized that the granting of an indulgence does not alleviate any sins, but

237 Cf. DH 1835.

238 Paul VI, *Apostolic Constitution* Indulgentiarum doctrina *(January 1, 1967)*. Abbreviated as ID in the following.

239 John Paul II, *Bull of Indiction of the Great Jubilee of the Year 2000* Incarnationis mysterium (November 29, 1998). Abbreviated as IM in the following.

merely redeems the temporal punishment for sins, although the penitential disposition of the indulgences has the power to redeem sins. He clearly emphasized that the punishments "from which we must be purified" (IM no. 9) are to be understood as the internal consequences of sin, the overcoming of which requires both the personal commitment of the individual and the sacramental action of the Church. Although man is acquitted of his sins in the Sacrament of Penance, his failure has caused wounds that can heal only slowly. "The indulgences mark steps on this path of healing"[240] without replacing or absolving from the path of conversion and healing. The pope, thus, views temporal punishments for sin primarily existentially and the indulgence as an aid for the conversion and renewal of man. It is not a matter of a quantitatively measurable reduction of temporal punishments for sins, but rather an existential process in which the penitent, beyond confession, strives to perfect the inner purification insofar as he accepts the consequences of his sins and works them out. Such a spiritual theology of indulgences renders impossible any indication of time and measure, as was customary in the medieval practice of indulgences.

The "treasures of the Church" would lend themselves as a support and an encouragement in the search for a spiritual renewal of life and in the purification of troubled relationships. Pope John Paul II expressly emphasized that the treasures of the Church mean nothing other than that all are connected with one another in the supernatural unity of the mystical body and that, for this reason, it "establishes among the faithful a marvellous exchange of spiritual gifts, in virtue of which the holiness of one benefits others" (IM no. 10). This exchange applies especially to those Christians who would leave behind an abundance of love, of endured suffering, of purity and truth, in which others would be included and, thereby, uplifted (cf. ibid.). The Church treasure is, therefore, not a physical reality that is freely available. Rather it is about the "personal love of Christ and the saints" that is alive in the Church.[241] This love would enable the active participation in the work of salvation. Pope John Paul II introduced a reform, which not only considers spiritual penance as a "valid way" towards the perfection of an inner purification, but also "forms of personal sacrifice," such as the material or voluntary support of religious or diaconal projects as well as abstinence from the pleasures of consumption (IM Conditions no. 4).

240 N. N., "Papst warnt vor Missverständnissen des Ablasswesens," *KNA/Ökumenische Information* 41 (October 5, 1999), 4.
241 Beinert, Wolfgang, "Vom Sinn des Ablasses," *Prediger und Katechet* 122 (1983), 742.

4.3.3 Ecumenical Rapprochements

Just as, according to Reformation theology, sin carries its punishment within itself, insofar as it causes a negative reality, which is contrary to God's will, and that has an irrevocable after-effect, so, according to Catholic theology, the "evil habits, acquired through a bad life"[242] are not simply rectified with the forgiveness of sins. The after-effects of sin have a negative effect beyond the sacramental reconciliation, "following from the very nature of sin";[243] they are to be dealt with, with the help of divine grace. Ecumenically it is undisputed that the forgiveness of sins after penance requires an existential betterment. Human repentance must be thought of as always having been included in Christ's satisfaction. Only in this way does repentance not appear as a work of man, but as an act of God's grace with the purpose of maturing and coming to terms with the consequences of sin. Indeed, the individual path of conversion amounts to more than the acceptance of canonical penitential requirements, but they do express the penitent's fundamental inner readiness to repent.

One can speak of a great progress, when Pope John Paul II focuses on the therapeutic-medical aspect of indulgences rather than the legal one: "Indulgences [. . .] are a kind of medicine, depending on the extent to which a human being is open to a deep and honest conversion."[244] Wolfgang Beinert sums up this therapeutic aspect as follows: "Just as a doctor puts a broken bone back together and splints it so that it grows together, so the Church brings the sinner and God together, so that there can be fellowship again."[245] For a better understanding on the Catholic side, one should refrain from legal-material ideas in favor of a therapeutic-ethical concept of penance and the institution of indulgences. It should be emphasized even more clearly that indulgences are a special form of piety and do not contribute to the justification of the sinner, but rather presuppose it, and do not imply any ecclesiastical right to dispose of the fruits of penance and divine grace. In addition, the idea of atonement and penal suffering should be avoided, and penance should be applied more to the concrete consequences of the sins. "The demands for indulgences will [. . .] have to face up to the real instances in

---

242 DH 1690.
243 *CCC*, no. 1472.
244 N. N., "Papst warnt vor Missverständnissen des Ablasswesens," 4.
245 Beinert, "Vom Sinn des Ablasses," 742.

which individuals, groups, and peoples entangle themselves and others into perdition."[246]

The prayer of intercession contributes to the healing of the consequences of sin. Because nothing is remitted here, the highly misleading and ecumenically burdened term "indulgence" should be avoided and instead one should speak of the Church's assistance in the process of sanctification. "You can only take the keyword out of circulation so as not to block the serious factual question hidden behind it."[247] Lutheran theologians agree that the justification process is followed by a lifelong process of sanctification, with the aim of allowing the grace of baptism to counteract the consequences of sin. Ultimately, the practice of indulgences attempts nothing other than to make fruitful the healing and sanctifying influence of the Church as a representative community of solidarity for the healing of the painful, long-term consequences of sin. For all believers are connected to one another in the mystical body of Christ.[248] This living fellowship forbids interpreting sin and forgiveness individually instead of communally or ecclesiastically. Each exercise of faith is embedded in the common exercise of the whole Church. That is why, from the beginning, Christians, on the path of sanctification, have tried to help one another. The Church's prayer of intercession is part of this healing and sanctifying tradition.

Alongside all previous ecumenical agreements, the role of the Church represents the decisive controversial-theological point of contention. According to reformatory understanding, it is God alone who justifies the unholy, without any active involvement in the work of salvation on the part of human beings. However, the doctrine of indulgences and ecclesiastical treasure originate precisely from this: "it is part of the grandeur of Christ's love not to leave us in the condition of passive recipients, but to draw us into his saving work and, in particular, into his Passion" (IM no. 10). Herein exactly lies "the ultimate decisive reason for the inevitable contradiction of this entire decree with any reformatory understanding of what it means to be Christian."[249] Does the officially-authoritative prayer of intercession, in fact, authorize the Church to apply divine salvation? Because the Church neither has God's grace at its disposal, nor can it definitively

246 Fuchs, Ottmar, "Christlicher Umgang mit den 'Folgen der Sünde' im Horizont von Geschichte und Gesellschaft," in: Hans-Ulrich von Brachel / Norbert Mette (eds.), *Kommunikation und Solidarität*, Freiburg (CH): Edition Exodus, 1985, 190.

247 Pesch, Otto Hermann, "Der Ablass – Luthers unerledigte Anfrage," *Christ in der Gegenwart* 60 (2008), 321.

248 Cf. 1 Cor 12:26.

249 Kaufmann, Thomas / Ohst, Martin, "Unvereinbar oder inhaltsleer. Der päpstliche Ablass widerlegt die Rede vom Rechtfertigungs-Konsens," *epd-Dokumentation* 39 (1999), 2.

determine the remission of punishment for sin, the Church's legal authority to remit punishments for sin, now more than ever, should be denied and the institution of indulgences should be viewed as purely intercessory. "Logically, the concept of 'consequences of sin' makes it impossible to imagine an indulgence as being a 'remission' of the consequences of sin."[250] Furthermore, the differentiation between partial and plenary indulgences should be forgone, considering that the latter presents a particular problem even for Catholic theology, since it presumes a complete disposition, an overcoming of every "attachment to sin, even to venial sin" (ID norm no. 7). Although new indulgences are repeatedly tendered on the part of the Catholic Church, there is a lack of any fundamental magisterial reflection. By holding on to legal ideas, "the theological objections raised by Luther and the Reformation against the Roman Catholic doctrine of indulgences [. . .] have not yet become irrelevant."[251]

5 Prospects

A Christian theology of sin should not be concerned in a legal, moralizing and classifying manner with individual sinful acts, but rather with the inner and fundamental moral attitude of man. It is within his freedom to make a fundamental decision about himself, which manifests itself gradually in a multitude of particular deeds. The fundamental decision is more than the sum of the individual deeds, it is a matter of personal disposition. Sin, in the proper sense of the word, occurs when a person in their freedom negates their own gratitude and, thus, their acknowledgement of God, i.e., they turn against God, the very basis of human freedom, and, in that respect, against themselves. Talking about sin is not an end in itself, rather it reveals the potential for salvation, which God has given man.

> He who deals with sin holds a key to the discovery of humanity, which surpasses all empirical knowledge of all things factual and all normative controversy over ideals of humanity, because it does not relate to the good we do or must do in order to live humanely, but, first and foremost, to the good things that happen to us owing to God, so that we can live from a promise that we are unable to exhaust.[252]

---

250 Hintzen, Georg, "Der Ablass: ein innerkatholisches Problem. Plädoyer für eine Revision der kirchlichen Ablasslehre und -praxis," *Catholica* 54 (2000), 303.
251 Benrath, "Ablaß," 363.
252 Dalferth, *Sünde*, 389.

Man's fundamental decision can find its way into the particular acts of freedom with varying degrees of intensity. Depending on the divisiveness of the human being within himself, both that which is his own and that which is foreign merge into his deed, the person is present in the act itself to different degrees, which must have an effect on moral judgment. This means that the traditional distinction between venial and grave sin is based on the intensity of one's personal involvement. Although actions emblematically indicate a person's moral attitude, it is, nevertheless, difficult to make concrete statements about the degree to which individual actions relate to the fundamental attitude of the person. Therefore, it cannot be said with absolute certainty "where guilt, in the Christian sense, occurs."[253] For only man's deeds are visible, but not his heart. Even the individual human being can be aware of his own moral disposition only in a non-thematic and non-reflexive way; it eludes his direct access, which is why the final determination of man's moral constitution is reserved for God alone, who "looks at the heart" of man (1 Sam 16:7).

If sin is understood as the negative overall disposition of human existence before God, as a willful rejection of the divine love, which reveals itself through Jesus Christ, it does not imply a personal restricted view of the concept of sin. Because being human is just as much about existing with others as it is about existing in the world. Therefore, if a person resists the divine gift of salvation, this not only affects him, but also his fellow men and the environment. Every abuse of freedom also affects the freedom of others. Sin is, therefore, not an individual concern; it creates objective realities that are socially and historically relevant. In order to make people aware of this communal character of sin, one, today, sometimes speaks of "social sin."[254] The term "social sin" not only indicates the social effects of personal sin, but also represents everything that contradicts the divine plan in the social structure (unjust structures, institutionalized violence, etc.) and negatively affects the individual. In this context, John Paul II also spoke of "structures of sin."[255] The traditional Church theology on sin, which all too often was focused solely on the external facts of the individual sins, is corrected by emphasizing the transpersonal dimension of sin. In the end, however, what matters is the personal depth of the life decision before God, which determines the life of the individual and always has social effects – for good and for bad.[256]

253 Rahner, Karl, "Schuld, Vergebung und Umkehr im christlichen Glauben," in: Albert Görres / Karl Rahner, *Das Böse. Wege zu einer Bewältigung in Psychotherapie und Christentum*, Freiburg i.Br.: Herder, ²1983, 217.

254 Cf. John Paul II, *Apostolic Exhortation* Reconciliatio et paenitentia *(December 2, 1984)*, no. 16.

255 Cf. John Paul II, *Encyclical* Sollicitudo rei socialis *(December 30, 1987)*, no. 36.

256 This text was translated from German into English by Rebecca Parker.

Copyright

Bibliography

Abbott, Walter M. / Gallagher, Joseph (eds.), *The Documents of Vatican II*, London et al.: Geoffrey Chapman, 1967.

Althaus, Paul, *Die christliche Wahrheit. Lehrbuch der Dogmatik*, 2 vols., Gütersloh: Mohn, 1947/48.

Althaus, Paul, "Zur Lehre von der Sünde," in: id., *Theologische Aufsätze*, Gütersloh: Bertelsmann, 1929, 51–73.

Augustine, *De peccatorum Meritis et Remissione libri III* (PL 44, 109–200).

Augustine, *In Johannis Evangelium Tractatus CXXIV* (PL 35, 1379–1976).

Augustine, *Contra secundam Iuliani responsionem imperfectum opus* (PL 45, 1049–1612).

Beck, Heinrich, *Reinkarnation oder Auferstehung. Ein Widerspruch?*, Innsbruck: Resch, 1988.

Bede the Venerable, *Historia Ecclesiastica* (PL 95, 23–290).

Beinert, Wolfgang, "Vom Sinn des Ablasses," *Prediger und Katechet* 122 (1983), 741–74.

Benjamin, Walter, "On the Concept of History," in: id., *Selected Writings*, vol. 4: *1938–1940*, trans. Edmund Jephcott et al., Howard Eiland / Michael W. Jennings (eds.), Cambridge, MA / London: Harvard University Press, 2003, 389–400.

Benrath, Gustav Adolf, "Ablaß," in: *Theologische Realenzyklopädie*, vol. 1, Berlin / New York: De Gruyter, 1993, 347–64.

Berkenkopf, Christian, *Sünde als ethisches Dispositiv. Über die biblische Grundlegung des Sündenbegriffs*, Paderborn et al: Ferdinand Schöningh, 2013.

The Book of Concord. The Confessions of the Evangelical Lutheran Church, trans. Charles Arand et al., Robert Kolb / Timothy J. Wengert (eds.), Minneapolis: Fortress Press, 2000.

Boros, Ladislaus, *The Mystery of Death*, trans. Gregory Bainbridge, New York: Herder and Herder, 1965.

Brunner, Emil, *Dogmatics*, vol. 2: *The Christian Doctrine of Creation and Redemption*, trans. Olive Wyon, Philadelphia: The Westminster Press, 1952.

Brunner, Emil, *Man in Revolt. A Christian Anthropology*, trans. Olive Wyon, Philadelphia: The Westminster Press, 1939.

Catechism of the Catholic Church, London: Burns & Oates, 1999.

Dalferth, Ingolf U., *Sünde. Die Entdeckung der Menschlichkeit*, Leipzig: Evangelische Verlagsanstalt, 2020.

Denzinger, Heinrich, *Compendium of Creeds, Definitions, and Declarations on Matters of Faith and Morals*, Peter Hünermann / Robert Fastiggi / Anne Englund Nash (eds.), San Francisco: Ignatius Press, 2012.

Drewermann, Eugen, *Psychoanalyse und Moraltheologie*, vol. 1: *Angst und Schuld*, Mainz: Matthias-Grünewald-Verlag, ^{2}1983.

Drewermann, Eugen, *Strukturen des Bösen. Die jahwistische Urgeschichte in exegetischer, psychoanalytischer und philosophischer Sicht*, 3 vols., Paderborn: Schöningh, ^{2}1979/80.

Drewermann, Eugen, "Sünde, Schuld," in: Peter Eicher (ed.), *Neues Handbuch theologischer Grundbegriffe*, vol. 4, Munich: Kösel, 1985, 148–55.

Eichrodt, Walter, "Sünde im AT," in: Herbert Haag (ed.), *Bibel-Lexikon*, Zurich et al.: Benziger, [3]1982, 1664–1672.

Finkenzeller, Josef, "Eschatologie," in: Wolfgang Beinert (ed.), *Glaubenszugänge. Lehrbuch der Katholischen Dogmatik*, vol. 3, Paderborn: Schöningh, 1995, 525–671.

Fransen, Piet, "Karthago, Synode v. 418," in: *Lexikon für Theologie und Kirche*, vol. 6, Freiburg i.Br.: Herder, [2]1961, 3–4.

Fransen, Piet, "Die sog. II. Synode von Orange," in: *Lexikon für Theologie und Kirche*, vol. 7, Freiburg i.Br.: Herder, [2]1962, 1188–89.

Fuchs, Ottmar, "Christlicher Umgang mit den 'Folgen der Sünde' im Horizont von Geschichte und Gesellschaft," in: Hans-Ulrich von Brachel / Norbert Mette (eds.), *Kommunikation und Solidarität*, Freiburg (CH): Edition Exodus, 1985, 179–97.

Gnilka, Joachim, *Ist 1 Kor 3,10–15 ein Schriftzeugnis für das Fegfeuer?*, Düsseldorf: Triltsch, 1955.

Gregory the Great, *Dialogorum libri quatuor* (PL 77, 149–430).

Greshake, Gisbert, *Stärker als der Tod. Zukunft – Tod – Auferstehung – Himmel – Hölle – Fegefeuer*, Mainz: Matthias-Grünewald-Verlag, [11]1991.

Greshake, Gisbert, *Tod – und dann? Ende – Reinkarnation – Auferstehung. Der Streit der Hoffnungen*, Freiburg i.Br.: Herder, 1988.

Häring, Bernhard, *Frei in Christus. Moraltheologie für die Praxis des christlichen Lebens*, vol. 1, Freiburg i.Br.: Herder, 1989.

Häring, Hermann, *Die Macht des Bösen. Das Erbe Augustins*, Zurich et al.: Benziger / Mohn, 1979.

Heim, Karl, *The World: Its Creation and Consummation. The End of the Present Age and The Future of the World in The Light of the Resurrection*, trans. Robert Smith, Philadelphia: Muhlenberg Press, 1962.

Hintzen, Georg, "Der Ablass: ein innerkatholisches Problem. Plädoyer für eine Revision der kirchlichen Ablasslehre und -praxis," *Catholica* 54 (2000), 297–305.

Hoping, Helmut, *Freiheit im Widerspruch. Eine Untersuchung zur Erbsündenlehre im Ausgang von Immanuel Kant*, Innsbruck: Tyrolia, 1990.

Huizing, Klaas, *Schluss mit Sünde! Warum wir eine neue Reformation brauchen*, Hamburg: Kreuz, 2017.

Joest, Wilfried, *Dogmatik*, vol. 1: *Die Wirklichkeit Gottes*, Göttingen: Vandenhoeck & Ruprecht, 1984; vol. 2: *Der Weg Gottes mit den Menschen*, Göttingen: Vandenhoeck & Ruprecht, 1986.

John XXIII, "Opening Speech to the Council," in: Walter M. Abbott / Joseph Gallagher (eds.), *The Documents of Vatican II*, London et al.: Geoffrey Chapman, 1967, 710–19.

John Paul II, *Apostolic Exhortation* Reconciliatio et paenitentia (December 2, 1984).

John Paul II, *Bull of Indiction of the Great Jubilee of the Year 2000* Incarnationis mysterium (November 29, 1998).

John Paul II, "Bull of Indiction of the Jubilee for the 1950th anniversary of the Redemption *Aperite Portas Redemptori* (January 6, 1983)," *AAS* 75/I (1983), 89–106.

John Paul II, *Encyclical* Sollicitudo rei socialis (December 30, 1987).

Jüngel, Eberhard, "Evangelischer Glaube und die Frage nach dem ewigen Leben," in: *Das Wesen des Christentums in seiner evangelischen Gestalt. Eine Vortragsreihe im Berliner Dom*, Neukirchen: Neukirchener, 2000, 112–32.

Kaufmann, Thomas / Ohst, Martin, "Unvereinbar oder inhaltsleer. Der päpstliche Ablass widerlegt die Rede vom Rechtfertigungs-Konsens," *epd-Dokumentation* 39 (1999), 1–2.

Kehl, Medard, "Neue Hoffnung für den Kosmos. Über das Heraustreten der Erde aus dem Schatten des Menschen," *Salzburger theologische Zeitschrift* 1 (1997), 15–23.

Kinder, Ernst, “Sünde und Schuld, dogmengeschichtlich,” in: *Religion in Geschichte und Gegenwart*, vol. 6, Tübingen: Mohr, ^{3}1986, 489–94.
Kirchenamt der Evangelischen Kirche in Deutschland / Sekretariat der Deutschen Bischofskonferenz (eds.), *Verantwortung wahrnehmen für die Schöpfung. Gemeinsame Erklärung des Rates der Evangelischen Kirche in Deutschland und der Deutschen Bischofskonferenz*, Gütersloh: Mohn, ^{2}1985.
Küng, Hans, *Eternal Life? Life After Death as a Medical, Philosophical, and Theological Problem*, trans. Edward Quinn, New York et al: Doubleday, 1985.
Limbeck, Meinrad, “Sünde im NT,” in: Herbert Haag (ed.), *Bibel-Lexikon*, Zurich et al.: Benziger, ^{3}1982, 1672–74.
Luther, Martin, “Disputation Against Scholastic Theology,” in: id., *Career of the Reformer: I*,Luther’s Works 31, Harold J. Grimm (ed.), Philadelphia: Muhlenberg Press, 1957, 9–16.
Luther, Martin, “Heidelberg Disputation,” in: id., *Career of the Reformer: I*, Luther’s Works 31, Harold J. Grimm (ed.), Philadelphia: Muhlenberg Press, 1957, 39–70.
Luther, Martin, “Ninety-Five Theses or Disputation on the Power and Efficacy of Indulgences,” in: id., *Career of the Reformer: I*, Luther’s Works 31, Harold J. Grimm (ed.), Philadelphia: Muhlenberg Press, 1957, 25–33.
Luther, Martin, *On the Freedom of a Christian. With Related Texts*, trans./ed. Tryntje Helfferich, Indianapolis / Cambridge: Hackett Publishing Company, 2013.
Luther, Martin, *Werke. Kritische Gesamtausgabe* [= WA], Weimar: Hermann Böhlau, 1883ff.
Lutheran World Federation / Catholic Church, *Joint Declaration on the Doctrine of Justification*. Available online under the following link: https://www.lutheranworld.org/sites/default/files/Joint%20Declaration%20on%20the%20Doctrine%20of%20Justification.pdf (September 25, 2023).
Merkt, Andreas, *Das Fegefeuer. Entstehung und Funktion einer Idee*, Darmstadt: Wissenschaftliche Buchgesellschaft, 2005.
Moltmann, Jürgen, *The Coming of God. Christian Eschatology*, trans. Margaret Kohl, Minneapolis: Fortress Press, 1996.
Moser, Tilmann, *Gottesvergiftung*, Frankfurt a. M.: Suhrkamp, 1976.
Nietzsche, Friedrich, *Dawn. Thoughts on the Presumptions of Morality*, trans. Brittain Smith, The Complete Works of Friedrich Nietzsche 5, Stanford, CA: Stanford University Press, 2011.
Nietzsche, Friedrich, “Ecce homo,” in: id., *The Case of Wagner. Twilight of the Idols. The Antichrist. Ecce Homo. Dionysius Dithyrambs. Nietzsche Contra Wagner*, trans. Adrian Del Caro et al., The Complete Works of Friedrich Nietzsche 9, Stanford, CA: Stanford University Press, 2011, 211–313.
N. N., “Papst warnt vor Missverständnissen des Ablasswesens,” *KNA/Ökumenische Information* 41 (October 5, 1999), 4.
Paul VI, *Apostolic Constitution* Indulgentiarum doctrina *(January 1, 1967)*.
Pesch, Otto Hermann, “Der Ablass – Luthers unerledigte Anfrage,” *Christ in der Gegenwart* 60 (2008), 321–22, 329–30.
Pesch, Otto Hermann, *Frei sein aus Gnade. Theologische Anthropologie*, Freiburg i.Br.: Herder, 1983.
Pesch, Otto Hermann, “Rechtfertigung, Ökumenischer Dialog,” in: Wolfgang Thönissen et al. (eds.), *Lexikon der Ökumene und Konfessionskunde*, Freiburg i. Br.: Herder, 2007, 1132–40.
Pieper, Josef, *The Concept of Sin*, trans. Edward T. Oakes, South Bend, IN: St Augustine’s Press, 2001.
Rahner, Karl, *Foundations of Christian Faith. An Introduction to the Idea of Christianity*, trans. William V. Dych, New York: Crossroad, 1982.
Rahner, Karl, “Schuld, Vergebung und Umkehr im christlichen Glauben,” in: Albert Görres / Karl Rahner, *Das Böse. Wege zu einer Bewältigung in Psychotherapie und Christentum*, Freiburg i.Br.: Herder, ^{2}1983.

Ritschl, Albrecht, *Die christliche Lehre von der Rechtfertigung und Versöhnung*, 3 vols., Bonn: Adolph Marcus, [2]1882–1883.
Sand, Alexander, "Sünde, Gesetz und Tod. Zum Menschenbild des Paulus," in: Norbert Lohfink et al., *Zum Problem der Erbsünde. Theologische und philosophische Versuche*, Essen: Ludgerus, 1981, 53–104.
Scheffczyk, Leo, "Adams Sündenfall. Die Erbschuld als Problem gläubigen Denkens heute," *Wort und Wahrheit* 20 (1965), 761–76.
Scheffczyk, Leo, "Das Dogma von der Erbsünde. Biblische Grundlagen – Geschichtliche Entwicklung – Bedeutung für die Gegenwart," in: Rudolf Schnackenburg (ed.), *Die Macht des Bösen und der Glaube der Kirche*, Düsseldorf: Patmos, 1979, 107–19.
Scheffczyk, Leo, "Die Erbschuld zwischen Naturalismus und Existentialismus. Zur Frage nach der Anpassung des Erbsündendogmas an das moderne Denken," *Münchener Theologische Zeitschrift* 15 (1964), 17–57.
Scheffczyk, Leo, "Sünde," in: Heinrich Fries (ed.), *Handbuch theologischer Grundbegriffe*, vol. 2, Munich: Kösel, 1963, 597–606.
Scheffczyk, Leo, "Versuche zur Neuaussprache der Erbschuld-Wahrheit," *Münchener Theologische Zeitschrift* 17 (1966), 253–60.
Schleiermacher, Friedrich, *The Christian Faith*, H. R. MacKintosh / J. S. Stewart (eds.), vol. 1, New York / Evanston: Harper & Row, 1963.
Schoonenberg, Piet, "Der Mensch in der Sünde," in: Johannes Löhrer / Magnus Feiner (eds.), *Mysterium salutis. Grundriß heilsgeschichtlicher Dogmatik*, vol. 2: *Die Heilsgeschichte vor Christus*, Einsiedeln et al.: Benziger, 1967, 845–941.
Schoonenberg, Piet, *Man and Sin. A Theological View*, trans. Joseph Donceel, Notre Dame, IN: University of Notre Dame Press, 1965.
Stendahl, Krister, "Sünde und Schuld im NT," in: *Religion in Geschichte und Gegenwart*, vol. 6, Tübingen: Mohr, [3]1986, 484–89.
Teilhard de Chardin, Pierre, "Note on Some Possible Historical Representations of Original Sin," in: id., *Christianity and Evolution*, trans. René Hague, New York: Harcourt Brace Jovanovich, 1971, 45–55.
Thomas Aquinas, *Summa Theologica*, trans. Fathers of the English Dominican Province, 3 vols., New York et al.: Benziger Brothers, 1947.
Vögtle, Anton, "Sünde im NT," in: *Lexikon für Theologie und Kirche*, vol. 9, Freiburg i. Br.: Herder, [2]1964, 1174–77.
Vrienzen, Theodorus Christian, "Sünde und Schuld im AT," in: *RGG*, vol. 6, Tübingen: Mohr, [3]1986, 478–82.
Weger, Karl-Heinz, *Erbsünde heute*, Munich: Don Bosco, 1972.
Weger, Karl-Heinz, "Erbsündentheologie heute. Situation, Probleme, Aufgaben," *Stimmen der Zeit* 181 (1968), 289–302.
Weger, Karl-Heinz, *Theologie der Erbsünde. Mit einem Exkurs Erbsünde und Monogenismus von Karl Rahner*, Quaestiones disputatae 44, Freiburg i.Br.: Herder, 1970.
Weger, Karl-Heinz, "Zur Diskussion um die Erbsünde," *Herder Korrespondenz* 21 (1967), 76–88.
Wellershoff, Dieter, *Der Himmel ist kein Ort*, Cologne: Kiepenheuer & Witsch, 2009.
Wickler, Wolfgang, "Biologische Deutung der Erbsünde," in: Rudolf Schnackenburg (ed.), *Die Macht des Bösen und der Glaube der Kirche*, Düsseldorf: Patmos, 1979, 98–106.
Zenger, Erich, "Zum biblischen Hintergrund der christlichen Erbsündentheologie," in: Siegfried Wiedenhofer (ed.), *Erbsünde – was ist das?*, Regensburg: Pustet, 1999, 9–33.

Suggestions for Further Reading

Böttigheimer, Christoph / Dausner, René (eds.), *Die Erbsündenlehre in der modernen Freiheitsdebatte*, Quaestiones disputatae 316, Freiburg i. Br.: Herder, 2021.

Dalferth, Ingolf U., *Sünde. Die Entdeckung der Menschlichkeit*, Leipzig: Evangelische Verlagsanstalt, 2020.

Enxing, Julia, *Schuld und Sünde (in) der Kirche. Eine systematisch-theologische Untersuchung*, Ostfildern: Grünewald, 2018.

Knop, Julia, *Sünde, Freiheit, Endlichkeit. Christliche Sündentheologie im theologischen Diskurs der Gegenwart*, Regensburg: Pustet, 2007.

McCall, Thomas H., *Against God and Nature: The Doctine of Sin*, Wheaton, IL: Crossway Books, 2019.

Mynatty, Hormis, "The Concept of Social Sin," *Louvain Studies* 16 (1991), 3–26.

Schumacher, Thomas, *Eine kurze Geschichte der Sünde. Biblische, geistesgeschichtliche und theologische Perspektiven,* Munich: Pneuma, 2021.

Ayman Shabana

The Concept of Sin in Islam

> Oh, my servants who have transgressed and wronged themselves, do not despair and lose hope in God's mercy, for God forgives all sins. Indeed, He is most forgiving most merciful.
> Qur'ān 93:53

> Abū Hurayrah reported that the Prophet said: "By the One in whose Hand is my soul, if you did not sin, God would replace you with other people who would sin and ask God for forgiveness and he will then forgive them."[1]

> All he could have; I made him just and right, Sufficient to have stood, though free to fall.
> John Milton, *Paradise Lost*

Sin is one of the most loaded and multivalent words. Linguistically, it denotes moral denunciation and condemnation, especially from a religious perspective. Understanding the full meaning of the term, however, would require close and careful analysis of related terms and concepts within the context of the moral-religious universe in question. The task is compounded in the case of comparative linguistic or religious studies because the wider meaning of key moral terms cannot be gained from word-for-word translation. By contrast in these cases greater attention should be devoted to clarifying and elucidating the broader semantic meaning(s) of key moral terms within the context of their own traditions.[2] This chapter aims to situate the concept of sin in Islam by examining its meaning; scriptural roots; and significance for important theological, legal and broader ethical questions. Ultimately, the chapter seeks to highlight the role of this important concept in the development of the Islamic normative tradition.

1 Meaning of Sin in the Arabic and Islamic Context

In the Arabic language several terms are connected with the concept of sin and each of them refers to one of its possible meanings. At least three main senses can be distinguished in the Islamic normative tradition. At the broadest level, the

1 al-Nawawī, Yaḥyā ibn Sharaf, *Ṣaḥīḥ Muslim bi Sharḥ al-Nawawī*, 18 vols., Cairo: al-Maṭbaʿah al-Miṣriyyah bi al-Azhar, 1929, 17:64–65 (kitāb al-tawbah, bāb suqūṭ al-dhunūb bi al-istighfār tawbah).
2 Cf. Izutsu, Toshihiko, *Ethico-Religious Concepts in the Qur'ān*, Montreal: McGill-Queen's University Press, 2002, 25.

https://doi.org/10.1515/9783111319452-003

first sense of sin denotes an act of disobedience against divine law or command, which is indicated by the Arabic terms *maʿṣiyah* and *ʿiṣyān* along with their various derivatives.[3] The second sense underscores its religious-ethical connotation as an act or deed that denotes moral wrong (misdeed) in the form of infraction or violation of a religious-moral injunction. The third sense of sin underscores its legal connotations as an ethical-legal infraction or crime, which refers primarily to the stipulated punishments or *ḥudūd* such as adultery or murder. Words such as *fāḥishah* and *faḥshāʾ* are used to refer to this meaning of sin, as is the case in 4:15–16 and 17:32, where the former is used to refer to adultery. The two terms are generally used to denote something that is abominable, detestable, or repugnant, whether in the case of words or actions.[4] Similarly, the term *jurm* is also used to denote the general meaning of sin, similar to *dhanb* or *ithm*, but often with reference to its ethical-legal connotation, especially in the case of another derivative of the same root, which is *jarīmah* (commonly translated in English as crime).[5]

The most common use of sin usually occurs in connection with its second sense as a religious-moral wrong, which is indicated by terms such as *khaṭaʾ*, *khaṭīʾah*, *ithm*, *dhanb*, *wizr* or *sayyiʾah*. The word *khaṭāʾ* stands for a mistake or something done in error, which is the opposite of what is right or correct. Another related word is *khiṭʾ*, which is used to denote intentional wrong in comparison with *khaṭaʾ*, which denotes lack of intent or premeditation. The word *khaṭīʾah* denotes an intentional infraction (*al-dhanb ʿan ʿamd*). It is, therefore, closer in meaning to *khiṭʾ* than *khaṭaʾ*, especially with reference to the existence of prior intent

---

3 The term *maʿṣiyah* itself is mentioned in the Qurʾān twice in 58:8–9. A synonymous verbal noun (*ʿiṣyān*) is mentioned in 49:7. Additionally various derivatives in different verbal forms are used about 30 times, see ʿAbd al-Bāqī, Muḥammad Fuʾād, *al-Muʿjam al-Mufahras li-Alfāẓ al-Qurʾān al-Karīm*, Cairo: Dār al-Ḥadīth, 2001, 569. This section draws in part on my chapter "The Concept of Sin in the Qurʾān in Light of the Story of Adam," in: Lucinda Musher / David Marshall (eds.), *Sin, Forgiveness, and Reconciliation*, Washington, DC: Georgetown University Press, 2016, 40–65.

4 Cf. Ibn Fāris, Aḥmad, *Muʿjam Maqāyīs al-Lughah*, ed. ʿAbd al-Salām Hārūn, 6 vols., Beirut: Dār al-Fikr lil-Ṭibāʿah wa al-Nashr wa al-Tawzīʿ, 1979, 4:478; Ibn Manẓūr, Jamāl al-Din Muḥammad, *Lisān al-ʿArab*, 18 vols., Beirut: Dār Ṣādir, 2008, 11:134; al-Zubaydī, Muḥammad Murtaḍā al-Ḥusaynī, *Tāj al-ʿArūs min Jawāhir al-Qāmus*, ed. Nawwāf al-Jarrāḥ, 10 vols., Beirut: Dār Ṣādir, 2011, 8:41–42; al-Rāghib al-Iṣfahānī, Abū al-Qāsim Ḥusayn ibn Muḥammad, *al-Mufradāt fī Gharīb al-Qurʾān*, ed. Muḥammad Sayyid Kilānī, Beirut: Dār al-Maʿrifah, n.d., 40–41. For references to these two terms in the Qurʾān, see ʿAbd al-Bāqī, *al-Muʿjam al-Mufahras*, 624.

5 Cf. Ibn Fāris, *Muʿjam Maqāyīs al-Lughah*, 1:446; Ibn Manẓūr, *Lisān al-ʿArab*, 3:129; al-Zubaydī, *Tāj al-ʿArūs*, 2:337. Although neither the term *jurm* nor its derivative *jarīmah* is mentioned in the Qurʾān, several other derivatives are frequently used, especially the verbal form *ajrama* and nominal form *mujrim* (both singular and plural forms), see ʿAbd al-Bāqī, *al-Muʿjam al-Mufahras*, 203–04.

or premeditation.[6] The word *ithm* is derived from the root that denotes slowness and also delay. Its moral connotation indicates slowness in doing what is good or lagging behind what is good.[7] The word stands for an act that involves transgression of norms (*fiʿl mā lā yaḥill*).[8] Similarly, the word *dhanb* is used to refer to an act of disobedience or a religious-moral violation, often synonymously with other related terms such as *ithm* or *jurm*.[9] The word *wizr* stands for a load or burden, especially if it is heavy. It is used to describe a misdeed due to its impact on the individual and that is why it is often used synonymously with *ithm* and *dhanb*.[10] The word *sayyiʾāh* (adjective in the feminine form) and *sayyiʾ* (masculine form) stem from the root that denotes ugliness.[11] It also denotes the act of doing bad or to spoil. These two terms are also used to denote a misdeed or a violation.[12]

One useful way to trace these different terms in the Qurʾān is to examine them in combination with their opposites. For example, the word for obedience (*ṭāʿah*) occurs only three times in the Qurʾān, but several other verbal derivatives are used repeatedly, often in comparison with the term *maʿṣiyah* (disobedience) and its derivatives.[13] The word *sayyiʾah* for bad deed (pl. *sayyiʾāt*) is often compared to its opposite *ḥasanah* (pl. *ḥasanāt*). Similarly, the word *sharr* (evil), which is also used to denote a religious-moral wrong, is contrasted with its opposite *khayr* as in 99:7–8. Moreover, the word *munkar* (wrong or evil) is also often con-

---

6 Cf. Ibn Fāris, *Muʿjam Maqāyīs al-Lughah*, 2:198; Ibn Manẓūr, *Lisān al-ʿArab*, 5:96–97; al-Zubaydī, *Tāj al-ʿArūs*, 3:721–22. The term *khaṭaʾ* and its derivatives are mentioned 12 times in the Qurʾān, while the term *khaṭīʾah* is mentioned 10 times in both singular and plural forms, see ʿAbd al-Bāqī, *al-Muʿjam al-Mufahras*, 288.

7 Cf. Ibn Fāris, *Muʿjam Maqāyīs al-Lughah*, 1:60.

8 Cf. Ibn Manẓūr, *Lisān al-ʿArab*, 1:56–57. It is also said to stand for a legal violation, which is lesser than a *ḥadd*, see al-Zubaydī, *Tāj al-ʿArūs*, 1:95–96. The term *ithm* is mentioned in the Qurʾān 35 times, see ʿAbd al-Bāqī, *al-Muʿjam al-Mufahras*, 15.

9 Cf. Ibn Fāris, *Muʿjam Maqāyīs al-Lughah*, 2:361; Ibn Manẓūr, *Lisān al-ʿArab*, 6:45; al-Zubaydī, *Tāj al-ʿArūs*, 4:311. The term *dhanb* is used 39 times in the Qurʾān in different singular and plural forms, see ʿAbd al-Bāqī, *al-Muʿjam al-Mufahras*, 339.

10 Cf. Ibn Fāris, *Muʿjam Maqāyīs al-Lughah*, 6:108; Ibn Manẓūr, *Lisān al-ʿArab*, 15:202; al-Zubaydī, *Tāj al-ʿArūs*, 10:765. The term *wizr* and its derivatives are mentioned about 25 times, see ʿAbd al-Bāqī, *al-Muʿjam al-Mufahras*, 840.

11 Cf. Ibn Fāris, *Muʿjam Maqāyīs al-Lughah*, 3:113.

12 Cf. Ibn Manẓūr, *Lisān al-ʿArab*, 7:292; al-Zubaydī, *Tāj al-ʿArūs*, 5:524. The term *sayyiʾah* is mentioned in the Qurʾān over 50 times in different forms, see ʿAbd al-Bāqī, *al-Muʿjam al-Mufahras*, 453–54.

13 In 4:81, 24:53, and 47:21, see ʿAbd al-Bāqī, *al-Muʿjam al-Mufahras*, 528–29.

trasted with its opposite *ma'rūf* (good), which is captured in one of Islam's fundamental moral principles; namely, *al-amr bi al-ma'rūf wa al-nahy 'an al-munkar* (commanding good and forbidding evil).[14] Occasionally some of these terms are combined as is the case in 4:112, where the terms *khaṭī'h* and *ithm* are mentioned in conjunction to each other. In other occasions they appear in combination with other related terms as is the case in 49:7, where *'iṣyān* (disobedience) is combined with *kufr* (infidelity or ingratitude) and *fusūq* (transgression), or in 8:33, where the word *ithm* is combined with *baghy* (infringement). More often, however, they are contrasted with their opposites. The term *sayyi'ah* is particularly important due to its frequency either on its own or in contrast to its opposite *ḥasanah*.

These three broad senses of sin are not always separated from each other. In fact, their usage often reveals a significant degree of overlap. For example, a *ḥadd* infraction in the case of adultery or theft is considered both a crime in the Islamic legal sense because it has a stipulated punishment in this world according to *sharī'ah* but it also signifies an act of religious-moral wrong because it entails disobedience to a divine command. On the other hand, a *ma'ṣiyah* or *dhanb* such as lying, cheating, or breaking a promise involves disobedience to divine injunctions but might not have a worldly punishment. Punishment for sin in this sense is relegated to God in the Hereafter.

One of the most famous classifications of sins in the Islamic normative tradition is their division into major or grave (*kabīrah*, pl. *kabā'ir*) and minor or lesser (*ṣaghīrah*, pl. *ṣaghā'ir*) sins. The term *kabā'ir* is mentioned in the Qur'ān in three places: 4:31, 42:37, and 53:32. In 4:31 it is indicated that avoidance of major sins could provide grounds for the forgiveness of other (minor) sins. In his commentary on the Qur'ān, the early exegete al-Ṭabarī (d. 310/923) indicates the different interpretations given to the term *kabā'ir*, which include views that specify a particular limit or number, while others give an open-ended range of moral wrongs. For example, according to one view, which is attributed to several successors via the Companion 'Abd Allāh ibn Mas'ūd (d. 32/650), they include all the condemned practices mentioned in the thirty verses of surah al-Nisā' (no. 4) that precede the

---

14 For references to *munkar* in the Qur'ān, see 'Abd al-Bāqī, *al-Mu'jam al-Mufahras*, 811 and for references to *ma'rūf*, see 'Abd al-Bāqī, *al-Mu'jam al-Mufahras*, 563. For a detailed account on the principle of commanding good and forbidding evil in the Islamic tradition, see Cook, Michael, *Commanding Right and Forbidding Wrong in Islamic Thought*, Cambridge: Cambridge University Press, 2000.

verse in which the term is mentioned.[15] Another narration, also attributed to Ibn Mas'ūd, specifies four major sins: associating partners with God (*shirk*), despair of God's forgiveness (*al-qunūṭ min raḥmat Allāh*), loss of hope in God's mercy (*al-ya's min rawḥ Allāh*), and the feeling of security from God's plotting (*al-amn min makr Allāh*).[16] According to another view, attributed to 'Alī ibn Abī Ṭālib, the major sins are seven in number. These are: associating partners with God, murder, slander, usurpation of an orphan's property, consumption of usury, fleeing from the battlefield, and leading a bedouin lifestyle after Hijrah (immigration to Medina).[17] Most of these sins are also mentioned separately in the Qur'ān.[18] According to a variant narration, attributed to Ibn 'Umar, they are nine: associating partners with God, murder, fleeing from the battlefield, slander, consumption of usury, usurpation of an orphan's property, causing mischief in the Holy mosque, black magic, and ingratitude to one's parents.[19]

While the term *kabā'ir* is used to denote major sins such as polytheism, and the term *fawāḥish* is used to refer to sins for which a stipulated punishment (*ḥadd*) has been indicated (especially illicit sexual relationship), other types of sins are usually categorized as minor sins. This is illustrated by 53:32, which distinguishes between *kabā'ir* and *fawāḥish* on the one hand and another category described as *lamam*. The usage of the term in classical Arabic culture refers to something that is closely connected to something else.[20] It is also interpreted as smaller, lesser, or minor sins.[21] The linguistic structure of the verse makes several interpretations possible depending on the meaning of the particle *illā*. If it is taken to denote connected exception (*istithnā' muttaṣil*), the term *lamam* would refer to the broader category of the major sins covering both *kabā'ir* and *fawāḥish*. In this case it would mean those sins committed by Muslims before their conversion to Islam or those committed before repentance. On the other hand, if *illā* is taken to denote disconnected exception (*istithnā' munqaṭi'*), the term *lamam*

---

15 Cf. al-Ṭabarī, Abū Ja'far Muḥammad ibn Jarīr, *Tafsīr al-Ṭabarī: Jāmi' al-Bayān 'an Ta'wīl Āy al-Qur'ān*, ed. 'Abd Allāh ibn 'Abd al-Muḥsin al-Turkī, 26 vols., Cairo: Dār Hajar, 2001, 6:640. See also Riḍā, Muḥammad Rashīd, *Tafsīr al-Qur'ān al-Ḥakīm, al-Mushtahir bi Tafsīr al-Manār*, 12 vols., Cairo: Dār al-Manār, 1947, 5:46–47.

16 Cf. al-Ṭabarī, *Tafsīr al-Ṭabarī: Jāmi' al-Bayān*, 6:648.

17 Cf. al-Ṭabarī, *Tafsīr al-Ṭabarī: Jāmi' al-Bayān*, 6:643; 'Abd al-Razzāq ibn Hammām al-Ṣan'ānī, *Tafsīr 'Abd al-Razzāq*, ed. Maḥmūd Muḥammad 'Abduh, 3 vols., Beirut: Dār al-Kutub al-'Ilmiyyah, 1999, 1:447–49.

18 See, for example, 6:151–52; 17:23–38; 25:68.

19 Cf. al-Ṭabarī, *Tafsīr al-Ṭabarī: Jāmi' al-Bayān*, 6:646.

20 Cf. al-Ṭabarī, *Tafsīr al-Ṭabarī: Jāmi' al-Bayān*, 22:69.

21 Cf. Riḍā, *Tafsīr al-Qur'ān al-Ḥakīm*, 5:48.

would mean another category of sins lesser than *kabā'ir* and *fawāḥish*. According to this view, which al-Ṭabarī supports, it would stand for sins other than those for which a stipulated worldly or otherworldly punishment is indicated.[22]

2 Sin in Islam's Foundational Sources

Keeping in mind the above list of terms that are associated with the concept of sin in the Arabic and Islamic context, this section will examine their usage in the Qur'ān and the Prophetic tradition or Sunnah. More particularly, it will survey some of the most prominent invocations of these terms, which can in turn clarify the role of this important concept in defining and shaping Islamic morality. This survey will focus on these points: nature, definition, and typologies; connections and relations to other key concepts; and impact on the status and fate of the believer.

2.1 Sin: Nature, Definition, and Typologies

In 41:34 the Qur'ān declares that a good deed (*ḥasanah*) is not equal to a bad deed (*sayi'ah*), and then gives the admonition to do what is best. Since these two terms are often compared or contrasted, it would be helpful to examine them side by side. Similarly, references to believers and their qualities as well as actions often appear in relationship to those belonging to those who are featured as their opponents. The status or fate of one party is usually indicated in contradistinction to the other and their accounts are almost always cast along parallel pathways. Occasionally the Qur'ān posits rhetorical questions concerning the (dis)similarity between these two groups, while leaving the logical answer to be deduced by the reader. For example, in 38:28 the Qur'ān asks about the possibility of equating those who believe and do good deeds with those who do mischief on earth or equating those who are pious with the transgressors. In the same vein, in 78:35 the Qur'ān posits the question whether those who submit to God (*Muslimīn*) and those who are evildoers (*mujrimīn*) should be equated. Moreover, in 45:21 the Qur'ān addresses the sinful, or those who are given to the commission of sins, and asks whether they act

22 Cf. al-Ṭabarī, *Tafsīr al-Ṭabarī: Jāmi' al-Bayān*, 22:63–67.

with the assumption that their desert, either in this life or ultimately in the hereafter, would be similar to those who believe and do good deeds.[23]

We can start this exploration of the concept of sin in the Qur'ān with the verses that specify the acts that qualify as examples or instances of sin, especially the major ones. This is best illustrated by the passages that list certain actions that are described either as *kabā'ir* (sing. *kabīrah*) or *fawāḥish* (sing. *fāḥishah*). For example, in 7:151–52, several actions are categorized as prohibited by God: associating partners with God; ingratitude to one's parents; killing one's own children for fear of poverty; murder outside the boundaries of the law; appropriating the wealth of orphans; cheating in transactions through manipulation of the units of measurement; and statements amounting to injustice, even if against one's own kin. Commentaries on the Qur'ān often emphasize the importance of this passage in light of the various reports that are traced to the Prophet and his companions. For example, the famous companion Ibn ʿAbbās (d. 68/687) noted that this passage constitutes the core of divine commandments that are referred to in 3:7 as conspicuous regulations (*muḥkamāt*).[24] They have never been abrogated as they are reiterated in all the moral-religious traditions across human history and they are also said to echo the Ten Commandments given to Moses.[25]

In addition to the actions listed above, the first verse in this passage (7:151) points out an important dimension of sin; namely, its division into two main types: external and internal. This part of the verse underscores the importance of avoiding all types of sins (*fawāḥish*), both public or explicit (*mā ẓahar*) as well as hidden or implicit (*mā baṭan*). Two main interpretations have been given to this part of the verse. The first emphasizes the generic import of the linguistic structure, covering the explicit as well as implicit dimensions of these actions. Accordingly, the explicit sins include all acts of disobedience. The implicit sins would include what is held

---

23 This comparative pattern is quite common throughout the Qur'ān. Examples are not limited to believers or Muslims on the one hand and disbelievers or polytheists on the other. They also include ones that involve additional contextual descriptions such as: the dwellers of Paradise (*aṣḥāb al-jannah*) and the dwellers of the Fire (*aṣḥāb al-nār*) (8:44–50); those who will experience happiness in the hereafter (*al-ladhina su'idu*) and those who will experience misery (*al-ladhina shaqū*) (11:105–08); those who will receive their written record of actions, in the hereafter, with their right hands (*man utya kitābahu bi-yamīnih*) and those who will receive it with their left hands (*bi shimālih*) (69:19–29) or from behind their backs (*warā'a ẓahrih*) (84:7–14); or the company of the right (*aṣḥāb al-yamīn*) and the company of the left (*aṣḥāb al-shimāl*) (56:27–48).

24 Cf. al-Ṭabarī, *Tafsīr al-Ṭabarī: Jāmiʿ al-Bayān*, 9:667–68.

25 Cf. al-Qurṭubī, Muḥammad ibn Aḥmad, *al-Jāmiʿ li-Aḥkām al-Qur'ān wa al-Mubayyin limā Taḍammanahu min al-Sunnah wa Āy al-Furqān*, ed. ʿAbd Allāh ibn ʿAbd al-Muḥsin al-Turkī, 24 vols., Beirut: Mu'ssassat al-Risālah, 2006, 9:106.

internally in one's heart.[26] The second draws on the special connection between the term *fāḥishah* and illicit sexual relationship in the form of fornication or adultery (*zinā*). It is said to refer to the pre-Islamic Arabian practice of denouncing illicit sexual relations in public, while condoning them if they are done in private. By contrast, the passage bans the action regardless of whether it is done in an open setting, as was the case with brothels in pre-Islamic Arabia, or secretly.[27]

In a similar passage in 17:23–39, the Qur'ān reiterates most of the actions mentioned in 7:151–52 and adds a number of additional ones. The passage can be divided into three main sections, including three sets of injunctions. The first covers several fundamental principles such as: monotheistic belief in God; honoring parents; and dutifulness to relatives as well as supporting the poor and the needy in moderation and without extravagance. The second denounces several practices such as: killing one's children for fear of poverty; illicit sexual relations; and appropriation or mismanagement of the wealth owned by orphans. The third includes a number of exhortations such as: commitment to one's promises and agreements; justice and honesty in transactions, as manifested in the proper and equitable handling of the units of measurement; ascertaining one's sources of knowledge; responsible use of one's faculties, especially hearing and sight; and avoidance of arrogance and haughtiness, as demonstrated in how a person walks or treats others in general. The passage concludes with a declaration that these sins – involved either in the negligence of the commandments or commission of the prohibitions within this text – are detested by God.[28]

Since, as noted above, words denoting sin are often mentioned in combination with or in comparison with their opposites, the Qur'ānic definition of sin can

26 Cf. al-Qurṭubī, *al-Jāmī' li-Aḥkām al-Qur'ān*, 9:108.

27 Cf. al-Rāzī, Fakhr al-Dīn Muḥammad ibn 'Umar, *Tafsīr al-Fakhr al-Rāzī al-Mushtahir bi al-Tafsīr al-Kabīr wa Mafātīḥ al-Ghayb*, 32 vols., Beirut: Dār al-Fikr lil-Ṭibā'ah wa al-Nashr wa al-Tawzī', 1981, 13:245. According to another opinion, public sins (*fawāḥish*) refer to the prohibited types of relationships and those amounting to incest (as mentioned in 4:23), especially those involving close female relatives such as mothers and mothers in law. Hidden sins, on the other hand, refer to adultery or fornication. According to yet another opinion, public sins refer to the consumption of wine, while implicit sins refer to adultery or fornication, see al-Ṭabarī, *Tafsīr al-Ṭabarī: Jāmi' al-Bayān*, 9:659–61. Reference to these two dimensions of sin is also made in an earlier verse in the same chapter (7:120), see also al-Ṭabarī, *Tafsīr al-Ṭabarī: Jāmi' al-Bayān*, 9:516–19. In one narration attributed to the famous successor 'Ikrimah (d. 105/723), explicit sins are those that involve injustice to people, while hidden ones refer to fornication and theft because they are done in secrecy, see Riḍā, *Tafsīr al-Qur'ān al-Ḥakīm*, 8:187–88.

28 Cf. al-Ṭabarī, *Tafsīr al-Ṭabarī: Jāmi' al-Bayān*, 14:600–01; al-Qurṭubī, *al-Jāmī' li-Aḥkām al-Qur'ān*, 13:83–84; al-Rāzī, *Tafsīr al-Fakhr al-Rāzī al-Mushtahir bi al-Tafsīr al-Kabīr wa Mafātīḥ al-Ghayb*, 20:213.

also be gleaned from passages that explain terms associated with the good and its different forms. A clear example is 2:177, in which the term *birr* is defined. The linguistic meaning of the term is said to capture the broadest meaning of the good. In its origin, the word is derived from *barr*, which stands for shore or land. It is compared to the sea or ocean in terms of its vast and expansive boundaries. The religious-moral scope of the term covers all actions that enable the individual to draw near to God by means of good deeds and moral behavior.[29] The passage indicates that the good cannot be limited to the mere offering of prayer, or rituals, in a perfunctory manner. By contrast, it should be rooted in and driven by a firm belief in the fundamentals of faith: monotheistic belief in God, the Last Day, His angels, His Books, and His messengers. It should also be demonstrated by concrete evidence through: offering financial support, despite one's attachment to one's own wealth (to relatives, orphans, the needy, wayfarers, those who ask for help, and those who seek to free themselves); establishment of prayer; payment of charity; fulfilling promises; showing patience in times of distress, hardship, or during intense battles.[30] The verse is described as one of the most comprehensive statements of faith due to its inclusion of numerous theological, legal, and moral principles.[31] Ultimately, however, by elucidating this general meaning and scope of *birr*, it can also serve as an indication of its outer contours and interface with sin. Therefore, one can only get a clearer view of the larger picture that the Qur'ān draws for sin after placing this passage, and similar ones, next to the other passages that address sin more closely.

In the same vein, the Qur'ānic conception of sin can also be gathered from passages that offer descriptions of the qualities of the believers. The Qur'ān does not only use the term for believers (*al-mu'minūn*), but it uses a number of other related terms that denote other various qualities such as: those who submit (*al-muslimūn*), those who are pious (*al-muttaqūn*), those who show humility (*al-khāshi'ūn*), those who offer prayer (*al-muṣallūn*), those who fast (*al-ṣā'imūn*), those who tell the truth (*al-ṣādiqūn*), those who offer charity (*al-mutaṣaddiqūn*), those who are devoutly obedient (*al-qāniṭūn*), those who are patient (*al-ṣābirūn*), and those who remember God (*al-dhdhākirūn*).[32] These descriptive passages, similar to 7:151–52 and 17:23–39, often include a combination of commandments, to be followed, and infractions, to be avoided. Two instances can be highlighted here. The first is 23:1–11, which is the opening passage of the chapter (al-Mu'minūn). It

29 Cf. al-Rāghib al-Iṣfahānī, *al-Mufradāt fī Gharīb al-Qur'ān*, 40–41; Riḍā, *Tafsīr al-Qur'ān al-Ḥakīm*, 2:110.

30 Cf. al-Ṭabarī, *Tafsīr al-Ṭabarī: Jāmi' al-Bayān*, 3:74.

31 Cf. al-Qurṭubī, *al-Jāmī' li-Aḥkām al-Qur'ān*, 3:59.

32 Most of these qualities are mentioned in 33:35. Other similar passages include 70:22–35.

begins with a statement indicating the good fortune of the believers. It then proceeds to spell out the qualities by means of which the believers, and those who follow their example, are able to reach this position. These qualities include: establishment of prayer with humility and perseverance;[33] refraining from idle talk; offering charity; preservation of private parts by not engaging in illicit sexual relations; and maintaining trusts with honesty. The passage concludes with the ultimate reward that the believers will obtain in the Hereafter; namely, admission into the promised paradise.

The second is 25:63–75, which also includes descriptions of God's servants. They are depicted as those who: walk with modesty; when aroused by the ignorant, they do not lose their peace; engage in night vigil and pray for protection from the Hellfire; spend in moderation, being neither miserly nor extravagant; do not associate partners with God; do not violate the sanctity of human life, outside the boundaries of the law; do not partake in false testimony or idle talk; and when they are reminded of God's signs, they pay heed. The passage includes grave warning that commission of the noted infractions would be grounds for severe and humiliating punishment in the Hereafter. However, the door for reconciliation is not shut, for those who sincerely repent and do good deeds. The passage also concludes by indicating the reward that the servants of God will receive in the Hereafter in the form of admission into paradise.[34]

Similarly, references to sin in the Qur'ān can be explored by tracing passages that provide description of disbelievers or people noted as deserving worldly or otherworldly punishment. Again, the Qur'ān does not only use the word *al-kāfirūn*, which is commonly translated as disbelievers, infidels, or those who are ungrateful. As noted above in the case of believers, the Qur'ān uses several other terms that denote their various qualities such as: the polytheists (*al-mushrikūn*), those who commit injustice (*al-ẓālimūn*), those who transgress (*al-fāsiqūn*), the hypocrites (*al-munāfiqūn*), and those who are evildoers (*al-mujrimūn*). For example, in 74:41–53 several actions are noted as causing severe punishment in the Hellfire: negligence of prayer; refraining from feeding the needy; engaging in idle talk; casting doubt on the Day of Judgment; and ignoring admonition.

This brief survey of the nature and types of sin in the Qur'ān should not be seen as exhaustive but only as illustrative and representative. A fuller or more

---

33 Other references in the Qur'ān indicate the specific role of prayer on the believer's ability to guard against sin. For example: "Recite what has been revealed to you from the Book and establish prayer for it drives away from abominable sin (*faḥshā'*) and that which is deemed ugly (*munkar*); remembrance of God is greater and God knows what you do" (29:45).

34 Other references to the qualities of believers that earn them ultimate reward in the hereafter include 51:15–19, 55:46–78, 56:10–38; and 70:22–35.

comprehensive survey falls beyond the scope of this chapter and would require a more systematic exploration in association with the terms highlighted above, in addition to other related ones. The same should also be said about surveying the concept in the larger corpus of the Sunnah, which is far more expansive than the Qur'ānic text. In fact, numerous Prophetic reports address the different types of sin in connection with the various Arabic terms associated with it. Some of the most prominent examples include the ones that specify the grave sins and they often reiterate most of what was mentioned above; namely, associating partners with God, murder, ingratitude to one's parents, false testimony, magic, gambling, theft, intoxication, slander, and false oath.[35]

2.2 A Broader View of Sin

Apart from enumerating the various types of sin, the scriptural sources do also address a number of points that clarify the ways in which sins affect one's life, both in this world and the next. These points include, for example: the scope of responsibility for sin, how sin is accounted for, the wider impact of sin, and also the possibility of repentance. First of all, the Qur'ān is quite clear on the individual scope of responsibility for sin, which is reiterated in several passages as a general principle. For example, in 41:46, the Qur'ān proclaims that whoever does good (*'amila ṣāliḥ^an^*), he (alone) shall receive due reward and whoever does bad (*asā'a*), he (alone) shall incur due consequences.[36] The conclusion of the verse emphasizes divine justice, which governs this process of accounting. In a similar verse (45:15), the same principle is stated with a reminder about ultimate return to God, when full justice will be served.[37] This principle is also rendered differently by another phrase, which appears in several places throughout the Qur'ān; namely, no (sinning) soul shall be held responsible for the sin of another (*lā taziru wāzirat^un^ wizr ukhrā*).[38] Moreover, this principle is often expressed in connection with the verb denoting acquisition

35 See, for example, ibn Ḥajar al-'Asqalānī, Aḥmad ibn 'Alī, *Fatḥ al-Bārī bi Sharḥ Ṣaḥīḥ al-Bukhārī*, 13 vols., Beirut: Dār al-Ma'rifah, n.d., 10:405; al-Nawawī, *Ṣaḥīḥ Muslim bi Sharḥ al-Nawawī*, 2:79–88 (kitāb al-imān, bāb al-kabā'ir wa akbaruhā). For other related Prophetic reports, see al-Ṭabarī, *Tafsīr al-Ṭabarī: Jāmi' al-Bayān*, 6:651–61; al-Qurṭubī, *al-Jāmī' li-Aḥkām al-Qur'ān*, 6:263–65.

36 Cf. al-Ṭabarī, *Tafsīr al-Ṭabarī: Jāmi' al-Bayān*, 20:454; al-Qurṭubī, *al-Jāmī' li-Aḥkām al-Qur'ān*, 18:432.

37 Cf. al-Ṭabarī, *Tafsīr al-Ṭabarī: Jāmi' al-Bayān*, 21:83; al-Qurṭubī, *al-Jāmī' li-Aḥkām al-Qur'ān*, 19:152

38 Cf. al-Ṭabarī, *Tafsīr al-Ṭabarī: Jāmi' al-Bayān*, 10:48–9. It is mentioned in 6:164; 17:15; 35:18; 39:7; and 53:38.

of actions (*kasab*), which, as discussed below, became subject to serious theological debates in the Islamic tradition.[39] In 6:164 these two phrases are mentioned next to each other, and the meaning is said to apply primarily to the religious and other-worldly reward.[40] If individual responsibility is upheld in the Qur'ān as a general principle, shared responsibility is sometimes noted in case sin is committed collectively. For example, narratives of the earlier Prophets reveal that divine punishment of entire communities often came as a result of their obstinacy, violation of divine instructions, and only after ample forewarning – as demonstrated in the stories of Prophets Nūḥ (Noah), Hūd, Ṣaliḥ, and Lūṭ (Lot).

Another important point is how sin is accounted for, also often in comparison to a good deed (*ḥasanah*). In order to encourage the performance of good deeds, the Qur'ān points out that their reward is compounded. The increase is sometimes noted as double, ten times, or more. By contrast the return for sin is often expressed as only single. For example, in 6:160, it is mentioned that a good deed is rewarded ten times, while a bad deed is counted as one and then compensated as such. The linguistic structure is generic and will accordingly cover good and bad deeds more broadly. With reference to the context of the verse, however, commentators noted that the good deed here stands for faith while the bad deed stands for disbelief.[41] The compounding of good deeds, in contradistinction to bad deeds, is also confirmed in several Prophetic reports that indicate the difference in the recording and also how these acts are evaluated. Some also underscore the role of one's intention during the stage preceding the action itself. For example, according to one report on the authority of the companion Ibn ʿAbbās, if a person considers doing a good deed without actually doing it, it will be recorded as a full good deed. If he proceeds and does it, it will be recorded as ten good deeds and it could also be doubled up to seven hundred or more times. Conversely, if he considers doing a bad deed without doing it, it will be recorded as a good deed. If he does it, it will be recorded as one single bad deed. The phrasing of the report denotes that the Prophet's statement is based on divine revelation, which justifies its classification among a special category of aḥādīth that are described as *qudsiyyah*.[42]

---

39 For references to this verb and its derivatives in the Qur'ān, see ʿAbd al-Bāqī, *al-Muʿjam al-Mufahras*, 707–08.

40 Cf. al-Qurṭubī, *al-Jāmīʿ li-Aḥkām al-Qur'ān*, 9:145; Riḍā, *Tafsīr al-Qur'ān al-Ḥakīm*, 8:245–6. For the debate on whether the reward of actions by the living can reach the dead, see ibid. 8:247–70.

41 Cf. al-Ṭabarī, *Tafsīr al-Ṭabarī: Jāmiʿ al-Bayān*, 10:36–44; al-Qurṭubī, *al-Jāmīʿ li-Aḥkām al-Qur'ān*, 9:136–37; Riḍā, *Tafsīr al-Qur'ān al-Ḥakīm*, 8:233.

42 Cf. Ibn Ḥajar al-ʿAsqalānī, *Fatḥ al-Bārī bi Sharḥ Ṣaḥīḥ al-Bukhārī*, 11:323 (kitāb al-riqāq, Bab man hamma bi ḥasant[in] aww sayi"ah). For this report and several similar ones, see also al-Nawawī, *Ṣaḥīḥ Muslim bi Sharḥ al-Nawawī*, 2:149 (kitāb al-imān).

While references to the compounding of good deeds do not always mention specific examples, occasionally, however, certain acts of benevolence are highlighted. This is particularly the case with charity and spending money for charitable causes. Here also some verses indicate the reward with a specific rate of increase more explicitly, while others leave the reward and its range open. For example, in 2:261, which describes the reward for those who spend for the sake of God, it is indicated that reward is doubled up to seven hundred times. On the other hand, in 2:245, which describes the reward for those who offer God a good loan (*qarḍ*^{an} *ḥasan*^{an}), it is indicated that the reward would be compounded many times (*aḍʿāf*^{an} *kathīrah*).[43] Explanations given for the compounding of reward for specific deeds, particularly charity, often relegate this to divine knowledge and wisdom. They also allude to the underlying motives of the individual and the extent to which actions are meant sincerely for the sake of God, without ulterior or worldly reasons. When these acts are done with the right attitude and intention, they would be rewarded immensely and generously. Furthermore, charity is often singled out because it does not only benefit the giving individual alone but also others.[44]

In addition to the accountability for sin in the hereafter, the scriptural sources also often address its wider implications on one's life in this world. This includes both the internal psychological state as well as the various external aspects. For example, in 20:124, it is indicated that whoever turns away from God's reminders, his life will be extremely hard. The Arabic term used is *ḍank*, which denotes tightness and misery. Life in this verse is said to refer to the hereafter, to the grave, and also this worldly life.[45] Conversely, other passages describe the impact of good deeds on the type of life that the person lives. For example, in 16:97 it is indicated that those who believe and do good deeds will be given a good life (*ḥayāt*^{an} *ṭayyibah*). Similarly, life in this verse may cover life in this world or ultimately in the hereafter. Al-Qurṭubī lists several opinions of companions and successors on the

---

43 Offering God a good loan is a metaphor that is used to refer to the various charitable causes, see al-Ṭabarī, *Tafsīr al-Ṭabarī: Jāmiʿ al-Bayān*, 4: 650, 4:428. It is used in several other passages as well in 5:12, 57:11,18, 64:17, 57:11, and 73:20. On the simile of charitable spending as offering a loan to God, it is noted that it is meant to encourage people to do it; namely, helping the poor and the needy is depicted as giving to God himself. Moreover, the description of this type of giving as a loan gives the indication that the payback is certain in the same way a lender expects to receive his money from the debtor, see al-Qurṭubī, *al-Jāmiʿ li-Aḥkām al-Qurʾān*, 4:223–24.

44 Cf. Ibn Ḥajar al-ʿAsqalānī, *Fatḥ al-Bārī bi Sharḥ Ṣaḥīḥ al-Bukhārī*, 11:326; Riḍā, *Tafsīr al-Qurʾān al-Ḥakīm*, 8:233.

45 Cf. al-Rāghib al-Iṣfahānī, *al-Mufradāt fī Gharīb al-Qurʾān*, 299; al-Ṭabarī, *Tafsīr al-Ṭabarī: Jāmiʿ al-Bayān*, 16:192–93; al-Qurṭubī, *al-Jāmiʿ li-Aḥkām al-Qurʾān*, 14:157–58.

meaning of life in this verse. According to one opinion it is ultimate reward in the hereafter. The other opinions refer to several possibilities that pertain to this worldly domain, which include: lawful provision; contentment; guidance to the performance of different types of obedience; and happiness, especially one that comes through experiencing the sweetness of faith.[46] The impact of sin on one's life is also highlighted in 42:30, where it is noted that whatever befalls the individual of misfortune (*muṣībah*), it is the result of what they have done. Again, the linguistic structure is quite generic and therefore various interpretations were suggested. For example, according to one explanation, it covers any type of adversity that affects the individual in his person, family, or wealth. According to another interpretation, however, it covers the stipulated penalties. The meaning then would be whatever punishment you receive, it is because of what you have done.[47]

This verse is also related to the passage in 99:7–8, according to which whoever does the scale of an atom of good would be rewarded accordingly. And whoever does the scale of an atom of evil would likewise be rewarded accordingly. The context of the entire passage refers to the hereafter and that is why several commentators noted that it pertains to ultimate reward then for all deeds, including the tiniest ones as small as atoms. Other commentators, however, relying on the general linguistic scope, noted that it applies to reward in this worldly life as well. Accordingly, a distinction is made between believers and disbelievers. For believers, while the reward for bad deeds is shown in this world in the form of adversities in one's person, family, or wealth, the reward for good deeds is stored until the hereafter. On the other hand, for the disbelievers, while the reward for good deeds is shown in this world in the form of prosperity in one's person, family, or wealth, the reward for bad deeds is stored until the hereafter.[48] Similarly, 30:41 refers to the appearance of corruption (*fasād*) in the land (*barr*) and in the sea (*baḥr*) because of people's (bad) deeds. It indicates that this is meant (by God) to let people taste the result of some of their actions, so they may return in repentance. While some commentators are of the opinion that reference here is to the pre-Islamic context, others support a more general interpretation. For example,

---

46 Cf. al-Ṭabarī, *Tafsīr al-Ṭabarī: Jāmiʿ al-Bayān*, 14:350–55; al-Qurṭubī, *al-Jāmīʿ li-Aḥkām al-Qurʾān*, 12:423–24.

47 Cf. al-Ṭabarī, *Tafsīr al-Ṭabarī: Jāmiʿ al-Bayān*, 20:512–14; al-Qurṭubī, *al-Jāmīʿ li-Aḥkām al-Qurʾān*, 18:477–80.

48 Cf. al-Ṣanʿānī, *Tafsīr ʿAbd al-Razzāq*, 3:449; al-Ṭabarī, *Tafsīr al-Ṭabarī: Jāmiʿ al-Bayān*, 24:562–69; al-Qurṭubī, *al-Jāmīʿ li-Aḥkām al-Qurʾān*, 22:421–25. This verse is also featured in several Prophetic reports, in which the Prophet described it as uniquely comprehensive (*al-jāmiʿah al-fadhdhah*), see Ibn Ḥajar al-ʿAsqalānī, *Fatḥ al-Bārī bi Sharḥ Ṣaḥīḥ al-Bukhārī*, 5:46 (kitāb al-musāqah, bab shurb al-nās wa saqy al-dawabb min al-anhār); al-Nawawī, *Ṣaḥīḥ Muslim bi Sharḥ al-Nawawī*, 7:67 (kitāb al-zakāh).

Ibn ʿAbbās noted that the term *fasād* stands for drought or lack of blessing because of people's bad deeds.[49]

Consequences of sin do not only cover impact on one's life in this world or in the hereafter, but several scriptural references also touch on the impact of sin on the state of one's faith. On this point some Prophetic reports question the faith of the perpetrator of certain sins. For example, according to one report that is narrated by Ibn ʿAbbās: "The adulterer does not commit adultery while he is a believer and a thief does not commit theft while he is a believer." When Ibn ʿAbbās was asked about the meaning of this statement, he noted that sin does not severe one's faith forever. But, after committing a sin, one can regain one's faith with sincere repentance.[50] Another report includes a similar, although longer, statement that includes reference to drinking wine and usurpation of wealth.[51] Commentators on this report gave several interpretations on the extent to which sin can undermine one's relationship with God. For example, in his commentary on Ṣaḥīḥ Muslim, al-Nawawī notes that it means that a believer will not commit these sins while in a state of complete faith. The title of the chapter in which the report is recorded indicates that acts of disobedience decrease one's faith. This view is supported by other Prophetic reports that indicate that sins do not necessarily result in total negation of faith or denial of salvation on the part of the sinner in the hereafter.[52] Moreover, in line with the various scriptural references that support the forgiveness of all sins except disbelief, al-Nawawī notes that this also includes grave sinners, who may be forgiven if they repent. Even if they die without sincere repentance, it would be up to God to either punish them or forgive them.[53] In addition to this interpretation that suggests a lesser degree of faith, al-Nawawī also records several

---

49 Cf. al-Ṭabarī, *Tafsīr al-Ṭabarī: Jāmiʿ al-Bayān*, 18:508–14; al-Qurṭubī, *al-Jāmīʿ li-Aḥkām al-Qurʾān*, 16:442.

50 Cf. Ibn Ḥajar al-ʿAsqalānī, *Fatḥ al-Bārī bi Sharḥ Ṣaḥīḥ al-Bukhārī*, 12:81 (kitāb al-ḥudūd, bab al-sāriq ḥina yasriq).

51 The report is narrated by another companion – Abū Hurayrah: "the adulterer does not commit adultery while he is a believer, the drinker of wine does not drink wine while he is a believer and a thief does not commit theft while he is a believer, the usurper of unlawful property (by force while people are staring at him), does not do that while he is a believer." Ibn Ḥajar al-ʿAsqalānī, *Fatḥ al-Bārī bi Sharḥ Ṣaḥīḥ al-Bukhārī*, 12:58 (kitāb al-ḥudūd, bab al-zinā wa shurb al-khamr wa qala Ibn ʿAbbās: yunzaʿ minhu nūr al-Imān fī al-zinā).

52 For example, in one report, narrated by the companion Abū Dharr, the Prophet noted that if a person dies while maintaining his monotheistic belief in God, he will be admitted to paradise. When Abū Dharr exclaimed even if that person committed sins such as adultery or theft, the Prophet confirmed that he will still be admitted to paradise. See Ibn Ḥajar al-ʿAsqalānī, *Fatḥ al-Bārī bi Sharḥ Ṣaḥīḥ al-Bukhārī*, 10:283 (kitāb al-libas, bab al-thiyāb al-bīḍ).

53 Cf. al-Nawawī, *Ṣaḥīḥ Muslim bi Sharḥ al-Nawawī*, 2:41–42 (kitāb al-Imān, bāb bayān nuqṣān al-Imān bi al-maʿāṣī).

other possible interpretations. For example, according to one interpretation, negation of faith as a consequence of sin occurs only in the case of sinners who deny and challenge the prohibition of these sinful acts. According to another interpretation, which is attributed to Ibn Jarīr al-Ṭabarī, sinners are deprived of the honorific epithet of faith and are instead described and defined by the sins they commit (e.g., thief, adulterer, or transgressor). Other interpretations, similar to the one given by Ibn ʿAbbās noted above, suggest that upon the commission of sin, the light of faith or one's propensity for discernment (*baṣīrah*) is suspended. Apart from these various interpretations that were suggested, some scholars were of the view that the meaning of the statement in this report is ambiguous (*mushkil*) and that it has to be accepted as it is without any effort to give a particular interpretation.[54]

The theme of repentance is quite common in the Qur'ān, often following verses of warning, punishment, and retribution. Almost all the passages cited above concerning sin and its punishment are followed by others that include some mention of repentance. Particularly, references to repentance and the possibility thereof are expressed in the form of exception (*istithnā'*). A case in point is 25:63–75, which covers the description of the servants of God as well as punishment for those who are guilty of the commission of the sins highlighted. Immediately thereafter, a clear statement is made about an exception that can be granted to those who repent (*illā man taba*) (25:70). What is interesting to note here is that often repentance is combined with other indications of the need that it should be coupled with deep faith (*āmana*) and performance of good deeds (*ʿamilā ʿamal*^{an} *ṣāliḥ*^{an}), almost as a prereq-

54 In his commentary on this report in Ṣaḥīḥ al-Bukhārī, Ibn Ḥajar al-ʿAsqalānī includes several other interpretations. While these interpretations underscore the need to safeguard against sin, they emphasize the possibility of forgiveness in the hereafter subject to divine will. As the discussion below on major sins shows, these interpretations are in line with the attitude of the Ashʿarī school on the status of the grave sinner, as opposed to the attitudes of both al-Khawārij and the Muʿtazilah school. See Ibn Ḥajar al-ʿAsqalānī, *Fatḥ al-Bārī bi Sharḥ Ṣaḥīḥ al-Bukhārī*, 12:60–63. See also al-Ṭabarī, Abū Jaʿfar Muḥammad ibn Jarīr, *Tahdhīb al-Āthār*, ed. Maḥmūd Muḥammad Shākir, 4 vols., Cairo: Maṭbʿat al-Midanī, 1982, 2:605. After reviewing the various narrations of this report, al-Ṭabarī also recorded the various views on its meaning. For example, according to one view, the actual statement denies that a believer would commit these sins (*lā yazniyanna mu'min wa lā yasriqanna mu'min*), see al-Ṭabarī, *Tahdhīb al-Āthār*, 2:623. According to another interpretation, negation of faith applies only in the case of a person who questions the prohibition of these sins. If the person, however, does not question such prohibition, he is considered only sinful but that does not deny his status as a believer. This view is supported by other traditions indicating the primacy of a montheistic belief for the achievement of salvation, despite the commission of sins, see al-Ṭabarī, *Tahdhīb al-Āthār*, 2:624–40. According to another interpretation, which al-Ṭabarī supports, commission of these sins would result in the removal of the title of a believer (a description of praise) and its substitution with other descriptions (of blame) such as hypocrite (*munāfiq*) or transgressor (*fāsiq*), see al-Ṭabarī, *Tahdhīb al-Āthār*, 2:640–43, 2:650.

uisite or concrete evidence to show seriousness on the part of the sinner by taking action to correct their ways. The interpretation of the verse is placed within its immediate and also thematic context. Since it occurs following mention of murder and illicit sex, it is also related to other similar thematic references. Based on certain sources, one opinion is that this verse applies mainly to infractions committed prior to Islam and that it was abrogated, especially in the case of murder, by a later reference in 4:93. While this view is attributed to Ibn ʿAbbās, other opinions also attributed to Ibn ʿAbbās indicate that there are no limitations to repentance.[55]

The general scope and applicability of repentance can also be supported by other broader references to the theme of repentance in the Qur'ān. One of the most general references to the theme of repentance is 39:53, which is quite explicit on the possibility of forgiveness for all types of sin: "oh my servants who have transgressed and wronged themselves, do not despair and lose hope in God's mercy for God forgives all sins. Indeed, He is most forgiving most merciful." Similar to the previous verse, some commentators limited its scope to early converts to Islam, especially those who were concerned about the sins they committed prior to their conversion and whether they can be forgiven. Other opinions, however, emphasized the general applicability of the verse also for sinning Muslims.[56]

3 Sin within Theological Debates

3.1 Drawing the Boundaries of Early Theological Orientations

The concept of sin was at the center of early theological debates within the Islamic tradition. These theological debates, which were critical in defining the boundaries of the various theological orientations (and subsequently schools), were also connected with early political disagreements.[57] In particular, these dis-

55 Cf. al-Ṭabarī, *Tafsīr al-Ṭabarī: Jāmiʿ al-Bayān*, 17:511–12, 7:350; al-Qurṭubī, *al-Jāmīʿ li-Aḥkām al-Qur'ān*, 15:481, 7:40.

56 Cf. al-Ṭabarī, *Tafsīr al-Ṭabarī: Jāmiʿ al-Bayān*, 20:224–31; al-Qurṭubī, *al-Jāmīʿ li-Aḥkām al-Qur'ān*, 18:293–96. The companion Ibn ʿUmar is reported as saying that this is the most hope-inspiring verse in the Qur'ān. Ibn ʿAbbās responded by noting that the most hope-inspiring passage is in 13:6: "Indeed your Lord showers people with forgiveness despite their wrongdoing."

57 Sources on early theological disputes often trace them to a Prophetic report indicating that the earlier nations of the People of the Book were divided into seventy-one or seventy-two sects. Similarly, Muslims would also be divided but into seventy-three sects. According to one narration, all of them will be in the Hellfire except one – and this one represents the mainstream of the community (*al-Jamāʿah*), see Abū Dāwūd Sulaymān ibn al-Ashʿath al-Sijstānī, *Sunan Abī*

agreements ensued the events of the civil war during the reign of the fourth caliph ʿAlī ibn Abī Ṭālib (d. 40/660) and the confrontation with the then governor of Syria and later the founder of the Umayyad dynasty, the companion Muʿāwiyah ibn Abī Sufyān (d. 60/680). Controversies started after the death of the third caliph ʿUthmān (d. 35/655) who was assassinated by a group of rebels on the grounds of claims of corruption and nepotism. The assassination of ʿUthmān stirred a major dispute between those who sided with the newly installed Caliph and those who sought to avenge the blood of the slain Caliph. Although ʿAlī himself was against the assassination of ʿUthmān and also wanted to punish the perpetrators, the disagreement was mainly about the priority between restoring order first or rather punishing the murderers of ʿUthmān, a view which was upheld mainly by ʿUthmān's own kinsfolk from the Umayyads. An initial confrontation between ʿAlī on one side and Talḥah ibn ʿUbayd Allāh (d. 36/656), al-Zubayr ibn al-ʿAwwām (d. 36/656), and the Prophet's wife ʿĀʾishah (d. 58/678) on another side in what became known as the battle of the Camel in 36/656, with reference to the Camel on which she was mounting, resulted in the victory of ʿAlī and his allies.[58] Subsequently, another confrontation took place one year later between ʿAlī and his allies against Muʿāwiyah and his allies in Ṣiffīn in 37/657. After a period of intense fighting with major losses on both sides, the sources indicate that while the army headed by ʿAlī was about to achieve victory, a proposition was made by Muʿāwiyah to resort to arbitration and to end the dispute accordingly. Although ʿAlī was inclined to finish the battle once and for all, a group within his troops were of the view of accepting the offer to settle the dispute through arbitration. The controversy surrounding the decision to submit to arbitration and also how it ended gave birth to one of the earliest theological debates concerning sin. After accepting the offer

Dāwūd, ed. Shuʿayb al-Arnaʾūṭ and Muḥammad Kāmil Qurabalalī, 7 vols., Damascus: Dār al-Risālah, 2009, 7:5–7. See also al-Baghdādī, ʿAbd al-Qāhir ibn Ṭāhir ibn Muḥammad, *al-Farq bayna al-Firaq*, ed. Muḥāmmad Muḥyī al-Dīn ʿAbd al-Ḥamīd, Beirut: al-Maktabah al-ʿAṣriyyah, 1995, 8, 4–11. As noted by the editor of al-Baghdādī's book, while some authors did overlook the report or even deemed it inauthentic, others were careful to enumerate seventy three sects and also elaborate on the characteristics of the saved sect, which represents the mainstream. See al-Baghdādī, *al-Farq bayna al-Firaq*, 318; al-Shahrastānī, Muḥammad ibn ʿAbd al-Karīm Ibn Abī Bakr Aḥmad, *al-Millal wa al-Niḥal*, ed. Amīr ʿAlī Mahannā and ʿAlī Ḥasan Fāʿūr, 2 vols., Beirut: Dār al-Maʿrifah, 1993, 1:104–06.

58 Cf. al-Ṭabarī, Muḥammad ibn Jarīr, *Tārīkh al-Ṭabar: Tārīkh al-Umam wa al-Mulūk*, ed. Nawwāf al-Jarrāḥ, 6 vols., Beirut: Dār Ṣadir, 2008, 3:858; al-Masʿūdī, ʿAlī Ibn al-Ḥusayn Ibn ʿAlī, *Murūj al-Dhahab wa Maʿādin al-Jawhar*, ed. ʿAfīf Nāyif Ḥāṭūm, 4 vols., Beirut: Dār Ṣādir, 2010, 2:229–31.

of arbitration, another group of 'Alī's supporters argued that this decision amounted to sin (*dhanb*) that requires repentance.[59]

The group that objected to 'Alī became known as the seceders (*al-khawārij*) and one of their main principles was developed in light of their firm and unwavering definition of sin. For them, the sin that 'Alī committed by accepting arbitration amounted to disbelief (*kufr*). Although they were later divided into several subgroups, one of their shared views remained connected with the destiny of the grave sinner (*murtakib al-kabīrah*), who, according to them, would be liable to eternal punishment in the Hellfire.[60] One of their subgroups upheld the view that the charge of *kufr* applies in the case of the unspecified sins. On the other hand, for the specified sins in the case of certain infractions such as theft or adultery, the specified term only should be used (e.g., thief or adulterer). In his famous work on early theological orientations, the famous theologian and founder of one of the most important theological schools in the Islamic tradition Abū al-Ḥasan al-Ash'arī (d. 324/936) noted that only the subgroup known as al-Najadāt does not share this view with regard to the grave sinner. Instead, they note that the term *kufr* in the case of the grave sinner stands for ingratitude (*kufr ni'mah*) rather than disbelief (*kufr dīn*).[61]

In opposition to the radical view of al-Khawārij on sin and the destiny of the grave sinner, another theological group, which was known as al-Murji'ah, argued that commission of a sin does not affect one's status as a believer and that a grave sinner should not be considered a disbeliever. Again, they were divided into several subgroups but their attitude on sin remained one of their most important shared views. The meaning of the term Murji'ah was interpreted in light of its linguistic origin, which can denote one of two possibilities – both are also related to their view on sin. The first is postponement (*irjā'*); namely, the destiny of the grave sinner is deferred and can only be known with certainty in the hereafter. The second is giving hope (*i'ṭā' al-rajā'*); namely, the grave sinner can still entertain hope in God's mercy. One of the famous statements attributed to them indicates that sin does not harm with faith in the same way that obedience does not benefit with disbelief (in terms of ultimate destiny in the hereafter).[62]

---

59 Cf. al-Ṭabarī, *Tārīkh al-Ṭabar*, 3:908.

60 According to al-Baghdādī, they were divided into 20 (sub)groups, see al-Baghdādī, *al-Farq bayna al-Firaq*, 73–74.

61 Cf. al-Ash'arī, al-Abū al-Ḥasan 'Alī ibn Ismā'īl, *Maqālāt al-Islāmiyyīn, wa Ikhtilāf al-Muṣallīn*, ed. Muḥāmmad Muḥyī al-Dīn 'Abd al-Ḥamīd, 2 vols., Cairo: Maktabat al-Nahḍah al-Miṣriyyah, 1950, 1:156–57; al-Shahrastānī, *al-Millal wa al-Niḥal*, 1:131–33.

62 Cf. al-Ash'arī, *Maqālāt al-Islāmiyyīn*, 1:197–201; al-Shahrastānī, *al-Millal wa al-Niḥal*, 1:161; al-Baghdādī, *al-Farq bayna al-Firaq*, 202.

Between the extreme view of al-Khawārij and the lenient view of al-Murji'ah, one of the main views on sin that emerged during the early phase of the Islamic theological tradition was developed by al-Mu'tazilah,[63] as one of their fundamental principles.[64] This principle is known as the Middle Position (*al-manzilah bayna al-manzilatayn*), according to which the grave sinner is neither a disbeliever nor a believer but he should be regarded in an intermediary position between these two, which can be described as transgression (*fisq*).[65] This principle is connected with the other principle of promise and threat (*al-wa'd wa al-wa'īd*), which emphasizes the generic scope of both reward and punishment, as indicated by the scriptural references.[66] They argued, in light of these textual indicators, that if a believer died in a state of obedience, he would deserve due reward, as promised. By contrast if

---

63 Several reasons are given to explain why they were called al-Mu'tazilah (from the root that means to separate, isolate, or retire). According to one view, they were called Mu'tazilah because of their unique view on the grave sinner, whom they called *fāsiq*, see al-Baghdādī, *al-Farq bayna al-Firaq*, 115. The more famous narration traces the name to a particular incident between Wāṣil ibn 'Aṭā' (arguably the founder of al-Mu'tazilah) and his teacher al-Ḥasan al-Baṣrī. Accordingly, when a person once asked al-Baṣrī about the fate of the grave sinner, Wāṣil answered before his teacher and noted that the grave sinner is in an intermediary position. He reportedly then left the study circle of his teacher and retired to another corner of the mosque and started explaining his opinion. Thereupon, his teacher remarked that Wāṣil has separated himself from us (*i'tazalana* Wāṣil), see al-Baghdādī, *al-Farq bayna al-Firaq*, 116–20; al-Shahrastānī, *al-Millal wa al-Niḥal*, 1:61–62; Rahman, Fazlur, *Islam*, Chicago: University of Chicago Press, 2002, 88.

64 The sources include different versions of these principles, depending on the various subgroups and also the historical development of the ideas of al-Mu'tazilah in general. For example, al-Shahrastānī lists a subgroup known as al-Wāṣiliyyah – attributed to Wāṣil ibn 'Aṭā' – who emphasized four principles. In addition to the middle position (with reference to the grave sinner), the other three are: negation of divine attributes; one's ability to determine destiny (*qadar*); judging who was at fault during the tumultuous events that involved the fighting between the companions, from the assassination of 'Uthmān to the assassination of 'Alī and including the two battles of the Camel and Siffīn. The Mu'tazilāh are also described, mainly by their critics, as *qadariyyah*, with reference to the second prinicple noted here. Interestingly, an epistle supporting this view on destiny was attributed to al-Ḥasan al-Baṣrī, published in 'Imārah, Muḥāmmad (ed.), *Rasā'il al-'Adl wa al-Tawḥīd*, Cairo: Dār al-Shurūq, 1988, 109–22. Al-Shahrastānī, however, refers to this epistle, which al-Ḥasan al-Bāṣrī wrote to 'Abd al-Malik ibn Marwān, and questions its provenance. He supports the view that it may have been written by Wāṣil ibn 'Aṭā' instead, as it it is in line with his opinions, see al-Shahrastānī, *al-Millal wa al-Niḥal*, 1:61.

65 Cf. 'Abd al-Jabbār ibn Aḥmad al-Asadābādī, *Sharḥ al-Uṣūl al-Khamsah*, ed. 'Abd al-Karīm 'Uthmān, Cairo: Maktabat Wahbah, 1996, 701–18; ibn Ḥazm, Abū Muḥammad 'Alī ibn Aḥmad, *al-Faṣl fī al-Milal wa al-Ahwā' wa al-Niḥal*, ed. Muḥammad Ibrāhīm Naṣr and 'Abd al-Raḥmān 'Umayrah, 5 vols., Beirut: Dār al-Jīl, n.d., 3:273.

66 Eventually the fundamental principles of the Mu'tazilah school became known as the five main priniciples (*al-uṣūl al-khamsah*). According to the famous articulation of al-Qāḍī 'Abd al-Jabbār (d. 415/1025), they include: monotheism, justice, promise and threat, the middle position,

he died in a state of disobedience following the commission of a grave sin and without repentance, he would be subject to eternal punishment in the hellfire, but such punishment would be lesser than the punishment for a disbeliever.[67] In response to this view of al-Muʿtazilah, Abū al-Ḥasan al-Ashʿarī supported the view that the fate of the grave sinner who died without repentance would be up to God – He may forgive him, avail him from the intercession of the Prophet, or punish him in a manner suitable for and equal to the sin he committed. Eventually, however, he will be admitted into paradise with God's mercy because a believer will not be subject to eternal punishment, similar to a disbeliever.[68]

These differences on the destiny of the grave sinner have to be placed within the broader historical context of the Islamic theological tradition. They also have to be studied in connection with other relevant and related theological concepts. For example, the question of sin was part of larger discussions on divine names and attributes, especially as far as conceptualizations of the role and scope of human freedom are concerned. In connection with theological discussions on divine will, one of the important questions that were debated was whether all actions, including human actions, are subject to God's will. More particularly, in the case of actions characterized as examples of evil or instances of sin, whether these also are willed by God. For the Muʿtazilah, following their principle on divine actions amounting to what is best (*al-aṣlaḥ*), evil and sinful actions are not and cannot be

---

and commanding the good and forbidding the evil, see ʿAbd al-Jabbār ibn Aḥmad al-Asadābādī, *Sharḥ al-Uṣūl al-Khamsah*.

67 Cf. al-Ashʿarī, *Maqālāt al-Islāmiyyīn*, 1:305; al-Shahrastānī, *al-Millal wa al-Niḥal*, 1:57–58. Some sources indicate that this was not a view that was unanimously upheld by all the divisions of al-Muʿtazilah. Some, for example, noted that God can still forgive grave sinners even without repentance, see al-Baghdādī, *al-Farq bayna al-Firaq*, 116.

68 Cf. al-Shahrastānī, *al-Millal wa al-Niḥal*, 1:114–15. al-Ashʿarī was inititally a follower of the Muʿtazilah before he started criticizing their views. Several narrations are also recorded to explain his conversion from Muʿtazilism. According to one famous narration, the change of heart followed a debate with his teacher Abū ʿAlī Muḥammad ibn ʿAbd al-Wahhāb al-Jubāʾī on the scope of divine will and its impact on human freedom. See al-Ashʿarī, *Maqālāt al-Islāmiyyīn*, 1:217; al-Taftazānī, Saʿd al-Dīn Masʿūd ibn ʿUmar, *Sharḥ al-ʿAqāʾid al-Nasafiyyah*, ed. Aḥmad Ḥijāzī al-Saqqā, Cairo: Maktabat al-Kulliyāt al-Azhariyyah, 1987, 11; Taj al-Dīn ʿAbd al-Wahhāb ibn ʿAlī al-Subkī, *Ṭabaqāt al-Shāfiʿiyyah al-Kubrā*, ed. ʿAbd al-Fattāḥ Muḥammad al-Ḥulw and Maḥmūd Muḥammad al-Tanāḥī, 10 vols., Cairo: Dār Iḥyāʾ al-Kutub a-ʿArabiyyah, n.d., 3:347; al-Ghazālī, Abū Ḥamid Muḥammad ibn Muḥammad, *Iḥyāʾ ʿUlūm al-Dīn*, ed. ʿAbd al-Muʿṭī Amīn Qalʿjī, 5 vols., Beirut: Dār Ṣādir, 2010, 1:154; Rahman, *Islam*, 91. Eventually his critique paved the way for a new theological orientation, which became known as the Ashʿarī school of theology. In general, the Ashʿarī school aimed to reconcile extreme rationalism and extreme literalism and, together with the Maturidī school, played an important role in shaping mainstream sunnism across Islamic history. For a review of these early theological debates, see Wolfson, Harry Austryn, *The Philosophy of the Kalam*, Cambridge: Harvard University Press, 1976.

willed by God.[69] In response, the Ash'arī school argued that this view will have negative implications on divine power, since according to this view, these actions would fall beyond the scope of divine control. Therefore, the Ash'arī school argued that all actions are subject to divine will, including what appears to be evil or sinful actions.[70] Answering this critique, the Mu'tazilah school distinguished between two types of actions. The first includes actions that are subject to divine will exclusively and these do occur for sure according to that divine will. The second includes actions that are subject to the will of others (apart from God). In the case of this second category agents are given the freedom to exercise their own will, without necessarily negating divine will.[71] As al-Ghazālī notes on this point, the disagreement revolves around the meaning and criteria of moral valuation and the definition of the good and the evil (*al-ḥasan wa al-qabīḥ*).[72] While for the Mu'tazilah moral values can be defined on objective grounds, the Ash'aris argue that they depend on intended objectives. Moreover, human criteria for the good and the evil do not apply to God since He cannot be thought of as acting on the basis of these criteria and objectives. To clarify this further, a distinction is made between natural or physical attributes (e.g., colors) and moral values. While the first are fixed and cannot be disputed, the second can be subject to disagreement in view of attending circumstances or relevant considerations.[73] As is the case with other theological debates, dis-

69 Cf. al-Asadabādī, Abd al-Jabbār b. Aḥmad, *al-Mughnī fī Abwāb al-Tawḥīd wa-l-'Adl*, ed. Maḥmūd Muḥammad Qāsim, 16 vols. (volume on Divine Will), Cairo: n.p., n.d., 218.

70 Cf. al-Juwaynī, 'Abd al-Malik ibn 'Abd Allāh, *Kitāb al-Irshād ilā Qawāṭi' al-Adillah fī Uṣūl al-I'tiqād*, Cairo: Maktabat al-Khanjī, 2002, 237; al-Ghazālī, *Iḥyā' 'Ulūm al-Dīn*, 1:152–53.

71 Cf. al-Asadabādī, *al-Mughnī fī Abwāb al-Tawḥīd wa-l-'Adl*, 257.

72 Cf. al-Ghazālī, Abū Ḥāmid Muḥammad ibn Muḥammad, *al-Iqtiṣād fī al-I'tiqād*, ed. Anas Muḥammad 'Adnān al-Sharafāwī, Cairo: Dār al-Minhāj, 2019, 338–39. The two terms *ḥasan* (good) and *qabīḥ* (ugly) are used in three distinct ways. The first denotes what is in (dis)agreement with instinct or good nature as is the case with saving a drowning person or usurping someone's property. The second denotes an attribute of (im)perfection, which is considered worthy of praise/blame, mainly in this world, such as telling truth or lying. The third denotes an action that is considered worthy of praise/blame, both in this world and the next. Unlike the first two senses, which are unanimously acknowledged, the third one is disputed. While the Mu'tazilis accept it, the Ash'aris insist that reason cannot determine the criteria of the good/evil in this sense and that such criteria depend exclusively on revelation, see Zuhayr, Muḥammad Abū al-Nūr, *Uṣūl al-Fiqh*, 4 pts in 1 vol., Cairo: Dār al-Baṣā'r, 2007, 1:196. The Matūrīdī school agrees with the Mu'tazilis on the possibility of rational justification for moral values but they agree with the Ash'aris that legal obligation (*taklīf*) as well as otherworldly consequences remain dependent on revelation, see Muḥammad Abū Zahrah, *Uṣūl al-Fiqh*, Cairo: Dār al-Fikr al-'Arabī, 2004, 72.

73 Cf. al-Ghazālī, *al-Iqtiṣād fī al-I'tiqād*, 304–06. The exchange between the Mu'tazilis and the Ash'aris is captured in a debate between two of the chief representatives of these two schools: al-Qāḍī

cussions are often centered around the interpretation of relevant scriptural passages. While textual evidence is proffered by both sides, the Ashʿarī argument is primarily anchored in the texts that emphasize the primacy of divine will.[74]

Ultimately, a proper understanding of the various views on sin and the status as well as the destiny of the sinner should be related to the meaning of key terms such as faith (*Imān*) and its requirements or implications. For example, it was defined as: mere knowledge and belief in one's heart; admission with one's tongue; both knowledge in the heart as well as admission with the tongue; or knowledge in one's heart, admission with the tongue, and actual deeds with one's limbs. Therefore, it was used in these theological debates as the opposite of disbelief, transgression, or negligence of religious acts of obedience.[75] Similarly, views on sin depend on conceptualizations of reward and punishment and also the extent to which desert is deemed obligatory or categorical.[76]

ʿAbd al-Jabbār and Abū Isḥāq al-Isfrāyīnī (d. 418/1027). Reportedly ʿAbd al-Jabbār started by saying: "glory be to the one who has been absolved of sin." Al-Isfrayīnī responded by saying: "Glory be to the one in whose dominion nothing occurs without His permission." ʿAbd al-Jabbār remarked: "Does our Lord will disobedience?" al-Isfrayīnī responded: "Can our Lord be disobeyed despite His will?" ʿAbd al-Jabbār noted: "what if He withheld guidance from me and decreed misery on me – did He in this case do good or bad to me?" al-Isfrayīnī then noted: "if He withheld something that belongs to you, He would have done you bad but if He withheld from you something that belongs to Him, He could then grant His mercy to whom He chooses." See al-Subkī, *Ṭabaqāt al-Shāfiʿiyyah al-Kubrā*, 4:261–62. See also on this point Ormsby, Eric Linn, *Theodicy in Islamic Thought: The Dispute over al-Ghazali's Best of All Possible Worlds*, Princeton: Princeton University Press, 1984, 195.

74 Cf. al-Juwaynī, *Kitāb al-Irshād*, 254.

75 Cf. Ibn Ḥazm, *al-Faṣl fī al-Milal wa al-Ahwāʾ wa al-Niḥal*, 3:227–28, 255; al-Juwaynī, *Kitāb al-Irshād*, 396–98; al-Taftazānī, *Sharḥ al-ʿAqāʾid al-Nasafiyyah*, 71–80. Al-Ghazālī notes that the two terms *Islām* and *Imān* are sometimes used as synonyms and sometimes they are distinguished to differentiate between internal belief and external expression of this belief. After presenting three main views on the meaning of faith (belief in one's heart, belief in the heart and expression by the tongue, and belief in the heart, expression by the tongue, and actual deeds by the limbs), he distinguished six possible levels or degrees: combination of all three items; the first two items and some of the third, that is internal belief, verbal expression, and some deeds; the first two items only, that is internal belief, verbal expression, but without actual deeds; internal belief only, that is the case of someone who had internal faith in his heart but he died before expressing it verbally or practically; internal belief only, that is the case of someone who had internal faith in his heart but he never expressed it verbally or practically, despite having ample time prior to his death; and finally, verbal expression of faith with the tongue without faith in one's heart, which is the case of a hypcrite. Such a person is considered a disbeliever in terms of otherworldy consequences but should be treated as a Muslim as far as his status in this world is concerned. See al-Ghazālī, *Iḥyāʾ ʿUlūm al-Dīn*, 1:159–65.

76 Cf. al-Juwaynī, *Kitāb al-Irshād*, 381–83.

3.2 Major and Minor Sins

One of the main questions that emerges in early theological debates in connection with the theme of sin is the typology of sin, especially the difference between major and minor types. As noted above, this distinction is rooted in several scriptural references such as 4:31. Some early exegetes such as the companion Ibn ʿAbbās were of the opinion that all acts of disobedience amount to major sins, which can be forgiven with repentance. On the other hand, other interpreters supported the view of distinguishing major sins from minor ones in light of the scriptural references that mention more than one term for sin, occasionally in the same verse or passage, indicating a difference in kind or degree.

Subsequently, the various theological schools also elaborated on this question, including implications and consequences on one's status as well as destiny in the hereafter. For example, the recorded view of al-Khawārij is that any type of disobedience constitutes a major sin, for which the sinner deserves eternal punishment in the hellfire.[77] The other theological schools, on the other hand, mostly distinguish between major and minor sins, which can be supported by numerous textual references that use the two words *ṣaghīrah* and *kabīrah* to denote the difference between these two types of sins (e.g., 18:49 and 54:53).[78] There was a disagreement, however, on whether the category of major sins can always be distinguished from the category of minor sins. Many scholars, mainly within the Ashʿarī school, were of the view that these two categories cannot always be clearly distinguished. They argued that although some examples are indicated as major sins in several Prophetic reports, the boundaries between these two categories remain undetermined. This opinion, mainly with reference to 4:31, is based on the view that if the category of major sins is known for sure, and it is then known that avoidance of major sins does expiate minor sins, it would remove any inhibition associated with minor sins, especially when one knows that they will be forgiven – as long as major sins are avoided. Moreover, if major sins and minor sins are not clearly separated from each other, and if any infraction a person does may amount to a major sin, that would serve as enough deterrence for him not to commit such an infraction.[79] According to this view a minor sin is only considered minor in relationship to another bigger one.[80]

---

77 Cf. ʿAbd al-Jabbār ibn Aḥmad al-Asadābādī, *Sharḥ al-Uṣūl al-Khamsah*, 632.

78 Cf. al-Rāzī, *Tafsīr al-Fakhr al-Rāzī al-Mushtahir bi al-Tafsīr al-Kabīr wa Mafātīḥ al-Ghayb*, 10:76; Riḍā, *Tafsīr al-Qur'ān al-Ḥakīm*, 5:47, 8:188.

79 Cf. al-Rāzī, *Tafsīr al-Fakhr al-Rāzī al-Mushtahir bi al-Tafsīr al-Kabīr wa Mafātīḥ al-Ghayb*, 10:78–79.

80 Cf. al-Qurṭubī, *al-Jāmiʿ li-Aḥkām al-Qur'ān*, 6:263.

According to the Muʿtazilah school, the distinction between these two categories is clear.[81] Nonetheless, as noted by al-Qāḍī ʿAbd al-Jabbār, there was a disagreement within the school on whether the distinction between major and minor sins can be known not only on the basis of textual evidence but on the basis of rational evidence as well. For example, Abū ʿAlī al-Jubāʾī (d. 303/916) was of the view that the distinction is known primarily through textual evidence. Rationally, in his opinion, it would be difficult to distinguish between a major and a minor sin. According to this view, for the least act of disobedience, the sinner deserves two types of punishment and for the least act of obedience, the actor deserves one type of reward. The difference has to do with the nature and also position of the one against whom the sin is committed (i.e., God). In other words, the sin, even if minor, is considered major due to the fact that it is committed against the ultimate benefactor. Abū Hāshim al-Jubāʾī (d. 321/933), the son of Abū ʿAlī, argued that the difference between major and minor sins can also be known rationally, as can be seen in the difference between theft of 10 dirhams or another theft of only one.[82]

Moreover, the Muʿtazilah school also noted that major sins can be distinguished from minor sins with regard to the status of the perpetrator. According to this view, for each act of obedience there is a specified reward and conversely for each act of disobedience there is a specified penalty. If a person does an act of obedience and another act of disobedience, there can be three main possibilities. The first is when both reward and penalty are equal. This would result in a situation where they can cancel each other out and consequently the person would neither be subject to punishment nor deserving of reward. This possibility is ruled out due to textual evidence indicating that people would ultimately be either enjoying reward or suffering punishment. The second is the case of someone whose reward exceeds his penalty. In this case the exceeding reward would cancel the specified (smaller) penalty and that would leave a residual of the specified reward. This is the case of expiation (*takfīr*), by means of which a greater reward cancels a smaller penalty – and this is the example of the minor sin. The third possibility is the reverse case of someone whose penalty exceeds his reward and that would leave a residual of a specified penalty. This would be the opposite of expiation, which is called thwarting (*iḥbāṭ*) – and this is the example of a major sin. In response to this rational distinction between major and minor sins, the

81 Cf. al-Ashʿarī, *Maqālāt al-Islāmiyyīn*, 1:303.

82 Cf. ʿAbd al-Jabbār ibn Aḥmad al-Asadābādī, *Sharḥ al-Uṣūl al-Khamsah*, 632–34. Among the Ashʿaris, al-Juwaynī developed a view similar to the one attributed to Abu ʿAlī. He noted that all sins should be considered major not so much in view of the magnitude of the sin committed but rather of the one against whom the sin is committed, see al-Juwaynī, *Kitāb al-Irshād*, 391.

Ash'arī school retorted by criticizing the view that obedience necessitates reward or that disobedience necessitates punishment. According to this view, nothing can be held as obligatory on the part of God. Ultimately, however, both punishment and forgiveness of sins are not categorical but they are rather based on preponderance, hope, and ultimately divine will.[83] This difference is rooted in the main disagreement between the Mu'tazilī and the Ash'arī schools on divine justice and human freedom.

4 Sin within Juristic Discourses

Juristic discussions are often divided into two main divisions to distinguish theoretical and methodological questions from practical and concrete questions associated with particular legal issues. The first is the domain of legal methodology or *uṣūl al-fiqh*, while the second is the domain of substantive law or *fiqh* proper. Invocations of sin permeate juristic discussions in both divisions. Within theoretical and methodological discussions, sin is addressed at the broader conceptual level in terms of definition, typologies, and consequences. Within substantive juristic discussions sin is addressed at a more focused level with regard to certain legal issues or questions. *Fiqh* is primarily concerned with delineating the boundaries of what is allowed and what is not and one of its main objectives is to guard against the acquisition of a sin either through the commission of an infraction or the negligence of a religious duty. By definition, *fiqh* entails knowledge of practical sharī'ah-based rules, mainly on the basis of the scriptural indications. These sharī'ah-based rules reflect divine will with regard to the actions that legally-competent individuals undertake.[84]

---

83 Cf. al-Qurṭubī, *al-Jāmi' li-Aḥkām al-Qur'ān*, 6:262; al-Rāzī, *Tafsīr al-Fakhr al-Rāzī al-Mushtahir bi al-Tafsīr al-Kabīr wa Mafātīḥ al-Ghayb*, 10:77–8, 81; Riḍā, *Tafsīr al-Qur'ān al-Ḥakīm*, 5:47.

84 A sharī'ah rule or *ḥukm* (pl. *aḥkām*) is usually defined as the Lawgiver's qualification of the actions of legally-competent persons by way of command, optionality, or correlation (*khiṭāb Allāh al-muta'alliq bi-af'āl al-mukallafīn bi-al-iqtiḍā' aw al-takhyīr, aw al-waḍ'*). Command can be either positive or negative and can also be either categorical or uncategorical. Categorical positive command denotes an obligatory action while uncategorical positive command denotes a recommended action. Categorical negative command denotes a prohibited action while uncategorical negative command denotes a reprehensible action. Optionality stands for neutrality and correlation covers attending and relevant causes or stipulations for any given rule. See Abū Zahrah, *Uṣūl al-Fiqh*, 29–30; Zuhayr, *Uṣūl al-Fiqh*, 1:69; al-Khuḍarī, Muḥammad, *Uṣūl al-Fiqh*, Cairo: Dār al-Ḥadīth, 2003, 21. See also Kamali, Muhammad Hashim, *Principles of Islamic Jurisprudence*, Cambridge: Islamic Texts Society, 2003.

4.1 Sin and Legal Rules

A good place to start this exploration of sin within juristic discussions is the concept of a sharīʿah-based rule (*ḥukm sharʿī*), which is divided into two main types: enjoining (*taklīfī*) and correlative (*waḍʿī*). The first includes the five main categories that cover all the actions that a person does from the perspective of sharīʿah: obligatory, recommended, neutral, reprehensible, and prohibited.[85] The second covers any qualifications that pertain to the implementation of the first type and includes any relevant causes, conditions, or impediments. The definition of each of the five enjoining rules explains how it is articulated in relationship to sin. For example, the obligatory (*wājib*) stands for an act that is deemed mandatory. Renouncing an obligatory act is a sin that involves a sanction. Renunciation of the obligatory is censured and in this case the person is considered blameworthy from the perspective of sharīʿah.[86] By contrast, the prohibited (*ḥarām*) stands for an act that is censured and deemed forbidden. Commission of a prohibited act is a sin that involves a sanction and the perpetrator is considered blameworthy from the perspective of sharīʿah. The recommended (*mandūb*) stands for an act for which the person is praised but if undone the person is not blamed, unless the person intentionally undertakes the opposite of a recommended act – which itself is deemed an act of disobedience.[87] The reprehensible (*makrūh*) can include several degrees but it is generally considered lesser than the prohibited. While the

85 This fivefold classification of legal rules is the view of the majority of jurists. The Ḥanafis, however, add two additional rules, that are considered further subdivisions of both the obligatory (*wājib*) and the reprehensible (*makrūh*). Accordingly, the obligatory is distinguished from what is considered mandatory (*farḍ*), which is derived from a categorical evidence. The obligatory is, however, derived from a probable evidence. Similarly, reprehensibility is further divided into prohibitive reprehensibility (*karāhah taḥrīmiyyah*) and precautionary reprehensibility (*karāhah tanzīhiyyah*). The former is derived from a probable evidence, as opposed to the category of the prohibited, which is derved from a categorical evidence. This first catgory of the reprehensive, therefore, is considered the opposite of the *wājib* according to the Ḥanafī classification. See Abū Zahrah, *Uṣūl al-Fiqh*, 31–46; al-Khuḍarī, *Uṣūl al-Fiqh*, 35.

86 Cf. al-Zarkashī, Badr al-Dīn Muḥammad ibn Bahādir ibn ʿAbd Allāh, *al-Baḥr al-Muḥīṭ fī Uṣūl al-Fiqh*, ed. ʿAbd al-Sattār Abū Ghudah et al., 6 vols., Kuwait: Wizārat al-Awqāf wa a l-Shuʾūn al-Islāmiyyah, 2010, 1:176–77. The obligatory is further divided into two main categories in terms of its scope or applicability: individual and collective. The first applies to each legally-competent person (e.g., prayer and other ritual deeds) and if it is neglected the person acquires sin. The second applies to the Muslim community as is the case with the funeral prayer. If a part of the community undertakes this duty, it will be considered as fulfilled. But, if it is left undone, the community partakes in the sin that results from this negligence. See Abū Zahrah, *Uṣūl al-Fiqh*, 37–38.

87 Cf. al-Zarkashī, *al-Baḥr al-Muḥīṭ*, 1:284.

perpetrator of a reprehensible act is not blamed, avoidance of such an act is considered praiseworthy.[88] The neutral (*mubāḥ*) is the intermediary category that includes all the acts that are not deemed subject to obligation or prohibition in themselves. The ruling may vary depending on contextual factors that can change the evaluation of the act in question. For example, while a sale transaction is deemed neutral, it should not be given priority over something that is obligatory, such as the performance of the daily prayers.[89] In general the neutral is determined by several indications, which include: negation of sin (*ithm*), if undertaken; absence of explicit prohibition, or explicit permission.[90]

Therefore, the relationship between sin and these five legal rules depends on the qualification given to a certain act and the extent to which such an act involves violation of a divine command as is the case with omission or negligence of an obligation or commission of a prohibition. The relationship between sin on the one hand and either negligence of an obligatory act or commission of a prohibited act, however, is not coextensive. As the 14th century jurist al-Zarkashī (d. 794/1392) remarks, an important criterion for the consideration of a sin is knowledge and also intention. Therefore, if a person undertakes an act that is deemed forbidden

---

88 Cf. al-Zarkashī, *al-Baḥr al-Muḥīṭ*, 1:96; Abū Zahrah, *Uṣūl al-Fiqh*, 46.

89 Cf. al-Zarkashī, *al-Baḥr al-Muḥīṭ*, 1:275.

90 Cf. Abū Zahrah, *Uṣūl al-Fiqh*, 47. In addition to this fivefold classification (or sevenfold according to the Ḥanafīs) of the enjoining rules, the jurists also distinguish between the original or standard form of these rules (*ʿazīmah*) from situations that demand, require, or merit an exception or a concession (*rukhṣah*). These exceptional situations that warrant relaxation of the original rules are of different types: obligation (e.g., consumption of a prohibited item to save one's life); recommendation as is the case with shortening of prayer in case of travel; permission as is the case of certain transactions such as the sale of *salam*; and unrecommended or contrary to the optimal choice (*khilāf al-awlā*) as is the case with breaking the fast in Ramadan for a healthy person who can fast. See Zuhayr, *Uṣūl al-Fiqh*, 1:122–24. Another important typology of legal rules in terms of validity or lack thereof can also reveal the role of sin in the determination of whether a particular ruling is valid or not. The majority of jurists divide legal rules into two main categories: valid (*ṣaḥīḥ*) and invalid (*ghayr ṣaḥīḥ/ bāṭil*). The first stands for a ruling that fulfills all relevant conditions and stipulations, while the second is the one that does not meet these requirements. The Ḥanafī jurists, however, distinguish between invalidity (*buṭlān*) and defectiveness (*fasād*). Accordingly, invalidity denotes a defect in one of the pillars of the transaction in question. By contrast defectiveness denotes a defect in one of the related conditions or stipulations. The main difference becomes clear in contractual transactions. According to the majority view, invalid transactions are null and void in the sense that they do not give rise to claims, rights or entitlements. According to the Ḥanafī view, on the other hand, this is the case with invalid transactions only. While defective transactions are still considered lacking, they can establish certain entitlements, mainly in order to preserve the rights of those concerned. See al-Zarkashī, *al-Baḥr al-Muḥīṭ*, 1:320; Abū Zahrah, *Uṣūl al-Fiqh*, 62–65; al-Bukhārī, ʿAlāʾ al-Dīn ʿAbd al-ʿAzīz ibn Aḥmad, *Kashf al-Asrār ʿan Uṣūl Fakhr al-Islām al-Bazdawī*, 4 vols., Beirut: Dār al-Kutub al-ʿIlmiyyah, 1997, 1:380.

unknowingly or unintentionally, the deed remains forbidden but the sin is lifted. Conversely, if a person does an act that is deemed permissible, while under the impression that it was forbidden, the act remains permissible but the person acquires a sin due to his willingness to violate the rules, even in his mind.[91]

These prerequisites for the establishment of sin are often discussed under broader juristic themes such as legal accountability (*taklīf*) and legal capacity (*ahliyyah*). In order for a person to be considered fully accountable, he must fulfill the conditions for legal capacity, which usually include criteria such as maturity, sanity, and freedom of choice. In juristic terms, legal capacity stands for the ability to enter into agreements by means of which he can both receive rights or entitlements and also to discharge duties. From this perspective, legal capacity is divided into two main categories: original capacity (*ahliyyat wujūb*) and executive capacity (*ahliyyat adāʾ*).[92] The first (original) legal capacity stands for inherent capability by means of which an individual acquires a distinct identity and becomes eligible to engage in legal transactions. It is divided into two main types: incomplete or deficient original capacity, by means of which the person can only acquire certain rights and privileges as is the case with the fetus; and complete or full original capacity, by means of which the person can both acquire rights and discharge duties. The second (executive) legal capacity refers to the legal capability that allows the individual to exercise different religious-legal acts upon reaching the age of maturity. This category is also divided into two main types: deficient executive capacity, by means of which the person acquires limited capability to exercise different religious-legal acts as is the case with minors; and full executive capacity, by means of which the person acquires the capability to exercise all types of religious-legal transactions, which is attained upon reaching full majority.[93] The person is considered legally responsible as long as he is in possession of full legal capacity, but such capacity can be interrupted either temporarily or permanently due to certain impediments. The jurists discussed these impediments under the rubric of barriers

---

91 al-Zarkashī gives the example of a permissible act that is believed to be forbidden as the case of a person who establishes a relationship with his wife, while under the impression that she is another (stranger/unrelated) woman. On the other hand, the example of a forbidden act that is believed to be permissible is the case of a person who establishes a relationship with a (stranger/unrelated) woman, while under the impression that she is his wife. See al-Zarkashī, *al-Baḥr al-Muḥīṭ*, 1:256.

92 Cf. Abū Zahrah, *Uṣūl al-Fiqh*, 299. Kamali translates them as receptive legal capacity and active legal capacity, see Kamali, *Principles of Islamic Jurisprudence*, 450.

93 Cf. al-Bukhārī, *Kashf al-Asrār*, 4:335; al-Zarkashī, *al-Baḥr al-Muḥīṭ*, 1:342; al-Zarqā, Muṣṭafā, *al-Madkhal al-Fiqhī al-ʿĀmm*, 2 vols., Damascus: Dār al-Qalam, 2012, 2:785; al-Zuḥaylī, Wahbah, *Mawsūʿat al-Fiqh al-Islāmī wa al-Qaḍāyā al-Muʿāṣirah*, 14 vols., Damascus: Dār al-Fikr, 2012, 13:550.

(*ʿawāriḍ*) to full legal capacity, which they divided into two main types: natural (*samāwiyya*) and accidental (*ʿāriḍa*). The former includes: madness, imbecility, fainting, sleep, terminal illness, and slavery.[94] The latter includes: foolishness, intoxication, ignorance, mistake, and coercion.[95]

4.2 Sin and the Penal System

As noted above, the sin that attaches to the omission of an obligatory rule or commission of a prohibited rule is rooted in the act of disobedience to the divine command that inheres in these rules. The acquisition of a sin affects primarily the believer's standing before God both in this world and the next. Within the juristic context, however, in addition to the impact on the believer's standing before God, sin can also accrue certain penalties, as determined by sharīʿah in the case of the stipulated punishments.[96] In general, religious penalties include stated punishments either in this world (*ʿuqūbah*) or in the hereafter (*ʿiqāb*).[97] Worldly penalties include three main types: prescribed punishments (*ḥudūd*), retaliation (*qiṣāṣ*), and discretionary punishments (*taʿzīr*).[98] The prescribed punishments include the stipulated punishments stated in the scriptural sources for these acts: fornication, slander, drinking wine, theft, and highway robbery. Some disputed acts such as apostasy and sedition (*baghy*) are sometimes included. Retaliation stands for a punishment equal to an act of aggression, which covers aggression against one's life or any type of bodily injury.[99] Discretionary penalties stand for any unstated punishments that are imposed to redress a violation involving aggression against

94 One of the important reports in this regard is the one narrated by ʿAlī b. Abī Ṭālib (d. 40/661), which states: "The pen (responsibility) is lifted in the case of three: the mad person until he recovers, the sleeping person until he wakes up, and the minor until he reaches the age of maturity." See Abū Dāwūd al-Sijstānī, *Sunan Abī Dāwūd*, 6:452; Ibn Ḥajar al-ʿAsqalānī, *Fatḥ al-Bārī*, 9:388.

95 Cf. Abū Zahrah, *Uṣūl al-Fiqh*, 306–27. Some scholars add other items such as bankruptcy, see al-Zarqā, *al-Madkhal al-Fiqhī al-ʿĀmm*, 833. Others add more items such as forgetfulness and jesting, see *al-Mawsūʿah al-Fiqhiyyah*, 45 vols., Kuwait: Wizārat al-Awqāf wa a l-Shuʾūn al-Islāmiyyah, 2010, 7:161–67. See also al-Suyūṭī, Jalāl al-Dīn ʿAbd al-Raḥmān, *al-Ashbāh wa al-Naẓāʾir fī Qawāʿid wa Furūʿ Fiqh al-Shāfiʿiyyah*, Beirut: Dār al-Kutub al-ʿIlmiyyah, 1983, 187.

96 Cf. ʿAwdah, ʿAbd al-Qādir, *al-Tashrīʿ al-Jināʾī al-Islāmī Muqāran[an] bi al-Qānūn al-Waḍʿī*, 2 vols., Cairo: Maktabat Dār al-Turāth, 2003, 2:57.

97 Cf. *al-Mawsūʿah al-Fiqhiyyah*, 30:269.

98 This typology is based on the severity of the stated punishment. Other typologies are also suggested such as the one that is based on the intention of the perpetrator (e.g., intentional/premeditated and unintentional), see ʿAwdah, *al-Tashrīʿ al-Jināʾī al-Islāmī*, 1:67.

99 Cf. *al-Mawsūʿah al-Fiqhiyyah*, 33:259–81.

established rights due either to God or to people. They are primarily meant to ensure deterrence as well as reforming the criminal behavior of the perpetrator.[100]

This three-partite typology of crimes is considered significant for revealing important distinctions among these three categories. First, in terms of absolution or possibility thereof, this does not apply in the case of *ḥudūd*. Once a *ḥadd* crime is established, the stated punishment has to be implemented. In the case of *qiṣāṣ*, on the other hand, a punishment can be substituted by the payment of a monetary compensation (*diyah*). Similarly in the case of *taʿzīr*, punishment can be waived depending on the nature of the crime and also the parties involved. Second, in terms of the scope of the judge's power to amend the stated punishment, greater room exists in the case of *taʿzīr* while in the case of *qiṣāṣ*, it depends on the forgiveness of the victim, which can then allow for the possibility of a monetary compensation. In the case of *ḥudūd*, however, a judge does not have the power to amend the stated punishment. Third, in terms of the admission of mitigating factors, this applies mainly in the case of *taʿzīr* but not in the two categories of *ḥudūd* or *qiṣāṣ*. Fourth, in terms of admissible evidence, the standards are tighter in certain *ḥudūd*, which require their particular types of evidence. For example, in the case of adultery four male witnesses are needed to establish the crime. For the rest of the *ḥudūd* and *qiṣāṣ* crimes a minimum of two witnesses are needed. The standards of evidence in the case of *taʿzīr* crimes is generally lighter, for which one witness can be sufficient.[101]

This typology of crimes-punishments is closely connected to another important typology of legal rights (*ḥuqūq*). In general, the jurists use the word for right *ḥaqq* in two main ways. The first is its use as a synonym of a sharīʿah-based rule in light of its rootedness in it. From this perspective any right is derived primarily from a particular rule. The second is the action itself that is associated with a given rule or right. Within substantive law, the term is usually used to refer to what someone deserves. Rights have been subject to different types of classifications on the basis of several considerations such as: rights holders, entailment of public or private benefits, possibility of waiving a particular right, intelligibility of intended meaning or objective, differentiation between acts of worship or customary practices.[102] The most famous classification is the one undertaken from the perspective of rights holders. In general, rights are divided into four main types: pure rights of God, pure rights of people, mixed rights of God and people with a greater share for God, and mixed rights of God and people with a greater

100 Cf. *al-Mawsūʿah al-Fiqhiyyah*, 30:271.
101 Cf. ʿAwdah, *al-Tashrīʿ al-Jināʾī al-Islāmī*, 1:70–71.
102 Cf. *al-Mawsūʿah al-Fiqhiyyah*, 18:8–13.

share for people. God's rights mainly cover acts of worship as well as all the issues that involve public benefits, which do not belong to any person specifically. They have also been defined as rights that cannot be tolerated, suspended, or compensated. These include the stipulated punishments as well as various types of expiations.[103] People's rights, on the other hand, are those that belong to individuals in a more specific manner and they can be tolerated, waived, or compensated for. Religious penalties are categorized as belonging either to the domain of God's rights or the mixed rights of God and man. They involve God's rights since they entail a violation of a divine command, as is the case with fornication and theft. Similarly, they involve man's rights because they entail encroachment on other people's rights, as is the case with retaliation. They may still involve the mixed rights of God and man, as is the case with slander.[104]

Considering this typology of rights, especially in terms of their entailment of an exclusive or shared entitlement for God and/or for man, punishment for disobedience is classified into three main classes. The first covers the stipulated crimes and their punishments. Some jurists add an additional penalty by way of *taʿzīr* in addition to the execution of a *ḥadd* punishment.[105] The second involves

---

103 The Ḥanafī jurists include eight main categories under the exclusive rights of God: pure acts of worship; acts of worship that involve public benefit such as the obligatory alms; public benefit that involves an act of worship such as the alms levied on agricultural land; public benefit that involves the meaning of a sanction such as the case of the tax levied on conquered land (*kharāj*); rights that include both devotional and penal elements such as the stipulated expiations for certain infractions (e.g., the oath of repudiating a wife or *ẓihār*, breaking the fast in Ramadan, and breaking an oath); pure punishments such as the stipulated penalties (*ḥudūd*); partial punishments such as depriving a murderer from inheriting a related victim; and established right of God such as the share of a one-fifth of the spoils of war, see *al-Mawsūʿah al-Fiqhiyyah*, 18:15–18.

104 Cf. *al-Mawsūʿah al-Fiqhiyyah*, 30:270; al-Khuḍarī, *Uṣūl al-Fiqh*, 30–32. For further discussions on this issue see Ibn ʿAbd al-Salām, ʿIzz al-Dīn ʿAbd al-ʿAzīz, *al-Qawāʿid al-Kubrā al-Mawsūm bi Qawāʿid al-Aḥkām fī Iṣlāḥ al-Anām*, ed. Nazīh Kamāl Ḥammād and ʿUthmān Jumʿah Ḍumayriyyah, 2 vols., Damascus: Dār al-Qalam, 2000, 2:219; some jurists argued that all rights involve a right for God and, accordingly, rights are divided into three types excluding the exclusive rights of man, see al-Shāṭibī, Abū Isḥāq Ibrahīm ibn Mūsā, *al-Muwāfaqāt fī Uṣūl al-Sharīʿah*, ed. ʿAbd Allāh Darrāz, 4 vols., Cairo: al-Maktabah al-Tawfīqiyyah, 2003, 2:270–73, 2:318–21; al-Qarāfī, Shihāb al-Dīn Aḥmad ibn Idrīs, *Kitāb al-Furūq: Anwār al-Burūq fī Anwāʾ al-Furūq*, ed. Muḥammad Aḥmad Sarrāj and ʿAlī Jumʿah, 5 vols., Cairo: Dār al-Salām lil Ṭibāʿah wa al-Nashr wa al-Tawzīʿ, 2001, 1:269.

105 In general, a *ḥadd* punishment is considered sufficient but the jurists also allow the possibility of adding an additional penalty by way of *taʿzīr* if this is deemed beneficial for the public good. For example, the Mālikis include an additional penalty in the case of *qiṣāṣ* for the different types of injuries, other than murder. They argue that the *qiṣāṣ* punishment is meant to compensate for the initial act of aggression on the part of the perpetrator and this is the due right of the victim. The additional penalty is meant to serve as the right of society for the breach of law and order that the act of aggression caused. The Shāfiʿis include an additional penalty by way of *taʿzīr*

an expiation only, as is the case for breaking the fast by means of sexual intercourse during Ramadan. The third involves the different types of disobedience for which no stated punishment is indicated, and that includes most of the examples of disobedience. The applicable worldly punishment, if any, for this type of disobedience is only discretionary (by way of *taʿzīr*) on the basis of the act in question and also surrounding circumstances, which has to be evaluated by the judicial authority.

This third category of disobedience, for which there is no stated punishment or expiation, is also divided into three main types. The first covers situations involving a *ḥadd* crime but the applicable *ḥadd* punishment cannot be implemented due to the lack of certain stipulations. This covers, for example, the theft of an item whose value is below the designated amount (*niṣāb*), which serves as the threshold for the applicability of the stated punishment. The second also covers situations involving a *ḥadd* crime but the applicable *ḥadd* punishment cannot be applied because of doubt (*shubhah*). This is the case, for example, when close family members are involved in a *ḥadd* crime such as theft or murder, in which a *ḥadd* punishment is substituted by *taʿzīr*. The third and broadest type of disobedience covers infractions for which there is no stated punishment. Depending on the nature of the infraction and its impact on individual or collective rights, it can be subject to a discretionary penalty by way of *taʿzīr*. Examples of this type cover a wide array of infractions such as consumption of prohibited food (e.g., meat of unslaughtered/dead animals), betrayal of trust, cheating, false testimony, or bribery.[106]

This classification of sin in terms of applicability of a worldly punishment was occasionally used in juristic discussions to distinguish between major and minor sins. Following similar theological discussion on this distinction, as noted above, the jurists also disagreed on whether these two categories can be delineated. For example, the 13th century Mālikī jurist Shihāb al-Dīn al-Qarāfī (d. 684/1258) acknowledged the difficulty of drawing clear lines between major and minor sins. Despite this difficulty, he recognized the importance of understanding the difference between these two sets of infractions, which is crucial for the proper understanding of different legal issues especially in the case of Muftis and

in case the stated punishment is substituted by a payment of a monetary compensation (*diyah*), as is the case of a situation involving a father killing his son. The Shafiʿis also, as well as the Ḥanbalis, allow the possibility of hanging the amputated hand of a thief after the execution of the punishment, by way of *taʿzīr* as a form of deterrence against the crime of theft. The Ḥanafis add the additional penalty of banishment to the stated punishment for the unmarried person who commits fornication, by way of *taʿzīr*, as a form of deterrence against this crime. See ʿAwdah, *al-Tashrīʿ al-Jināʾī al-Islāmī*, 1:115–17.

106 Cf. ʿAwdah, *al-Tashrīʿ al-Jināʾī al-Islāmī*, 1:117.

judges. One example that he highlighted was the role of this distinction in evaluating the moral standing of witnesses, since commission of certain types of sins would preclude the person from serving as a witness in a judicial proceeding.[107]

Similar to the view of the 11th century Shāfi'ī theologian-jurist al-Juwaynī, noted above, some jurists did not emphasize the distinction between major and minor sins. According to this opinion, any act of disobedience amounts to a grave sin, since it constitutes an affront against the divine will. This opinion can be traced to an interpretation by Ibn 'Abbās on textual references to the term *kabīrah*. According to this interpretation all the deeds that God warned against constitute major sins, especially those against which the punishment of Fire is stipulated. When he was asked once if they are seven in number, he replied by saying that they are perhaps closer to seventy rather than merely seven.[108] In another narration he is reported to have said that they are perhaps closer to seven hundred.[109] Supporters of this opinion, however, did recognize that while some sins could discredit a person and impact his moral standing as a witness in court, some other smaller sins could somehow be tolerated.

The majority of jurists, on the other hand, argued for a distinction between major and minor sins, mainly in light of textual evidence both in the Qur'ān and also various Prophetic traditions. For example, some textual references indicate the role of ritual deeds in the forgiveness of minor sins. Accordingly, sins that can be forgiven through the performance of ritual and devotional deeds are considered minor, while those that cannot be forgiven by these devotional deeds are considered major.[110] This view was also supported by several legal arguments on the basis of associated implications and consequences. For example, some jurists noted that sins that result in greater harm should be distinguished from others that result in lesser harm. Clues for this distinction can be gleaned from textual

---

107 Cf. al-Qarāfī, *Kitāb al-Furūq*, 1:241.

108 Cf. al-Ṭabarī, *Tafsīr al-Ṭabarī: Jāmi' al-Bayān*, 6:651–61. See also al-Qurṭubī, *al-Jāmi' li-Aḥkām al-Qur'ān*, 6:263–65.

109 Cf. al-Suyūṭī, *al-Ashbāh wa al-Naẓā'ir*, 386.

110 Cf. al-Nawawī, *Ṣaḥīḥ Muslim bi Sharḥ al-Nawawī*, 2:85. For example, several Prophetic reports indicate that the five daily prayers, from one Friday prayer to the next, and from one month of Ramadan to the following one in the subsequent year – all these regular ritual deeds wipe out the minor sins that a person may commit, as long as major sins are avoided. Unlike minor sins, which can be forgiven through these devotional deeds, these reports show, as noted by al-Nawawī, that major sins would require sincere repentance in order for them to be forgiven. See al-Nawawī, *Ṣaḥīḥ Muslim bi Sharḥ al-Nawawī*, 3:112–17 (kitāb al-ṭahārah). See also Ibn Qayyim al-Jawziyyah, Abū 'Abd Allāh Muḥammad ibn Abī Bakr, *Madārij al-Sālikīn bayna Manāzil Iyyāka Na'budu wa Iyyāka Nasta'īn*, ed. Muḥammad al-Mu'taṣim bi-Allāh al-Baghdādī, 3 vols., Beirut: Dār al-Kitāb al-'Arabī, 2003, 1:321.

references that describe certain sins as major or most serious. Some other jurists make the distinction between major and minor sins on the basis of the stated punishment for the sin in question. Accordingly, sins that are punished by a stipulated *ḥadd* punishment can be qualified as major.[111] Similarly, the 13th century Shāfiʿī jurist al-ʿIzz ibn ʿAbd al-Salām (d. 660/1262) noted that major sins can be determined on the basis of the harm that they cause in addition to attached signs such as associated warning, curse, or stipulated punishment. Ibn ʿAbd al-Salām refers also to another important dimension in evaluating the gravity of a major sin, which is the attitude of the sinning person. This would be the case of a person who commits such a sin in a manner that betrays a sense of apathy or carelessness. Moreover, insistence or persistence even in the case of minor sins can be equated with the commission of a major sin. The criteria for persistence would depend on the extent to which this amounts to a repeated behavior on the part of the individual, especially one that denotes indifference or lack of remorse.[112] This view is in line with an earlier opinion by Ibn ʿAbbās, who is reported to have said: "no major sin with repentance, and no minor sin with insistence" (*lā kabīrah maʿa istighfār, wa-lā ṣaghīrah maʿa iṣrār*).[113]

In general, while some scholars used these criteria to distinguish major and minor sins but left the scope somehow open-ended, others developed extended lists of the infractions that should be qualified as major sins. For example, the 14th century Shāfiʿī jurist Tāj al-Dīn al-Subkī (d. 771/1370) compiled a list that includes more than 35 offenses that can be qualified as major sins, mainly as deduced from relevant textual references. The listed offenses are: murder, adultery, homosexuality, intoxication, theft and usurpation, slander, backbiting, false testimony, false oath, breaching family ties, mistreatment of one's parents, fleeing from the battlefield, unlawful consumption of an orphan's wealth, mishandling of weights and measurements, performance of the daily prayers earlier or later than their assigned times without a valid excuse, falsifying a Prophetic statement, hitting a Muslim, cursing the companions of the Prophet, withholding testimony, bribery, cuckoldry, calumny, withholding of alms, giving up hope in God's mercy, careless indulgence in disobedience and reliance on forgiveness (*al-amn min makr Allah*), taking oath to treat one's wife like one's mother (*ẓihār*), consumption of pork or dead animals, breaking the fast during the month of Ramadan without an excuse, unlawful acquisition of spoils, highway robbery, black magic, usury,

---

111 Cf. al-Qarāfī, *Kitāb al-Furūq*, 1:242–43.

112 Cf. Ibn ʿAbd al-Salām, *al-Qawāʿid al-Kubrā*, 1:32–34.

113 al-Ṭabarī, *Tafsīr al-Ṭabarī: Jāmiʿ al-Bayān*, 6:651–61. See also al-Qurṭubī, *al-Jāmiʿ li-Aḥkām al-Qurʾān*, 6:263–65.

and persistence on minor sins.[114] The 16th century Shāfiʿī jurist Jalāl al-Dīn al-Suyūṭī (d. 911/1505) added several other items that were recorded by other scholars such as: forgetting the Qur'ān – after memorizing it, having sexual intercourse with one's wife during the menstruation period, burning animals, for a wife to refrain from answering her husband's invitation to have intimate relationship with her, refraining from commanding the good and forbidding evil – while being capable of doing it, not cleaning oneself after urinating, intentionally causing harm in one's testament, withholding surplus water from the wayfarer, and use of golden or silver utensils.[115]

5 Sin and the Boundaries of Islamic Morality

Apart from purely theological as well as juristic discourses, broader ethical discussions on the concept of sin also played an important role in highlighting the wider contours of Islamic morality and subsequently shaping the field of Islamic ethics. A general survey of the two disciplines of *ādāb* (proper etiquettes) and *akhlāq* (character traits) reveals frequent invocations of sin – mainly in the second sense outlined in the introduction. This meaning of sin is associated with terms such as *ithm*, *dhanb*, *wizr* or *sayyi'ah*, which denote a moral wrong (misdeed) in the form of infraction or violation of a religious-moral injunction. Since, ultimately, the field of Islamic ethics is primarily concerned with conceptualizations of the good and the evil from the perspective of sharīʿah, these conceptualizations are often articulated in relationship to the definition, role, and implications of sin both in this world and the next.

The term *adab* (pl. *ādāb*) stands for good etiquettes or manners and within the religious context it denotes proper conduct or behavior, as inspired by the Prophetic model. In this sense, other terms are sometimes used to denote the

---

114 Cf. al-Subkī, Taj al-Dīn ʿAbd al-Wahhāb ibn ʿAlī, *Jamʿ al-Jawāmiʿ fī Uṣūl al-Fiqh*, ed. ʿAbd al-Munʿim Khalīl Ibrāhīm, Beirut: Dār al-Kutub al-ʿIlmiyyah, 2003, 70–72.

115 Cf. al-Suyūṭī, *al-Ashbāh wa al-Naẓā'ir*, 386. A more extended list can be found in a special treatise by the 14th century scholar al-Dhahabī, which includes 76 offenses qualified as major sins, see al-Dhahabī, Abū ʿAbd Allāh Muḥammad ibn Aḥmad ibn ʿUthmān, *Kitāb al-Kabā'ir wa Tabyīn al-Maḥārim*, Damascus: Dār ibn Kathīr, n.d. Similarly, the 14th century Ḥanbalī jurist Ibn Qayyim al-Jawziyyah developed a far more extensive list, extracted mainly from the various Prophetic reports that denote denunciation of certain actions, see Ibn Qayyim al-Jawziyyah, Abū ʿAbd Allāh Muḥammad ibn Abī Bakr, *Iʿlām al-Muwaqqiʿīn ʿan Rabb al-ʿĀlamīn*, ed. Abū ʿUbaydah Mashhūr ibn Ḥasan Āl-Salmān, 7 vols., Dammam: Dār Ibn al-Jawzī, 1423/2002, 6:569–84; Ibn Qayyim al-Jawziyyah, *Madārij al-Sālikīn*, 1:327–37.

same meaning such as *hady* (guided practice) or *sunnah* (repeated or habitual action). Each human activity has an *adab* or a proper way, according to which it should be done. Canonical books of the Prophetic traditions often include lengthy sections that detail this aspect of Islamic teachings, which aim to inspire Muslims to achieve full or near full compliance with the Prophetic model in the different aspects of one's life, even those that are not directly subject to legal jurisdiction. This includes, for example, the wide range of the ordinary aspects of life, which include how to dress, eat, drink, or interact with others. These ethics of action fall within the broader scope of Islamic morality that somehow differ from the other set of ethics of action that are discussed by the jurists within the scope of *fiqh*.

Disobedience within this broader meaning of ethics, which corresponds with the second meaning of sin, may occasionally overlap with the first and broadest sense that is mentioned in the introduction. One main distinction between these two meanings of sin and the third meaning that denotes its ethical-legal connotation pertains to their implications and consequences. Sin in this latter ethical-legal sense is usually addressed by the jurists within the context of determining the applicable punishment in this world, either by means of a stipulated (*ḥadd* or *qiṣāṣ*) or discretionary (*ta'zīr*) penalty. On the other hand, sin in the first two senses is mainly concerned with the religious consciousness and moral sensibility of the believer as it affects his relationship with God in the first place. Moreover, punishment for sin in this sense is primarily in the hereafter.

The term *akhlāq* (sing. *khuluq*) stands for characteristics or character traits. It shares its linguistic root with the word for creation (*khalq*) and this etymological relationship is often highlighted to indicate the lasting impact of these traits on one's personality. Moreover, these traits require repetition through habitual consistent practice over time in order for them to be established and become like second nature to the individual, which also make them quite difficult to change. As al-Ghazālī notes, while *khalq* refers to and denotes external shape, *khuluq* refers to and denotes internal constitution.[116] These ethics of character are primarily concerned with the characteristics that distinguish a moral person. Similar to its *ādāb* counterpart, textual evidence can be found in the scriptural sources, particularly in sections within the collections of Prophetic reports that address virtues or virtuous deeds (*faḍā'il al-a'māl*), often in comparison with their opposites or vices. Ultimately, detailed discussions on religious virtues such as piety (*taqwā*) or bashful-

116 Cf. al-Ghazālī, Abū Ḥamid Muḥammad ibn Muḥammad, *Kitāb al-Arba'īn fī Uṣūl al-Dīn*, ed. 'Abd Allāh 'Abd al-Ḥamīd 'Arwānī, Damascus: Dār al-Qalam, 2003, 179.

ness (*ḥayāʾ*) are often framed as qualities or states of the heart that safeguard the individual from the commission of sin.[117]

One of the most important genres within the wider domain of Islamic ethics that emphasize the importance of these virtuous deeds includes works that highlight the mystical-sufī dimension of the religious experience. Sufism is mainly concerned with the reinforcement of God-consciousness and strengthening one's personal connection with the divine. The sufī path often involves practical instructions on how one can achieve a deeper level of religiosity through certain routines involving remembrance of God as well as performance of supererogatory devotional practices. More particularly, for the purpose of sin, Sufism emphasizes a constant state of alertness that would entail not only avoidance of what is clearly prohibited but also refraining from indulgence or excessive partaking in what is essentially permissible through the practice of ethical values such as renunciation (*zuhd*) and precautionary abstention (*waraʿ*).[118]

In general, greater emphasis is often placed within the various ethical genres on the significance of the internal dimensions that drive human behavior towards virtues or vices. The significance of these internal dimensions for moral analysis and decision-making explains the predominance of moral psychology in ethical treatises, mainly in their exploration of the nature of the soul and its constituent parts. According to the classical exposition, the soul includes three main parts: rational, appetitive, and irascible. From this perspective moral action depends on the individual's ability to maintain proper balance between these three elements, ideally by ensuring that the rational power is superior to the other two. Maintaining the balance between these three powers is a prerequisite for the generation of these three main virtues: wisdom, temperance, and courage. These virtues correspond to the rational, appetitive, and irascible faculties of the soul and they represent the mean, or the middle point between two extremes (vices) for each of them. The fourth virtue is justice, understood in this context as the ideal balance between the other three main virtues. Although this moral psychology traces its roots to Greek moral philosophy, it was routinely adopted by Muslim ethicists across the Islamic normative tradition, occasionally with significant modification. Most importantly, Muslim ethicists sought to anchor their discus-

117 Cf. al-Māwardī, Abū al-Ḥasan ʿAlī ibn Muḥammad, *Adab al-Dunyā wa al-Dīn*, ed. Muṣṭafā al-Saqqā, Beirut: al-Maktabah al-Thaqāfiyyah, 1955, 241–42.

118 For detailed discussions on these and similar ethical values, see al-Ghazālī, *Iḥyāʾ ʿUlūm al-Dīn*; al-Muḥāsabī, Abū ʿAbd Allāh al-Ḥārith ibn Asad, *al-Riʿāyah li-Ḥuqūq Allāh*, ed. ʿAbd al-Ḥalīm Maḥmūd, Cairo: Dār al-Maʿārif, 2003; Zargar, Cyrus Ali, *The Polished Mirror: Storytelling and the Pursuit of Virtue in Islamic Philosophy and Sufism*, London: Oneworld Publications, 2017, 181–85.

sions on the soul as well as its capacity to generate the various virtues or vices mainly within Islamic scriptural sources.[119]

The internal dimension of sin is underscored in several textual references. For example, when the Prophet was once asked about the meanings of the two terms *birr* (good) and *ithm*, he noted that *birr* stands for good manners (*ḥusn al-khuluq*) and *ithm* denotes something you do not feel comfortable or at ease with in your heart (*mā ḥāka fī ṣadrik*).[120] Other references to the internal dimension of sin include ones that highlight the role of intention in assessing the moral value of an action. For example, according to a famous report, the Prophet is recorded as saying: "Actions are but by intentions and everyone's deeds should be judged on the basis of one's intention. If a person intends his immigration for the sake of God and His Prophet, it will be rewarded accordingly and if a person intends his immigration for a worldly reward or for a woman to marry, it will be rewarded accordingly."[121] Similarly, the role of the inner voice is highlighted in references that highlight the importance of the heart in the process of moral decision-

---

119 See, for example, the classical exposition given by Abū Ḥāmid al-Ghazālī in his magnum opus *Iḥyā' 'ūlūm al-Dīn*, which he divided into four main sections: ritual deeds (*'ibadāt*), customary deeds (*'ādāt*), saving virtues (*munjiyāt*), and destructive vices (*muhlikāt*). He also touched on this exposition in many of his other works, especially in *Mīzān al-'Amal* and *al-Arba'īn fī Uṣūl al-Dīn*. See also Ibn Miskawayh, Abū 'Alī Aḥmad ibn Muḥammad, *Tahdhīb al-Akhlāq*, ed. Qusṭanṭīn Zurayq, Beirut: al-Jāmi'ah al-Amrikiyyah fī Bayrūt, 1966, 26–27; al-Rāghib al-Iṣfahānī, Abū al-Qāsim al-Ḥusayn ibn Muḥammad, *Kitāb al-Dharī'ah ilā Makārim al-Sharī'ah*, ed. Abū al-Yazīd Abū Zayd al-'Ajamī, Cairo: Dār al-Salām lil-Ṭibā'ah wa al-Nashr wa al-Tawzī' wa al-Tarjamah, 2007, 74–95; al-Ghazālī, Abū Ḥamid Muḥammad ibn Muḥammad, *Mīzān al-'Amal*, ed. Sulaymān Dunyā, Cairo: Dār al-Ma'ārif, 2003, 232–33, 264; Walī Allāh al-Dihlawī, Aḥmad ibn 'Abd al-Raḥīm, *Ḥujjat Allāh al-Bālighah*, ed. Sa'īd Aḥmad Yūsuf, 2 vols., Beirut: Dār Ibn Kathīr, 2020, 1:179–83; Fakhry, Majid, *Ethical Theories in Islam*, Leiden: Brill, 1994, 62.

120 See al-Nawawī, *Ṣaḥīḥ Muslim bi Sharḥ al-Nawawī*, 16:110–11 (kitāb al-birr wa al-ṣilah wa al-adab, bāb tafsīr al-birr wa al-ithm). This report is narrated by Nawwās ibn Sam'ān. Other reports are in *Musnad Aḥmad* (no. 17999, 18001, and 18006) through Wābiṣah Ibn Ma'bad, according to which, when Wābiṣah approached the Prophet to ask him about these two terms, the Prophet noted that *birr* is what you feel comfortable with in your heart (*mā iṭma'anna ilayhi al-qalb*) and *ithm* is what you do not feel comfortable with, even if people tell you otherwise. The chains of transmission of these reports in Musnad Aḥmad, however, are criticized, see ibn Ḥanbal, Aḥmad, *Musnad al-Imām Aḥmad Ibn Ḥanbal*, ed. Shu'ayb al-Arnā'ūṭ et al., 50 vols., Beirut: Mu'ssassat al-Risālah, 2001, 29: 523–33.

121 al-Nawawī, *Ṣaḥīḥ Muslim bi Sharḥ al-Nawawī*, 13:53 (kitāb al-imārah, bāb bayan qadr thawab man ghazā fa Ghanim wa man lam yaghnam); Ibn Ḥajar al-'Asqalānī, *Fatḥ al-Bārī bi Sharḥ Ṣaḥīḥ al-Bukhārī*, 1: (kitab bad' al-waḥy, bab kayfa kana bad' al-waḥy), 1:9–18, 1:135 (kitab al-Imān, bāb mā jā' Inna al-a'māl bi al-niyyah wa al-ḥisbah). Due to the importance of intention in the various sharī'ah-based rules, it is considered one of the main maxims that govern these rules, see al-Suyūṭī, *al-Ashbāh wa al-Naẓā'ir*, 8–50; Ibn Nujaym, Zayn al-Dīn ibn Ibrāhīm ibn Muḥammad,

making, especially in cases of ambiguity or contestation. In such situations one's ability to take right moral decisions depends on one's capacity for internal discernment and introspection. This capacity, however, requires a specific state of the heart by means of which it is considered sound, alert, or healthy. According to a famous report, the Prophet is recorded as saying:

> The permissible is clear and the impermissible is clear. In between there are issues that are doubtful, not known to many people. Whoever steers clear of these doubtful issues, it would be safer for his religion and honor. This is the example of a shepherd who grazes his herd close to a precinct, and as he draws near the sheep will soon trespass into the precinct. Know then well that every king has his designated precinct and God's precinct consists of his prohibitions. Within the body there is a morsel, if it is sound the rest of the body will be likewise and if it is corrupt the rest of the body will be likewise – and this is the heart.[122]

Several scriptural references point out the negative impact of sin on this moral capacity of the heart to the extent that it can disable it. For example, in 83:14 the Qur'ān describes how the sinners' hearts get enveloped with a rusted cover (*rān*) as a result of the sins that they commit. In his commentary on this verse, al-Ṭabarī notes that the detrimental effects of sins gradually engulf the heart as they slowly accumulate. He compares the effect of sins on the heart to the intoxicating effect of wine on the intellect. This interpretation is supported by a report in which the Prophet is quoted as saying: "When the individual commits a sin, a small black dot gets marked on his heart. If he repents, the heart gets polished and the black dot is wiped. If he returns to sin, the black dot gets marked again and, with repetition of sins, it keeps growing until it covers the heart."[123]

This cleansing impact of repentance or of good deeds in general is ubiquitous in the textual sources (e.g., Qur'ān 4:31; 11:114). The reverse effect, however, is also indicated; that is, bad deeds can spoil good deeds. This is the case, for example, of good deeds that are done for ulterior reasons not sincerely for the sake of God. This is illustrated in the Qur'ān (2:264) by a person who gives money in charity but in order to show off as he keeps reminding the recipients of the favors he has done to them. Ultimately, the effort to avoid sins cannot be separated from the effort to do good and the struggle to acquire virtues cannot be isolated from the challenge of fighting vices. This is also the constant battle that the believer has to

---

al-Ashbāh wa al-Naẓā'ir 'lā Madhhab Abī Ḥanīfah al-Nu'mān, Beirut: Dār al-Kutub al-'Ilmiyyah, 1999, 23–47.

122 al-Nawawī, *Ṣaḥīḥ Muslim bi Sharḥ al-Nawawī*, 11:27 (kitāb al-musāqāh, bāb akhdh al-ḥalāl wa tark al-shubuhāt); Ibn Ḥajar al-'Asqalānī, *Fatḥ al-Bārī bi Sharḥ Ṣaḥīḥ al-Bukhārī*, 4:290 (kitab al-buyū', bāb al-ḥalāl bayyin wa al-ḥarām bayyin wa baynahumā mushtabihāt).

123 al-Ṭabarī, *Tafsīr al-Ṭabarī: Jāmi' al-Bayān*, 24:199–204.

fight and its outcome would determine not only his happiness in this world but also salvation in the hereafter.[124]

6 Concluding Remarks

This chapter aimed to provide a general overview of the concept of sin in Islam and to demonstrate the extent to which it played a fundamental role in the development of the Islamic normative tradition. Three main senses of sin have been distinguished in order to highlight its various religious, moral, and ethical-legal connotations. The chapter then proceeded to explore the specific resonance of this concept within the context of various theological, juristic, and ethical discourses. As the chapter illustrates, the concept of sin was at the center of key discussions and debates within each of these genres, which eventually gave these genres their distinctive character and identity. For example, one of the earliest theological questions was concerned with the definition and consequences of a major sin, and subsequently the fate of a grave sinner. The concept of sin was also closely connected to other theological questions involving divine names and attributes, divine justice, and human freedom. As noted above, opinions on these questions were critical in delineating the boundaries among the main theological orientations and schools. Similarly, juristic discourses reveal extensive discussions on the concept of sin both at the theoretical level in the field of legal methodology or *uṣūl al-fiqh* or at the practical level in the various juristic themes and issues. Beyond the specific theological and juristic fields, the chapter aimed also to situate the concept of sin within the wider domain of Islamic ethics and its various genres or sub-genres including philosophical ethics (*akhlāq*), religious-literary ethics (*ādāb*), or mystical-sufī ethics.

One of the important points that the chapter highlights is the rootedness and connectedness of the concept of sin in the Islamic tradition. Therefore, in order to achieve a deeper understanding of this concept, it has to be examined in light of the various associated terms – along with their opposites – in relationship to other related concepts, both in the foundational sources and across the Islamic normative heritage. For example, the concept of sin cannot be properly studied in isolation of concepts pertaining to faith and belief on the one hand or those pertaining to repentance, expiation, and reconciliation on the other. Ultimately, as

124 See Ibn Qayyim al-Jawziyyah, Abū ʿAbd Allāh Muḥammad ibn Abī Bakr, *Zād al-Maʿād fī hady Khayr al-ʿIbād*, ed. Shuʿayb al-Arnāʾūṭ and ʿAbd al-Qādir al-Arnāʾūṭ, 6 vols., Beirut: Muʾssassat al-Risālah, 1998, 3:372–75.

the lines by John Milton (cited at the beginning of the chapter) indicate, the concept of sin lies at the core of all theological reflections. While it illustrates the extent to which man can rebel against divine will, it also reveals the extent to which man has been endowed with the freedom to do that – if he so chooses.

Bibliography

'Abd al-Bāqī, Muḥammad Fu'ād, *al-Mu'jam al-Mufahras li-Alfāẓ al-Qur'ān al-Karīm*, Cairo: Dār al-Ḥadīth, 2001.

'Abd al-Jabbār ibn Aḥmad al-Asadābādī, *Sharḥ al-Uṣūl al-Khamsah*, ed. 'Abd al-Karīm 'Uthmān, Cairo: Maktabat Wahbah, 1996.

Abū Dāwūd Sulaymān ibn al-Ash'ath al-Sijstānī, *Sunan Abī Dāwūd*, ed. Shu'ayb al-Arna'ūṭ and Muḥammad Kāmil Qurabalalī, 7 vols., Damascus: Dār al-Risālah, 2009.

Abū Zahrah, Muḥammad, *Uṣūl al-Fiqh*, Cairo: Dār al-Fikr al-'Arabī, 2004.

al-Asadabādī, Abd al-Jabbār b. Aḥmad, *al-Mughnī fī Abwāb al-Tawḥīd wa-l-'Adl*, ed. Maḥmūd Muḥammad Qāsim, 16 vols. (volume on Divine Will). Cairo: n.p., n.d.

al-Ash'arī, al-Abū al-Ḥasan 'Alī ibn Ismā'īl, *Maqālāt al-Islāmiyyīn, wa Ikhtilāf al-Muṣallīn*, ed. Muḥāmmad Muḥyī al-Dīn 'Abd al-Ḥamīd, 2 vols., Cairo: Maktabat al-Nahḍah al-Miṣriyyah, 1950.

'Awdah, 'Abd al-Qādir, *al-Tashrī' al-Jinā'ī al-Islāmī Muqāran*[an] *bi al-Qānūn al-Waḍ'ī*, 2 vols., Cairo: Maktabat Dār al-Turāth, 2003.

al-Bukhārī, 'Alā' al-Dīn 'Abd al-'Azīz ibn Aḥmad, *Kashf al-Asrār 'an Uṣūl Fakhr al-Islām al-Bazdawī*, 4 vols., Beirut: Dār al-Kutub al-'Ilmiyyah, 1997.

Cook, Michael, *Commanding Right and Forbidding Wrong in Islamic Thought*, Cambridge: Cambridge University Press, 2000.

al-Dhahabī, Abū 'Abd Allāh Muḥammad ibn Aḥmad ibn 'Uthmān, *Kitāb al-Kabā'ir wa Tabyīn al-Maḥārim*, Damascus: Dār ibn Kathīr, n.d.

al-Ghazālī, Abū Ḥamid Muḥammad ibn Muḥammad, *Iḥyā' 'Ulūm al-Dīn*, ed. 'Abd al-Mu'ṭī Amīn Qal'jī, 5 vols., Beirut: Dār Ṣādir, 2010.

al-Ghazālī, Abū Ḥāmid Muḥammad ibn Muḥammad, *al-Iqtiṣād fī al-I'tiqād*, ed. Anas Muḥammad 'Adnān al-Sharafāwī, Cairo: Dār al-Minhāj, 2019.

al-Ghazālī, Abū Ḥamid Muḥammad ibn Muḥammad, *Kitāb al-Arba'īn fī Uṣūl al-Dīn*, ed. 'Abd Allāh 'Abd al-Ḥamīd 'Arwānī, Damascus: Dār al-Qalam, 2003.

al-Ghazālī, Abū Ḥamid Muḥammad ibn Muḥammad, *Mīzān al-'Amal*, ed. Sulaymān Dunyā, Cairo: Dār al-Ma'ārif, 2003.

Ibn 'Abd al-Salām, 'Izz al-Dīn 'Abd al-'Azīz, *al-Qawā'id al-Kubrā al-Mawsūm bi Qawā'id al-Aḥkām fī Iṣlāḥ al-Anām*, ed. Nazīh Kamāl Ḥammād and 'Uthmān Jum'ah Ḍumayriyyah, 2 vols., Damascus: Dār al-Qalam, 2000.

Ibn Fāris, Aḥmad, *Mu'jam Maqāyīs al-Lughah*, ed. 'Abd al-Salām Hārūn, 6 vols., Beirut: Dār al-Fikr lil-Ṭibā'ah wa al-Nashr wa al-Tawzī', 1979.

Ibn Ḥajar al-'Asqalānī, Aḥmad ibn 'Alī, *Fatḥ al-Bārī bi Sharḥ Ṣaḥīḥ al-Bukhārī*, 13 vols., Beirut: Dār al-Ma'rifah, n.d.

Ibn Ḥanbal, Aḥmad, *Musnad al-Imām Aḥmad Ibn Ḥanbal*, ed. Shu'ayb al-Arnā'ūṭ and others, 50 vols., Beirut: Mu'ssassat al-Risālah, 2001.

Ibn Ḥazm, Abū Muḥammad ʿAlī ibn Aḥmad, *al-Faṣl fī al-Milal wa al-Ahwāʾ wa al-Niḥal*, ed. Muḥammad Ibrāhīm Naṣr and ʿAbd al-Raḥmān ʿUmayrah, 5 vols., Beirut: Dār al-Jīl, n.d.
Ibn Manẓūr, Jamāl al-Din Muḥammad, *Lisān al-ʿArab*, 18 vols., Beirut: Dār Ṣādir, 2008.
Ibn Miskawayh, Abū ʿAlī Aḥmad ibn Muḥammad, *Tahdhīb al-Akhlāq*, ed. Qusṭanṭīn Zurayq, Beirut: al-Jāmiʿah al-Amrikiyyah fī Bayrūt, 1966.
Ibn Nujaym, Zayn al-Dīn ibn Ibrāhīm ibn Muḥammad, *al-Ashbāh wa al-Naẓāʾir ʿlā Madhhab Abī Ḥanīfah al-Nuʿmān*, Beirut: Dār al-Kutub al-ʿIlmiyyah, 1999.
Ibn Qayyim al-Jawziyyah, Abū ʿAbd Allāh Muḥammad ibn Abī Bakr, *Iʿlām al-Muwaqqiʿīn ʿan Rabb al-ʿĀlamīn*, ed. Abū ʿUbaydah Mashhūfr ibn Ḥasan Āl-Salmān, 7 vols., Dammam: Dār Ibn al-Jawzī, 1423/2002.
Ibn Qayyim al-Jawziyyah, Abū ʿAbd Allāh Muḥammad ibn Abī Bakr, *Madārij al-Sālikīn bayna Manāzil Iyyāka Naʿbudu wa Iyyāka Nastaʿīn*, ed. Muḥammad al-Muʿtaṣim bi-Allāh al-Baghdādī, 3 vols., Beirut: Dār al-Kitāb al-ʿArabī, 2003.
Ibn Qayyim al-Jawziyyah, Abū ʿAbd Allāh Muḥammad ibn Abī Bakr, *Zād al-Maʿād fī hady Khayr al-ʿIbād*, ed. Shuʿayb al-Arnāʾūṭ and ʿAbd al-Qādir al-Arnāʾūṭ, 6 vols., Beirut: Muʾssassat al-Risālah, 1998.
al-Juwaynī, ʿAbd al-Malik ibn ʿabd Allāh, *Kitāb al-Irshād ilā Qawāṭiʿ al-Adillah fī Uṣūl al-Iʿtiqād*, Cairo: Maktabat al-Khanjī, 2002.
Kamali, Muhammad Hashim, *Principles of Islamic Jurisprudence*, Cambridge: Islamic Texts Society, 2003.
ʿImārah, Muḥāmmad (ed.), *Rasāʾil al-ʿAdl wa al-Tawḥīd*, Cairo: Dār al-Shurūq, 1988.
Izutsu, Toshihiko, *Ethico-Religious Concepts in the Quran*, Montreal: McGill-Queen's University Press, 2002.
al-Khuḍarī, Muḥammad, *Uṣūl al-Fiqh*, Cairo: Dār al-Ḥadīth, 2003.
al-Masʿūdī, ʿAlī Ibn al-Ḥusayn Ibn ʿAlī, *Murūj al-Dhahab wa Maʿādin al-Jawhar*, ed. ʿAfīf Nāyif Ḥāṭūm, 4 vols., Beirut: Dār Ṣādir, 2010.
al-Māwardī, Abū al-Ḥasan ʿAlī ibn Muḥammad, *Adab al-Dunyā wa al-Dīn*, ed. Muṣṭafā al-Saqqā, Beirut: al-Maktabah al-Thaqāfiyyah, 1955.
al-Muḥāsabī, Abū ʿAbd Allāh al-Ḥārith ibn Asad, *al-Riʿāyah li-Ḥuqūq Allāh*, ed. ʿAbd al-Ḥalīm Maḥmūd, Cairo: Dār al-Maʿārif, 2003.
al-Nawawī, Yaḥyā ibn Sharaf, *Ṣaḥīḥ Muslim bi Sharḥ al-Nawawī*, 18 vols., Cairo: al-Maṭbaʿah al-Miṣriyyah bi al-Azhar, 1929.
Ormsby, Eric Linn, *Theodicy in Islamic Thought: The Dispute over al-Ghazali's Best of All Possible Worlds*, Princeton: Princeton University Press, 1984.
al-Qarāfī, Shihāb al-Dīn Aḥmad ibn Idrīs, *Kitāb al-Furūq: Anwār al-Burūq fī Anwāʾ al-Furūq*, ed. Muḥammad Aḥmad Sarrāj and ʿAlī Jumʿah, 5 vols., Cairo: Dār al-Salām lil Ṭibāʿah wa al-Nashr wa al-Tawzīʿ, 2001.
al-Qurṭubī, Muḥammad ibn Aḥmad, *al-Jāmiʿ li-Aḥkām al-Qurʾān wa al-Mubayyin limā Taḍammanahu min al-Sunnah wa Āy al-Furqān*, ed. ʿAbd Allāh ibn ʿAbd al-Muḥsin al-Turkī, 24 vols., Beirut: Muʾssassat al-Risālah, 2006.
al-Rāghib al-Iṣfahānī, Abū al-Qāsim al-Ḥusayn ibn Muḥammad, *Kitāb al-Dharīʿah ilā Makārim al-Sharīʿah*, ed. Abū al-Yazīd Abū Zayd al-ʿAjamī, Cairo: Dār al-Salām lil-Ṭibāʿah wa al-Nashr wa al-Tawzīʿ wa al-Tarjamah, 2007.
al-Rāghib al-Iṣfahānī, Abū al-Qāsim Ḥusayn ibn Muḥammad, *al-Mufradāt fī Gharīb al-Qurʾān*, ed. Muḥammad Sayyid Kilānī, Beirut: Dār al-Maʿrifah, n.d.
Rahman, Fazlur, *Islam*, Chicago: University of Chicago Press, 2002.
al-Rāzī, Fakhr al-Dīn Muḥammad ibn ʿUmar, *Tafsīr al-Fakhr al-Rāzī al-Mushtahir bi al-Tafsīr al-Kabīr wa Mafātīḥ al-Ghayb*, 32 vols., Beirut: Dār al-Fikr lil-Ṭibāʿah wa al-Nashr wa al-Tawzīʿ, 1981.

Riḍā, Muḥammad Rashīd, *Tafsīr al-Qur'ān al-Ḥakīm, al-Mushtahir bi Tafsīr al-Manār*, 12 vols., Cairo: Dār al-Manār, 1947.
al-Ṣanʿānī, ʿAbd al-Razzāq ibn Hammām, *Tafsīr ʿAbd al-Razzāq*, ed. Maḥmūd Muḥammad ʿAbduh, 3 vols., Beirut: Dār al-Kutub al-ʿIlmiyyah, 1999.
Shabana, Ayman, "The Concept of Sin in the Qur'ān in Light of the Story of Adam," in: Lucinda Musher / David Marshall (eds.), *Sin, Forgiveness, and Reconciliation*, Washington, DC: Georgetown University Press, 2016, 40–65.
al-Shahrastānī, Muḥammad ibn ʿAbd al-Karīm Ibn Abī Bakr Aḥmad, *al-Millal wa al-Niḥal*, ed. Amīr ʿAlī Mahannā and ʿAlī Ḥasan Fāʿūr, 2 vols., Beirut: Dār al-Maʿrifah, 1993.
al-Shāṭibī, Abū Isḥāq Ibrahīm ibn Mūsā , *al-Muwāfaqāt fī Uṣūl al-Sharīʿah*, ed. ʿAbd Allāh Darrāz, 4 vols., Cairo: al-Maktabah al-Tawfīqiyyah, 2003.
al-Subkī, Taj al-Dīn ʿAbd al-Wahhāb ibn ʿAlī, *Jamʿ al-Jawāmiʿ fī Uṣūl al-Fiqh*, ed. ʿAbd al-Munʿim Khalīl Ibrāhīm, Beirut: Dār al-Kutub al-ʿIlmiyyah, 2003.
al-Subkī, Taj al-Dīn ʿAbd al-Wahhāb ibn ʿAli, *Ṭabaqāt al-Shāfiʿiyyah al-Kubrā*, ed. ʿAbd al-Fattāḥ Muḥammad al-Ḥulw and Maḥmūd Muḥammad al-Tanāḥī, 10 vols., Cairo: Dār Iḥyā' al-Kutub a-ʿArabiyyah, n.d.
al-Suyūṭī, Jalāl al-Dīn ʿAbd al-Raḥmān, *al-Ashbāh wa al-Naẓā'ir fī Qawāʿid wa Furūʿ Fiqh al-Shāfiʿiyyah*, Beirut: Dār al-Kutub al-ʿIlmiyyah, 1983.
al-Ṭabarī, Abū Jaʿfar Muḥammad ibn Jarīr, *Tafsīr al-Ṭabarī: Jāmiʿ al-Bayān ʿan Ta'wīl Āy al-Qur'ān*, ed. ʿAbd Allāh ibn ʿAbd al-Muḥsin al-Turkī, 26 vols., Cairo: Dār Hajar, 2001.
al-Ṭabarī, Abū Jaʿfar Muḥammad ibn Jarīr, *Tahdhīb al-Āthār*, ed. Maḥmūd Muḥammad Shākir, 4 vols., Cairo: Maṭbʿat al-Midanī, 1982.
al-Ṭabarī, Abū Jaʿfar Muḥammad ibn Jarīr, *Tārīkh al-Ṭabar: Tārīkh al-Umam wa al-Mulūk*, ed. Nawwāf al-Jarrāḥ, 6 vols., Beirut: Dār Ṣadir, 2008.
al-Taftazānī, Saʿd al-Dīn Masʿūd ibn ʿUmar, *Sharḥ al-ʿAqā'id al-Nasafiyyah*, ed. Aḥmad Ḥijāzī al-Saqqā. Cairo: Maktabat al-Kulliyāt al-Azhariyyah, 1987.
Walī Allāh al-Dihlawī, Aḥmad ibn ʿAbd al-Raḥīm, *Ḥujjat Allāh al-Bālighah*, ed. Saʿīd Aḥmad Yūsuf, 2 vols., Beirut: Dār Ibn Kathīr, 2020.
Wolfson, Harry Austryn, *The Philosophy of The Kalam*, Cambridge: Harvard University Press, 1976.
Zargar, Cyrus Ali, *The Polished Mirror: Storytelling and the Pursuit of Virtue in Islamic Philosophy and Sufism*, London: Oneworld Publications, 2017.
al-Zarkashī, Badr al-Dīn Muḥammad ibn Bahādir ibn ʿAbd Allāh, *al-Baḥr al-Muḥīṭ fī Uṣūl al-Fiqh*, ed. ʿAbd al-Sattār Abū Ghudah, ʿAbd al-Qādir ʿAbd Allāh al-Ānī, ʿUmār Sulaymān al-Ashqar, Muḥammad Sulaymān al-Ashqar, 6 vols., Kuwait: Wizārat al-Awqāf wa a l-Shu'ūn al-Islāmiyyah, 2010.
al-Zarqā, Muṣṭafā, *al-Madkhal al-Fiqhī al-ʿĀmm*, 2 vols., Damascus: Dār al-Qalam, 2012.
al-Zubaydī, Muḥammad Murtaḍā al-Ḥusaynī, *Tāj al-ʿArūs min Jawāhir al-Qāmus*, ed. Nawwāf al-Jarrāḥ, 10 vols., Beirut: Dār Ṣādir, 2011.
al-Zuḥaylī, Wahbah,*Mawsūʿat al-Fiqh al-Islāmī wa al-Qaḍāyā al-Muʿāṣirah*, 14 vols., Damascus: Dār al-Fikr, 2012.
Zuhayr, Muḥammad Abū al-Nūr, *Uṣūl al-Fiqh*, 4 pts in 1 vol., Cairo: Dār al-Baṣā'r, 2007.

Suggestions for Further Reading

Draz, M.A., *The Moral World of the Qur'an*, trans. Daniella Robinson / Rebecca Masterton, London: I.B. Tauris, 2008.
Fakhry, Majid, *Ethical Theories in Islam*, 2nd ed., Leiden: Brill, 1994.
Izutsu, Toshihiko, *Ethico-Religious Concepts in the Quran*, Montreal: McGill-Queen's University Press, 2002.
Kamali, Mohammad Hashim, *Shari'ah Law: An Introduction*, Oxford: Oneworld Publications, 2008.

Christoph Böttigheimer / Konstantin Kamp

Epilogue

Sin is a topic that many people associate very closely with religion. In fact, the term is used almost exclusively in religious contexts and, to pick up on a widespread understanding in common parlance, refers to any transgression of a divine commandment. The concept of sin is equally central to the teachings of Judaism, Christianity, and Islam. To name just a few examples, in the traditions of all three religions there has been extensive reflection on the meaning of the word "sin," the different types of sin, the fate of the sinner, and ways to overcome sin.

Despite its centrality in the three monotheistic religions, however, the concept poses serious problems for many people today. In a secular society, the concept of sin has become increasingly incomprehensible. One of the main reasons for this is that the notion of sin, unlike guilt, presupposes the existence of a divine being. Furthermore, speaking of sin assumes that this divine being lays down commandments, the transgression of which is qualified as "sin." This is problematic not only for atheists and agnostics, but also for some believers who find it difficult to accept the idea of a God who issues commandments and insists on their observance. This immense loss of plausibility of the religious discourse on sin is probably due not least to the use of the term "sin" throughout history. For many people, particularly those from traditionally Christian areas, the term is historically loaded. According to a widespread accusation, talk of "sin" was often used in the past to control people. This, it is argued, is particularly evident in the extensive consideration of the punishments that the sinner faced.

It is a matter of fact that in all three monotheistic religions there has been, and to some extent still is, extensive reflection on the fate of the sinner. But is talk of sin really just an instrument of power used to oppress people? Or is the preoccupation with sin rather motivated by a deep concern for humanity, because what is considered sinful is also seen as hostile to life, and therefore people need to be protected from it? Moreover, can the possibility of sin not also be seen as an expression of human dignity, insofar as it presupposes that humans are free to choose for or against the divine commandments?

As these questions indicate, the study of sin goes right to the heart of religion. Hardly any other topic touches so clearly upon the relationship between God and man. Discussing sin addresses the question of what the content and goal of each respective religion actually is. Because sin is such a central topic, it is particularly interesting to examine how the various religions deal with this issue. Gaining a more precise understanding of sin in Judaism, Christianity, and Islam is an important prerequisite for interreligious dialog and can also be theologically helpful in

https://doi.org/10.1515/9783111319452-004

finding answers to the above-mentioned problems. For this reason, the present book brought together three articles that examine the understanding of the concept of sin in Judaism, Christianity, and Islam, respectively. In the following, the most important results of each article will be summarized and commonalities and differences in the understanding of the term will be explored.

The Concept of Sin in Judaism

As David Bashevkin points out in his article on the Jewish understanding of the term, sin is a multifaceted phenomenon already in the Hebrew Bible. Not only are there various terms that can all be translated as "sin" in English (namely *ḥeṭ*, *'aṿon* and *pesh'a*), but there are also different metaphors that express what sin is. For example, sin can be described as a burden that a person must bear, as debt, or as a missed opportunity. In rabbinic times, the different Hebrew terms for "sin" could also be associated with varying degrees of severity, depending on intent. Since *ḥeṭ* refers to an unintentional sin, it is considered relatively minor. In contrast, *'aṿon* and *pesh'a* are intentional and therefore more serious, with *pesh'a* being the most severe because it denotes an act committed explicitly in rebellion against God. Intention is so crucial that even sins otherwise considered very serious in Jewish tradition (such as murder or adultery) are described as *ḥeṭ* when committed unintentionally.

In addition to these three biblical terms, the Mishnah contains a further word for sin, *'averah*. Since *'averah* is derived from the verb *la'avor*, which can be translated as "to transgress" or "to cross over," the term specifically emphasizes the spatial dimension of sin. It indicates that a person who sins enters an area that is forbidden to them, and thus points to the fact that in the Mishnah the boundaries of what was legally permitted and forbidden were already much clearer than in biblical times. Furthermore, *'averah* also has a common root with the word *'avar*, which means "past." This connection underscores that sin also has a temporal dimension, as past sins can potentially be experienced as obstacles to repentance in the present. Jewish literature repeatedly emphasizes that past experiences should not prevent individuals from mending their ways in the present.

When examining sin more closely, one question to consider is where it originates. A Jewish answer to this question can be found in the story of Adam and Eve in the Bible (Gen 2:25–3:24), where eating from the Tree of the Knowledge of Good and Evil is mentioned as the first sin of humankind. Although the text raises several questions – such as what exactly the first sin consisted of – a particularly frequently discussed issue in Jewish literature is *when* the first sin was committed. While the prevailing interpretation in Christian theology is that the first sin occurred after the completion of creation, the Talmud sees sin as part of the process of creation itself. The main reason for this view is that otherwise it is impossible to explain how Adam, who according to rabbis such as Nahmanides (1194–1270) was naturally doing God's will before he sinned, could have sinned in the first place. With sin being a part of creation, the question arises as to what exactly was created through sin. For rabbinic commentaries, it is the notion of self that Adam acquires through sin, thereby no longer seeing himself as part of God. In other words, as a result of sin, Adam is endowed with free will.

Although it is a common view among Jewish polemicists of the Middle Ages that there is nothing comparable to the Christian doctrine of original sin in Judaism, on closer inspection things are actually far less clear. For example, while Jewish theology does not consider humans to be spiritually depraved, it assumes a physical transmission of the consequences of Adam's sin to his descendants. More importantly, the Talmud also speaks of the long-term consequences of Adam's sin, describing it as a kind of poisoning of human beings. Like Christian theology, Jewish tradition identifies an antidote to this poisoning, which does not, however, consist in a form of baptism, but in the revelation of the Torah on Mount Sinai. Lurianic Kabbalah, which is based on the teachings of Isaac Luria (1534–1572), goes even further by admitting that Adam's sin damaged the whole of creation and gave sin an active presence in the world. A crucial difference from the Christian doctrine of original sin, however, is that according to Kabbalistic belief, no redeemer is necessary to overcome sin; rather, each person, with divine help, can contribute to defeating sin and redeeming creation.

As indicated above, according to Jewish tradition, intention is crucial to speaking of sin. This raises the question of whether thoughts can also be sinful. Even though there are seemingly contradictory statements in the Talmud, the standard position of the rabbis is that thoughts can only be sinful in the case of prohibitions that explicitly refer to thoughts. Another question concerning the connection between sin and intention is whether it is permissible to commit a sin for the sake of a higher goal. The Talmud refers to such a sin as *'averah lishmah*, i.e., "sin for a purpose." In Jewish discussion, three different interpretations of the concept of *'averah lishmah* can be discerned. First, it can be understood as a principle of Jewish law (*halakhah*) that permits a sin for the sake of another commandment. Second, it can be interpreted as evidence that intent alone is decisive in qualifying an action as sin. In this interpretation, *'averah lishmah* is more like a philosophical idea that is potentially antinomian in character, since it can call into question the whole idea of law. Third, it can be seen as a principle that can only be invoked in certain cases after an act in order to legitimize it.

When analyzing the further development of the Jewish understanding of sin over the course of history, one can look, for example, at the movement called *Ḥaside Ashkenaz* that emerged in Germany in the 12th and 13th centuries. The aim of this mystical-pietistic movement was to deepen the understanding of God's will and to live according to it. The idea of repentance therefore played an important role in the movement. It developed the doctrine of a form of repentance called *teshuvah haba'ah* that allows one to avoid sin even when given the opportunity to sin. Another special feature of the movement was that its representatives, including above all Rabbi Eleazer of Worms (c. 1165–1238), attempted to determine exactly which repentance was necessary for which sin. This approach proved to be influential for several centuries and appears in the so-called *responsa*, a class of rabbinical literature consisting of letters in which rabbis respond to individual halakhic questions, which were subsequently circulated. Since the understanding of repentance dominant in *Ḥaside Ashkenaz* at times shows similarities to Christian ideas, it is possible that it was at least partially due to Christian influence.

A peculiar understanding of sin was developed by Shabbetai Tsevi (1626–1676), who was highly influential in the 17th century as a self-proclaimed messiah and founder of the Sabbatean movement. Tsevi resolutely disregarded Jewish law and took an antinomian position. He did so by interpreting the concept of *'averah lishmah*, discussed above, as a philosophical principle that permitted transgression of the law in light of the messianic age he claimed was dawning with him. He argued that the law evolved with his messianic revolution and lost its validity, at least in its pre-messianic understanding. Thus, with the arrival of the messianic age, what had previously been a sin was suddenly declared permissible and even the fulfillment of God's will.

Another movement that had a major impact on Judaism's understanding of sin was Hasidism, which can be traced back to Rabbi Israel ben Eliezer, known as the Baal Shem Tov (c. 1700–1760). At a time of poverty and increasing isolation of the rabbinical elite from the problems of ordinary people in Eastern Europe, Hasidism sought to open a path to God for those very ordinary people. Since Hasidism did not always adhere strictly to Jewish law, it was sometimes criticized as a kind of revival of Sabbateanism, especially by a group of traditional rabbis, the *mitnagdim*, who were highly critical of Hasidism. As the representatives of Hasidism place particular emphasis on the individual's relationship with God, sin and repentance are issues of utmost importance to them. However, a closer look reveals very different approaches, depending on the founding rabbi of a particular Hasidic community. Rabbi Elimelekh of Lizhensk (1717–1787), for example, stresses the need for a *tsadik*, i.e., a righteous teacher who helps sinners to overcome sin. In contrast, Rabbi Shneur Zalman of Liadi (1745–1812) focused on the repentance of the sinners themselves, because he believed that repentance strengthens the presence of God in the world, which had previously been weakened by sin. To name a last example, for Rabbi Naḥman of Bratslav (1772–1810), the idea of God's absence played an important role, allowing him to show empathy for sinners.

A radical form of Hasidism is represented by the school of Izbica, which goes back to Rabbi Mordekhai Yosef Leiner (1801–1854). It is considered controversial because it held the seemingly deterministic view that even bad things can be traced back to God. This raises the question of whether sin can also be described as willed by God and therefore religiously appropriate. If this were the case, it could potentially lead to antinomianism and the abrogation of the Jewish law. However, the rabbis of the school of Izbica did not draw this conclusion but maintained a largely traditional lifestyle. The apparent determinism in the theology of Izbica is therefore possibly to be understood as a doctrine that does not have equal significance for everyone but is primarily intended to provide comfort to those struggling with their sins. For despite their deterministic teaching, the rabbis of Izbica attach great importance to the need for every person to submit to a permanent process of self-evaluation in order to ensure that they are in harmony with the divine will.

A different approach to sin can be found in Reform Judaism, which emerged in Germany in the 19th century in the wake of the Enlightenment. It brought a new awareness of the development of Judaism throughout history, which led to significant changes in prayer and teaching and, above all, called into question the need for strict observance of traditional Jewish law. Whether Reform Judaism can be seen as a late consequence of Sabbateanism, in that it also interprets Judaism in a way other than through strict adherence to the law, can be left open here. In any case, the question of what constitutes sin arose anew for Reform Judaism if sin was not simply identical with a violation of the *halakhah*. Various answers were and are still being developed today, such as reinterpreting the concept of sin in ethical terms or understanding sin as a starting point for personal development.

Orthodox, non-Hasidic Judaism also continued to deal with the problem of sin. One example of this is the *responsa* literature of the Enlightenment period, which deals with sin in detail. Rabbi Yeḥezkel Landau (1713–1793), for example, emphasized that repentance does not consist of precisely defined works (such as fasting and other acts of asceticism), as it was often understood in the wake of *Ḥaside Ashkenaz*, but rather in a sincere confession and turning away from sin with one's whole heart. A similar understanding of repentance can also be found in Rabbi Moshe Sofer (1762–1839), who recommended adding an annual day of personal reflection and fasting to the process of repentance alongside confession, regret, and turning away from sin.

The *responsa* literature continued to be cultivated in the following period and offers important insights into the understanding of sin in Judaism. Letters from the 20th century are particularly interesting because they also raise questions that were not yet addressed in earlier times. For example, Rabbi Moshe Feinstein (1895–1986), one of the most important representatives of Orthodox Judaism in America, also answered questions about how to deal with extramarital affairs or homosexuality. His approach is characterized by strict adherence to traditional Jewish law, combined with practical empathy for all those struggling. An approach based even more strongly on empathy for human struggles and failure can be found in the personal correspondence of Rabbi Yitzḥak Hutner (1906–1980). He emphasized that spiritual development does not proceed in a straight line, but rather requires failure.

In contemporary Orthodox Judaism, the question of sin can still be a subject of controversial debate, particularly between Hasidic and non-Hasidic rabbis. One example of this is the dispute between Rabbi Moshe Weinberger and Rabbi Noach Shafran. The issue at stake is the question: does man, as Hasidism and Rabbi Weinberger claim, have a permanent spiritual connection to God, which results from God's love for all Jews and cannot be violated by sin? Or can this connection be broken by violations of the law, as Rabbi Shafran states? As this example shows, the exact understanding of sin is still a question of central importance in Judaism today.

The Concept of Sin in Christianity

In his article on the Christian understanding of sin, Christoph Böttigheimer points out that "sin" refers not only to a violation of norms, but primarily to the associated turning away and alienation from God (*aversio a Deo*). Because of its inherent connection to God, he argues, speaking of sin only makes sense in the context of faith. This notion is already evident in the Old Testament with its various terms for "sin" discussed above. Here, transgressions of the law described as "sin" are construed as violations of a divinely ordained order of life. Whether committed consciously or unconsciously, they are regarded as acts of rebellion against God. As such, they are closely linked to their consequences, which are seen as a form of divine punishment. According to a widespread conviction in the Old Testament, by this punishment, God holds individuals captive within the realm of sin they have entered through their evil deeds. The correlation between actions and outcomes is so profound that the underlying sin can even be discerned from a person's lack of well-being. Because sins disrupt the order established by God, they are perceived not only as individual transgressions but also as having communal repercussions. Although such an understanding of sin as a violation of the divine order tends to overlook the personal aspect of sin, it is nevertheless reflected in the prophets, who emphasize the individuality of guilt and conceive of sin as self-centeredness and inhumanity at the core of the human being.

The New Testament, like the Old Testament prophets, occasionally highlights the sinfulness of all Israel. At the heart of Jesus' proclamation of the Kingdom of God, however, is the offer of unconditional divine mercy that opens a new way for sinners and invites them to repent. The healing accounts illustrate Jesus' concern for the well-being of the whole person. Compared to the Old Testament prophets, the personal dimension of sin takes on even greater significance, as sin is now understood as a rejection of God's offer of love. This divine offer of love also has a profound social dimension, since the forgiveness that God grants to an individual also requires that person to forgive others. Consequently, sin is also a social reality. As an inadequate response to the divine offer of love, sin directly affects other people and has impacts on the entire creation. Furthermore, a characteristic feature of Jesus' teaching is the internalization of sin, which he understands as an inner turning away from God, thereby emphasizing the intentionality and freedom of the human decision for or against sin. Unlike in the Old Testament, Jesus no longer sees a connection between a person's lack of well-being and their sins.

Although for Paul, as in the Old Testament, sin is a transgression of the divine law, there are important differences with regard to the understanding of the law. For Paul, too, the law goes back to God and refers to what he has commanded. However, Paul contends that humans are inherently incapable of fulfilling the law's requirements. The law exposes humanity's true condition, aiding individuals in recognizing their sinfulness and understanding their reliance on divine salvation.

In the early Church, the concept of sin was primarily reflected in relation to the practice of penance. A distinction was made between mortal sins, which required a one-time public penance, and venial sins, which could be privately repented. With the rise of Iro-Scottish monasticism, auricular confession eventually became established, allowing for more frequent penance. Regarding the difference between mortal and venial sins, Thomas Aquinas (1225–1274), for instance, posits that the gravity of a sin depends on its subjective orientation. While a mortal sin involves a deliberate decision against God, a venial sin pertains to a misuse of created things. For Aquinas, sinfulness is thus entirely located in the human act itself, originating from the will. In this way, Aquinas departs from the Old Testament perspective of sin as an external force, favoring a more anthropocentric understanding of sin. Whereas Aquinas emphasized intention, in late scholasticism and early modern times, an approach centered on objective degrees of severity became dominant. This approach primarily addressed various types of sin and the corresponding penances in a casuistic manner. It was only after the Second Vatican Council (1962–65) that a more personal approach once again began to prevail, which, in line with the New Testament, understood sin as a disruption of the relationship between humans and God.

Regarding the origin of sin, the story of Adam and Eve in Genesis 3 serves as an equally important point of reference for Christian theology as it does for Judaism. Although this narrative was soon interpreted in Western Christian theology in terms of the doctrine of original sin, modern exegesis highlights its original purpose as an etiology. Understood in this way, the narrative does not present a comprehensive theological theory of sin and the universal sinfulness of humanity but rather illustrates how the evidently broken relationship with God came about. It portrays the act of eating from the Tree of the Knowledge of Good and Evil as a violation of a boundary established by God for humanity, which affects the original harmony of man and God as well as human relationships. While there are indications in the Old Testament that Adam's sin also affected his descendants, Paul's writings in the New Testament are the first to explicitly refer to a connection between the universal sinfulness of humankind and Adam's transgression.

Even though Paul assumes the sinfulness of all humanity, he does not speak of inherited guilt as the doctrine of original sin would later do. Instead, he portrays sin as a destructive force manifested in numerous individual sins. It affects all people and can be characterized as a failure to recognize human dependence on God. According to Paul, sin cannot be overcome by adherence to the law but only through embracing the grace of salvation in Jesus Christ. However, Paul's acceptance of the universality of sinfulness is not based on a theological theory of human nature as such. Rather, he infers the universality of sin from the universality of salvation offered to humanity through Jesus Christ.

Augustine is credited with developing the doctrine of original sin, which subsequently became integral to Western Christian theology. He posits that Adam's sin corrupted human nature, interpreting Rom 5:12 to suggest that all humans sinned "in him." This leads Augustine to conceptualize sin as transmitted through procreation, with Adam's sin inherited by all descendants, thereby making all of them guilty. Due to its corruption, humanity is totally dependent on divine grace. Consequently, baptism is necessary even for infants to cleanse the inherent guilt passed down from Adam's sin. Despite his formulation of original sin, Augustine also strives to maintain human freedom and accountability for sin. However, he cannot explain how human beings can be truly guilty without their sin being personally attributable to their freedom.

It is important to note that the Eastern Church does not accept the doctrine of original sin as developed by Augustine, affirming instead that certain consequences of Adam's sin, particularly mortality, are passed on to all human beings. In the West, however, original sin became an integral part of Christian theology. For instance, it was affirmed by the Synods of Carthage (418) and Orange (529), although the status of their decrees as universally accepted Church teachings remains disputed. Thomas Aquinas also defended the concept of original sin, locating it within the human soul and defining it as concupiscence, which leads humanity to deviate from its original righteousness. According to Aquinas, sin is passed on physically through the male sperm, as it encompasses the whole person due to the intimate connection between body and soul. Given the corruption of human nature by original sin, human beings are in need of divine grace to attain God as the last end of their life.

In the 16th century, both the Reformers and Catholic theologians upheld the doctrine of original sin, but with significant differences. Catholic theology posited that human nature was not entirely corrupted by original sin and that humans could cooperate with grace to some extent. In contrast, the Reformers argued that sin had completely destroyed humanity's relationship with God. Martin Luther (1483–1546) held that sinful humans were inherently contradictory to God, unable to contribute to their own salvation, and entirely dependent on divine grace. He maintained that justification was a passive process, whereby humans are declared righteous by God despite their ongoing sinfulness. The Council of Trent rejected this view, emphasizing instead that an inner renewal of humanity is possible through grace, beginning with baptism. By doing so, Trent presupposed the doctrine of original sin in its Augustinian form without delving too deeply into its nature. It stated that humanity has lost its true freedom through Adam's sin and is unable to turn to God without divine grace, but that after baptism, people regain the necessary freedom to resist concupiscence. Similar to Augustine's view, Trent asserted that Adam's sin is "transmitted by propagation, not by imitation" (DH 1513), implying a physical transmission, although the exact meaning of "propagation" is left unspecified.

Even though the Augustinian doctrine of original sin is still part of Catholic doctrine today, it is nevertheless maintained in a somewhat moderate form. Thus, in the "Catechism of the Catholic Church," for example, it is only referred to as sin in the analogous sense due to its pre-personal character. As the "Joint Declaration on the Doctrine of Justification" shows, original sin is still a controversial topic in ecumenical theology. Although Catholic and Lutheran theologians were able to find at least some common ground on this issue, the confessional differences could not be fundamentally overcome.

In recent theology, there have been a number of attempts to reformulate the doctrine of original sin under modern conditions. These attempts have, for example, resulted in an evolutionary approach that seeks to understand sin as the result of human development and is advocated by theologians such as Pierre Teilhard de Chardin (1881–1955) or Friedrich Daniel Ernst Schleiermacher (1768–1834). Also influential is a sociological-empirical approach that understands original sin as man's entanglement in a social context that is characterized by sin. Such an approach is represented, for example, by Albrecht Ritschl (1822–1889) or Piet Schoonenberg (1911–1999). Other interpretations of original sin that can be found in today's theology are a historical-empirical, an existential-transempirical, a depth-psychological, and a transcendental-historical approach.

In Christian theology, sin is not only an important topic at the beginning of humanity's existence, but also at its end. Christians expect Jesus Christ to return at the end of time and bring the Kingdom of God to completion. With Christ's second coming, earthly time will cease, and sin will be ultimately conquered. At the same time, according to Christian eschatology, humanity will face the Last Judgment. This is particularly important because it will bring justice to the oppressed and the victims of history. For Christians, the Last Judgment is, thus, an expression of hope for final justice, despite its frequent instrumentalization to threaten people. Ultimately, as Rev 21:5 states, at the end of time all things will be made new, signifying that Christ's return will bring renewal not only to humanity but to the entire creation.

The expectation of the Last Judgment is closely linked to the doctrine of purgatory held by the Roman Catholic Church. Even if the existence of a post-mortem place of purification cannot be directly deduced from the Bible, there are indications that can be interpreted in this way. Origen (185–253/54) explicitly advocates the idea of a purifying fire for deceased believers and can thus be regarded as one of the first proponents of a doctrine resembling purgatory. This doctrine received a divided reception among the Church Fathers, with some accepting and others rejecting it. As a result of the practice of prayer and the celebration of the Eucharist for the deceased, the assumption of a third place between heaven and hell became an integral part of Roman Church doctrine in the Middle Ages. To this day, the doctrine of the Catholic Church conceives of purgatory as an eschatological place for those who do not die sinless but are also not in a state of grave sin, serving to purify them before they can be accepted into heaven. From an ecumenical point of view, however, the doctrine of purgatory remains controversial because it is rejected by both Orthodox theology and the Reformers. For this reason, contemporary Catholic theologians seek to understand purgatory less as a third place between heaven and hell, and more as a process of purification that occurs after death through the encounter with divine love.

Another topic closely related to the concept of sin in Christianity is indulgences. Indulgences aim at the remission of temporal punishments for sins whose guilt has already been forgiven. They emerged as a consequence of auricular confession, which could be repeated frequently and required acts of penance to follow the absolution of sin. The practice of indulgences in this form in the Western Church dates back to the 11th and 12th centuries. Since the 13th century, the Church has held that it is possible to obtain indulgences for the deceased, attributing its authority to remit temporal punishments even after death to the so-called “treasury of grace” left to the Church by Christ and the saints. From the 14th century onwards, the practice of granting indulgences was finally separated from confession.

It is well known that the practice of indulgences was a major point of criticism of the Roman Church by the Reformers. Martin Luther considered indulgences to be unbiblical and potentially undermining the singularity of Christ’s work of redemption. He rejected the Church’s claim to be able to dispense grace. Instead, he believed that humans were fundamentally dependent on the grace of justification and that, therefore, their entire lives should be a process of repentance. As a consequence of the Reformers’ critique, the Council of Trent addressed abuses in the practice of indulgences but simultaneously reaffirmed the Church’s authority to grant them.

It was not until after the Second Vatican Council that the magisterium first attempted to develop a new approach toward indulgences. In 1967, Pope Paul VI reinterpreted indulgences as intercessory prayers that effect the remission of temporal punishments. He emphasized that indulgences are not merely formulas to be recited for certain effects but are intended to initiate a real process of renewal and growth in faith. Pope John Paul II further reflected theologically on indulgences, clarifying that they help to overcome the inner consequences of sin by promoting personal commitment and spiritual growth. He thus emphasized the existential character of indulgences. While this focus on the therapeutic effect of indulgences can be seen as progress, the Catholic practice of indulgences remains controversial in ecumenical dialogue. From a Lutheran perspective, it is problematic that indulgences emphasize a major contribution of the Church to the process of forgiveness, whereas for the Reformers it was clear that humans are justified by the grace of Christ alone. As the example of indulgences shows, the concept of sin is still a much-discussed theological issue in Christianity and is therefore of continuing relevance.

The Concept of Sin in Islam

Ayman Shabana’s chapter on the understanding of sin in Islam begins with an observation similar to those made in the two previous articles. As in Judaism and Christianity, the concept of sin in Islam is multifaceted. At least three different but closely related levels of meaning can be distinguished: First, the term "sin" can refer to a violation of a commandment; second, to something that is religiously and morally wrong; and third, in the legal sense, to a crime that must be punished accordingly. The latter level applies primarily to the so-called *ḥadd* crimes, i.e., acts such as murder or adultery, for which Islamic law has well-defined punishments that must be carried out in this life. In distinguishing between these three levels, it should be noted that they overlap to some extent. A crime in the sense of the third level is of course also morally and religiously wrong and violates a commandment. However, the distinction is useful because there are violations of commandments that are morally wrong but do not constitute crimes. In such cases, punishment is meted out by God in the afterlife.

Just as there are different levels to the concept of sin, there are also various Arabic words that can be associated with the English term "sin," such as *fāḥishah, jurm, dhanb, ithm,* or *khaṭaʾ*, to name a few. Each of these terms has different nuances of meaning and can be assigned to different layers of the concept of sin. Additionally, there are various terms that are semantically related to the concept of sin, such as *maʿṣiyah* (disobedience), *sayiʾah* (bad deed), and *munkar* (evil), among others.

When examining the Qur'ān, one can find a clear distinction between major sins, referred to as *kabāʾir* in Arabic, and minor sins, called *ṣaghāʾir*. Among the major sins, the term *fawāḥish* is used to denote those transgressions which are considered *ḥadd* crimes. Which specific acts are to be classified as major sins is a matter of debate and varies from one interpreter to another. Nevertheless, a generally accepted classification is that disregarding Islamic monotheism is always a major sin. In the Qur'ān, one can find a list of commandments in 7:151–152 that prohibit polytheism, ingratitude towards one's parents, murder, and several other actions. Similar lists appear in other sections of the Qur'ān, such as 17:23–39. Many commentaries regard the commandments in 7:151–152 as highly significant, noting their resemblance to the Ten Commandments and to the moral core of many other religions and traditions. Consequently, violations of these commandments are considered major sins. In addition to the distinction between major and minor sins, a closer analysis of the Qur'ān reveals a further differentiation between explicit and implicit sins. Again, the exact meaning of this distinction is not entirely clear, as different interpretations are upheld. For example, explicit sins can be understood as those committed in public and implicit sins as those committed in secret.

To gain a deeper understanding of what the Qur'ān means by sin, it is also worth examining how it describes goodness. Since sin is the opposite of goodness, one can indirectly infer what is meant by "sin." According to Qur'ān 2:177, goodness consists of firm faith in God and actions such as charity, prayer, and perseverance in times of distress. Therefore, sin can be interpreted as the lack of such faith and good deeds. Given that the ideal believer is repeatedly described in the Qur'ān (for instance, in 23:1–11) as someone who submits to God, is pious, humble, restrained, prays, and fasts, a sinner must be a person who does not submit to God, is haughty, and does not pray or fast, among other characteristics.

In addition, the Qur'ān clarifies several other points relevant to understanding the Islamic concept of sin. For example, it states that each person bears individual responsibility for their own sin, and that joint responsibility applies only when sins are committed together. Accordingly, sins are usually rewarded or punished individually. Another interesting point is that in Islam, the reward for good deeds in the hereafter is often considered much greater than the punishment for bad deeds, as stated, for example, in Qur'ān 6:160. Thus, good deeds are sometimes rewarded up to ten times, whereas bad deeds are only counted once. Among good deeds, works of charity are considered particularly meritorious. Sometimes even good intentions are classified as good deeds, while bad intentions are not treated as sins.

Besides the consequences in the afterlife, good deeds and sins are sometimes seen to affect one's life in this world, making it either lighter or heavier, respectively. However, according to some commentators, the effect may be different for believers and unbelievers. While unbelievers may experience the effects of their good deeds in this world, such as material prosperity, they do not suffer the punishments until the afterlife. For believers, it is the opposite: they may experience the consequences of their bad deeds in this life, while they are rewarded for their good deeds only in the hereafter.

Based on certain traditions of the Prophet Muḥammad, another point of discussion in early Islamic literature is the relationship between sin and faith. Ibn ʿAbbās (c. 619–687), for example, asserts that a sinner cannot be considered a believer at and after the moment of sin, but must first regain faith through repentance. Additionally, there are numerous other views on this issue held by Islamic authorities and scholars, such as the belief that sin diminishes faith without causing the sinner to lose it completely. As is well-known, while the Qur'ān frequently threatens sinners with punishment in the afterlife, it also emphasizes the importance of repentance. Repentance is portrayed as a means to avoid the divine punishment consequent to sin. However, repentance is not just a superficial attitude but must be linked to deep faith and action. Whether forgiveness can be obtained for all types of sin through repentance remains controversial.

One of the first controversies in Islamic theology concerning the concept of sin began shortly after the assassination of the third caliph, ʿUthmān (574–656). While political questions also played an important role in this controversy, the main theological issue was the question of the status of the grave sinner. Different positions clashed in this debate. The Kharijites (al-Khawārij) held a particularly radical stance, considering grave sin tantamount to disbelief and deserving of corresponding punishment in the afterlife. Consequently, they argued that grave sinners should not be regarded as believers. In contrast, a group called al-Murji'ah maintained that grave sin did not invalidate one's status as a believer and claimed that only in the hereafter could the fate of grave sinners be determined. They emphasized that even grave sinners could hope for God's mercy. The Muʿtazilites adopted a nuanced position, as they viewed grave sinners neither as believers nor unbelievers, ascribing to them an intermediate position instead. According to them, the punishment for grave sinners would be less severe than that for disbelievers, though it would still involve eternal hellfire. This position was criticized by Abū al-Ḥasan al-Ashʿarī (c. 873–935), the founder of the Ashʿarite school, who argued that while God was free to punish grave sinners, as believers they would not face eternal punishment.

Another controversial issue between the Muʿtazilites and the Ashʿarites was whether God wills sinful actions. At issue here is the relationship between God's omnipotence, goodness, and human freedom. According to the Muʿtazilites, since God only does what is good, sinful actions cannot be willed by God. The Ashʿarites, on the other hand, argued that this would be an unacceptable limitation of divine power. In response, the Muʿtazilites distinguished between acts that depend solely on the divine will and acts that involve the will of other beings, as is the case with sinful acts committed by humans. One problem with this debate, highlighted by al-Ghazālī (c. 1058–1111), is that both schools disagree on whether it is possible to objectively define what constitutes good and evil, or whether the goodness of an act depends on the intention behind it.

In early Islamic theology, further thought was given on the question of how to distinguish between major and minor sins. Again, there were different views on this issue. The Kharijites argued that all acts of disobedience were major sins. The other schools, by contrast, made a distinction between major and minor acts of disobedience, although there was no agreement on what exactly constitutes the difference between the two types. The Ashʿarites took the position that no clear distinction was possible between major and minor sins. While for the Muʿtazilites there was no doubt that there was a clear difference between major and minor sins, there were different positions on the question of whether this difference could only be determined on the basis of the Qur'ān or also by means of reason.

Further clarifications that are relevant for understanding the concept of sin in Islam can also be found in the legal discussions. For example, according to *sharī'ah*, a distinction is made between obligatory, recommended, neutral, reprehensible, and prohibited actions. In the case of obligatory acts, it is clear that their omission is seen as a sin. With prohibited acts, it is equally clear that performing them is a sin. The omission of recommended acts is not considered a sin unless one does the exact opposite of what is recommended, in which case it is a sin. Reprehensible acts are not necessarily sins, although their omission is preferable. Neutral acts are generally not sinful unless, for instance, they are prioritized over an obligatory action.

Whether an act is considered sinful generally depends on which of these five categories it is assigned to. Additionally, other criteria such as knowledge and intention can help to determine whether someone is committing a sin or not. For example, if a person does not know that their action is prohibited, the act is considered forbidden but not sinful. From a juristic perspective, legal accountability for one's own sins also depends on legal capacity, which is the condition for attributing rights to someone and requiring them to fulfill obligations. Only someone who has full legal capacity can be held responsible for his or her sins. Whether a person possesses legal capacity depends in turn on factors such as maturity, sanity, and freedom of choice.

As mentioned above, sinners are threatened with punishment in the afterlife if they do not repent. In addition, the *sharīʿah* also prescribes inner-worldly punishments for certain sins. There are different types of punishments: prescribed punishments, which must be applied in the case of the aforementioned *ḥadd* crimes (among them, for example, fornication, slander, or theft), retaliation, and discretionary punishments. A peculiarity of *ḥadd* crimes is that the prescribed punishment must be enforced once the sin is committed and cannot be replaced by another penalty or waived. This is different with retaliation, which means a punishment equal to the offense, and with discretionary penalties. In these cases, the penalty can also be replaced by another or, under certain conditions, mitigated by the judge. However, while *ḥadd* crimes must be punished more vigorously than other forms of sin, the burden of proof in these cases is also significantly higher.

In addition, Islamic legal discourse distinguishes transgressions according to whose rights they violate. There are four types of rights that can be violated by sin: rights exclusively pertaining to God, rights exclusively pertaining to human beings, mixed rights of God and human beings with a greater share for God, and mixed rights of God and human beings with a greater share for human beings. Religious punishments mainly concern offenses that affect the rights of God (whether they be God's rights alone or shared rights). Again, there are different forms of punishment depending on the transgression, such as fixed punishments for certain offenses, acts of penance, or, as in most cases, punishments to be determined by juristic authorities for actions for which there are no fixed punishments. It is worth mentioning that in Islamic legal discourse, attempts have also been made to define the difference between major and minor sins in terms of the respective forms of punishment. However, there is no clear consensus on where exactly to draw the line between these two types of sin.

In addition to legal discourse, Islamic ethics also addresses sin. Here, the discipline of *ādāb* aims at reflecting on the appropriate behavior of Muslims, modeled after the example of the Prophet Muḥammad. This includes issues such as clothing, food, and interaction with others. However, violations of such appropriate behavior are not sins in the legal sense but usually pertain to the second level of the concept of sin discussed above (i.e., being morally and religiously wrong). They are usually not punished in this world but only in the afterlife. Besides *ādāb*, Islamic ethics also includes the discipline of *akhlāq*, which deals with the character traits a believer should acquire through repeated practice over a long time. This term refers to virtues such as piety, which are rooted in the heart and help believers avoid sins. The cultivation of such virtues was particularly emphasized in Sufism, which developed practices to maintain a deeper connection with God. Among these practices, asceticism and renunciation were seen as especially important means of avoiding sins. In general, Islamic ethics devotes considerable attention to moral psychology and attempts to determine what drives people toward goodness and enables them to avoid sins. In doing so, Islamic ethics is partly influenced by Greek philosophy, but a focus on the inner self and its role in virtue and vice can also be substantiated by the Qurʾān and the prophetic tradition.

Similarities and Differences

Having discussed significant aspects of the understanding of sin in Judaism, Christianity, and Islam, we can now examine their commonalities and differences. A primary commonality, as crucial as it is evident, is that the concept of sin is multifaceted in all three religions. Both the Bible and the Qurʾān employ various terms to describe sin. Within the traditions of these religions, different levels of severity and diverse aspects of sin are distinguished, illustrating that the concept of sin encompasses ethical, legal, and, at times, even cosmological implications. Additionally, various schools of thought or denominations within each religion approach the phenomenon of sin differently. This suggests that while our initial understanding of sin as a transgression of a commandment captures an important aspect of the concept, it is by no means exhaustive. Instead, sin can be approached in numerous ways, such as viewing it primarily as a burden on individuals, as something that causes a turning away from God, or as a crime necessitating earthly punishment according to religious doctrines.

When looking at the nature of sin, a further similarity is apparent. In Judaism and Christianity in particular, the will to sin is decisive for committing a sin. Sin is therefore not just a violation of a God-given commandment but requires intention. While this aspect seems to be slightly less emphasized in the Islamic tradition, some legal scholars do also underscore its importance. This perspective is also indirectly reflected in Islamic jurisprudence, which asserts that only individuals possessing legal capacity – thus having the ability to freely choose whether to commit an act or not – can be held accountable for their actions.

Another interesting topic, where both similarities and differences can be observed, is the question of the origin of sin. All three monotheistic religions trace the first sin of humankind back to Adam and Eve. Judaism and Islam, however, reject the Christian doctrine of original sin as developed by Augustine, which posits that sin is transmitted physically to Adam's descendants and hence to all humanity. In contrast, Islam maintains that individuals fundamentally have the choice to resist sin in their lives. A detailed examination of Judaism reveals a nuanced and differentiated picture: even if the Christian doctrine of original sin has always been vehemently rejected in polemical literature, at least partially comparable ideas can be found in the Talmud and especially in Kabbalistic thought. Nevertheless, Judaism in all its strands denies the necessity of Christ or baptism, instead emphasizing the redeeming power of God's covenant made with Israel at Sinai.

One thing that Judaism and Christianity have in common is that both assume that the first sin brought about a kind of self-awareness, in that humans now see themselves as different from God. However, there are significant differences in how this self-awareness is evaluated. In Western Christian theology, particularly following Augustine, the first sin is seen as resulting in the loss of true freedom. Consequently, the first sin is not viewed as part of the creation process but rather as a disruption of God's fundamentally good creation. Judaism, at least according to the Talmud, takes an almost opposite view of the first sin: it is considered the origin of free will and, as such, is an integral part of the creation process itself.

A similarity between all three religions exists on a practical level. Judaism, Christianity, and Islam equally elaborate detailed considerations on how individuals can overcome sin. A significant method in combating sin is through repentance, often accompanied by ascetic practices. The importance of these practices is particularly underscored by movements that focus on a personal relationship with God, such as Kabbalah, Hasidism, Christian mysticism, certain branches of the Reformation, and Sufism, among others. Closely related to this is another common feature: In all three religions, there are extensive discussions of particular sins. In Judaism, such treatments are found particularly in responsa literature, in Christianity primarily in writings intended to lead to confession, as well as in casuistic approaches to moral theology, which were widespread especially in the early modern period, and in Islam primarily in legal literature.

At this point, a major difference in the treatment of the concept of sin becomes apparent: each religion seems to have its dominant approach to the phenomenon of sin. In Judaism, the approach varies depending on whether sin is treated from an orthodox or liberal perspective, with legal or ethical-moral approaches being prevalent. In Christianity, sin is mostly addressed within the context of overarching theological concepts, such as general considerations of salvation. Here, the discussion of individual sins plays, at best, a subordinate role today. In Islam, a predominantly legal and moral focus can be observed, with particular emphasis on individual sins and their relevance in juristic terms.

Finally, this highlights another difference. In Judaism, but especially in Islam, there is a much greater focus on the worldly consequences of sin. In contrast, the Christian approach to sin is more eschatologically oriented. Although there are religious actions – such as the practice of indulgences in the Roman Catholic Church – that can be interpreted as attempts to influence God's judgment, there is, at least today, hardly any religious punishment of sins by the institutions of the Church (with the exception of ecclesiastical penalties such as excommunication for specific sins). Instead, Christian theology views punishment in this world as primarily the responsibility of secular authorities. In Islam, by contrast, there are numerous sins that, according to Islamic law, must be punished in this world and in accordance with religious guidelines. Thus, in the context of sin, as in other fields, it becomes clear how differently the relationship between the secular and religious spheres can be defined in the individual religions.

Overall, then, sin is an area in which there are major commonalities on the one hand, but also important differences on the other. If there is one main commonality, it is perhaps how complex sin is and how seriously it is therefore taken in the individual religions. This complexity could serve as an interesting approach in interreligious dialogue: if the individual religions acknowledge that sin is a multifaceted phenomenon and that other religions also grapple with it seriously, the willingness to learn from one another might increase. Ultimately, it may be the very complexity of sin that brings the individual religions closer together.

List of Contributors and Editors

David Bashevkin is the director of education for NCSY, the youth movement of the Orthodox Union, and the Clinical Assistant Professor of Jewish Values at the Sy Syms School of Business at Yeshiva University. He completed rabbinic ordination at Yeshiva University's Rabbi Isaac Elchanan Theological Seminary, as well as a Master's degree at the Bernard Revel Graduate School of Jewish Studies focusing on the thought of Rabbi Zadok of Lublin under the guidance of Dr. Yaakov Elman. He completed his doctorate in Public Policy and Management at The New School's Milano School of International Affairs, focusing on crisis management. He has published four books, *Sin·a·gogue: Sin and Failure in Jewish Thought*, a Hebrew work *B'Rogez Rachem Tizkor* (trans. In Anger, Remember Mercy), *Top 5: Lists of Jewish Character and Character*, and *Just One: The NCSY Haggadah*. He is the host and founder of 18forty, a new Jewish media site. David has been rejected from several prestigious fellowships and awards.

Christoph Böttigheimer has held the Chair of Fundamental Theology at the Catholic University of Eichstätt-Ingolstadt since 2002. He studied Catholic theology at the Universities of Tübingen and Innsbruck (Austria), obtained his doctorate at the University of Munich in 1993 and habilitated there in 1996. He is the author of *Lehrbuch der Fundamentaltheologie*, one of the most well-received and influential textbooks in the field of fundamental theology in the German-speaking world. His works on fundamental theological issues and core questions of faith have been translated into several languages. Recently, a 4th edition of the textbook and a monograph entitled *Die Reich-Gottes-Botschaft Jesu. Verlorene Mitte christlichen Glaubens* (Herder, 2020) have been published. He is a member of numerous academic research and working committees, especially in the field of ecumenical dialogue and cooperation.

Ayman Shabana is Associate Professor of Theology and Islamic Studies at Georgetown University in Qatar. He received his Ph.D. from the University of California, Los Angeles, his MA from Leiden University in the Netherlands, and his BA from al-Azhar University in Egypt. His teaching and research interests include Islamic legal and intellectual history; Islamic law and ethics; religious studies and moral philosophy; applied ethics, human rights, and bioethics. He is the director of the Islamic Bioethics Project, which has been supported by three consecutive grants from Qatar National Research Fund's National Priorities Research Program. In 2012 he received the Research Excellence Award at the Qatar Annual Research Forum and during the academic year 2013-2014 he was a visiting research fellow at the Islamic Legal Studies Program at Harvard Law School. He is the author of *Custom in Islamic Law and Legal Theory* in addition to several book chapters and academic journal articles, which appeared in *Islamic Law and Society*, *Journal of Islamic Studies*, *Journal of Islamic Ethics*, *Journal of Religious Ethics*, *Journal of Qur'anic Studies*, *Zygon*, *Hawwa*, *Religion Compass*, *Sociology of Islam*, *The Muslim World*, and *Medicine Health Care and Philosophy*.

Konstantin Kamp is research assistant at the Chair of Theology in Processes of Transformation at the Catholic University of Eichstätt-Ingolstadt. He studied Catholic Theology and Philosophy in Tübingen, Munich, and Rome. His research interests include the tradition of negative theology, the relationship between theology and spirituality, Christology, and interreligious dialogue.

https://doi.org/10.1515/9783111319452-005

Index of Persons

'Abd al-Jabbār, al-Qāḍī 129
Abel 8
Abū Hurayrah 105
Adam 7–15, 19, 30, 61–62, 64–69, 73, 76–78, 82, 85, 152–153, 158–159, 167
'Ā'ishah 122
'Alī ibn Abī Ṭālib 109, 122–123
Althaus, Paul 78–79
Ambrosiaster 65
Anderson, Gary A. 1
Aquinas, Thomas 59–60, 69–70, 157, 159
al-Ash'arī, Abū al-Ḥasan 123, 125, 164
Augustine 10–11, 15, 59, 64–69, 73, 158–159, 167
Avraham Ibn David of Posquières (Rabbi) 12

Baal Shem Tov 25–27, 39, 42, 154
Beinert, Wolfgang 96
Benedict XII (pope) 88
Berkenkopf, Christian 53
Blankovsky, Yuval 18
Boniface II (pope) 68
Brill, Alan 32
Brunner, Emil 78–79

Cain 8
Calvin, John 89
Clement of Alexandria 87
Clement VI (pope) 92
Coudert, Allison 14
Cyprian 87
Cyril of Jerusalem 88

David (King) 25
Dessler, Eliyahu (Rabbi) 42
Drewermann, Eugen 81

Eiger, Leible (Rabbi) 30
Eleazer of Worms (Rabbi) 21–22, 37, 154
Elimelekh of Lizhensk (Rabbi) 27–28, 154
Engel, Yosef (Rabbi) 17
Eve 7–9, 12–13, 30, 152, 158, 167

Fairstein, Morris 30
Feinstein, Moshe (Rabbi) 38–39, 156
Fishman, Talya 22
Fraade, Steven 4

al-Ghazālī, Abū Ḥāmid Muḥammad ibn Muḥammad 126, 141, 164
Gregory of Nazianzus 88
Gregory of Nyssa 88
Gregory the Great 59

Ḥayyim of Volozhin (Rabbi) 26
Horowitz, Isaiah (Rabbi) 13
Hutner, Yitzḥak (Rabbi) 40–42, 156

Ibn al-'Awwām, al-Zubayr 122
Ibn Mas'ūd, 'Abd Allāh 108–109
Ibn 'Abbās 111, 116, 119–121, 128, 138–139, 163
Ibn 'Abd al-Salām, al-'Izz 139
Ibn 'Ubayd Allāh, Talḥah 122
Ibn 'Umar 109
Israel ben Eliezer (Rabbi) *See* Baal Shem Tov

Jacobs, Louis 27
Jesus Christ 13, 54–58, 62–64, 67–68, 70, 72, 77, 83–84, 89, 91–92, 94–97, 99, 157–158, 160–161, 167
Joest, Wilfried 78
John Chrysostom 88
John (evangelist) 56–57
John Paul II (pope) 51, 94–96, 99, 161
John the Baptist 54–55
John XXIII (pope) 51
al-Jubā'ī, Abū 'Alī 129
al-Jubā'ī, Abū Hāshim 129
al-Juwaynī, 'Abd al-Malik ibn 'abd Allāh 138

Knorr von Rosenroth, Christian 14

Lam, Joseph 1–2
Landau, Yeḥezkel (Rabbi) 36–37, 39, 155
Lasker, Daniel 12–13
Leibniz, Gottfried Wilhelm 15
Leiner, Gershon Ḥenokh (Rabbi) 29–30, 32
Leiner, Mordekhai Yosef (Rabbi) 29–31, 42, 155
Leiner, Yaakov (Rabbi) 29–30

https://doi.org/10.1515/9783111319452-006

Lewis, Clive Staples 8
Loew, Yehudah (Rabbi) 16–17
Lot 116
Luntschitz, Ephraim (Rabbi) 13
Luria, Isaac 14, 153
Luther, Martin 70–71, 74, 89, 93–94, 98, 159, 161

Magid, Shaul 29
Maimonides, Moses 6, 16
Mary 62
Maximus Confessor 88
Meir (Rabbi) 2–3
Melanchthon, Philip 89
Mendelssohn, Moses 34
Milton, John 105, 146
Moser, Tilmann 51
Moses 111
Muḥammad (prophet) 105, 111, 115–116, 119, 125, 128, 139–140, 143–144, 163, 166
Muʿāwiyah ibn Abī Sufyān 122

Naḥman of Bratslav (Rabbi) 27, 29, 155
Nahmanides 9, 153
Nathan of Gaza 24
al-Nawawī, Yaḥyā ibn Sharaf 119
Nietzsche, Friedrich 50
Noah 116

Origen 87–88, 160

Paul (apostle) 10, 56–58, 60, 62–64, 68–69, 85–87, 157–158
Paul VI (pope) 94, 161
Pelagius 11, 15, 68, 73–74
Pieper, Josef 49
Pius V (pope) 94

al-Qarāfī, Shihāb al-Dīn 137
al-Qurṭubī, Muḥammad ibn Aḥmad 117

Rabinowitz, Zadok ha-Kohen (Rabbi) 29–31, 42, 44
Rahner, Karl 77
Ra'avad *See* Avraham Ibn David of Posquières (Rabbi)
Rembaum, Joel 11
Ritschl, Albrecht 79–80, 160
Rosen, Michael 26

Schachter, Hershel (Rabbi) 19
Scheffczyk, Leo 76
Schleiermacher, Friedrich Daniel Ernst 77, 160
Scholem, Gershom 23–24, 34
Schoonenberg, Piet 79–80, 160
Schorr, Gedalia (Rabbi) 42
Shafran, Noach (Rabbi) 43–44, 156
Shneur Zalman of Liadi (Rabbi) 27–28, 154
Sofer, Moshe (Rabbi) 37–39, 155
Soloveitchik, Haym 21
al-Subkī, Tāj al-Dīn 139
al-Suyūṭī, Jalāl al-Dīn 140

al-Ṭabarī, Abū Jaʿfar Muḥammad ibn Jarīr 108, 110, 120, 144
Teilhard de Chardin, Pierre 77, 160
Tsevi, Shabbetai 23–25, 34, 154

Ussher, James 8
ʿUthmān (caliph) 122, 163

Van Helmot, Francis Mercury 14
Vital, Ḥayyim 14

Weger, Karl-Heinz 79–80
Weil, Yaakov ben Yehudah (Rabbi) 22–23
Weinberger, Moshe (Rabbi) 42–44, 156
Wickler, Wolfgang 77–78

Yehudah of Regensburg (Rabbi) 20–21

al-Zarkashī, Badr al-Dīn Muḥammad ibn Bahādir ibn ʿAbd Allāh 132
Zosimus (pope) 67
Zunz, Leopold 33
Zwingli, Huldrych 89

Index of Subjects

'averah 1, 4–6, 152
'averah lishmah 17–20, 24–25, 153–154
'avon 1–5, 152
antinomianism 18, 24–25, 30–31, 33–34, 43–44, 153–155
asceticism 37, 155, 166–167
Ash'arites 126–128, 130, 164

baptism 11–12, 65–66, 70, 72–74, 93, 97, 153, 158–159, 167
body 16, 64, 68–69, 73, 87, 89, 144, 159

Catechism of the Catholic Church 60, 67, 159
Catholic Tübingen School 60
Church 58, 66–67, 81–82, 88, 91–99, 161
commandment 6, 18–20, 24, 26, 30, 50, 52, 55, 57, 71, 106, 108, 111–113, 134, 136, 151, 153, 162, 166–167
concupiscence 69–73, 159
confession 2–3, 37, 58–59, 91–93, 95, 155, 157, 160–161, 167
conscience 49, 56, 60
Council of Ferrara-Florence 88
Council of Trent 66, 68, 70, 72–73, 89, 94, 159, 161
covenant 52–54, 167
creation 6, 8–10, 14, 19, 29, 55, 84–86, 153, 157, 167

determinism 30–32, 155
divine names 125, 145

Enlightenment 34, 37, 50, 155
Eucharist 88–89, 160
evil 11, 13–15, 40, 49, 53, 55–56, 58, 60–61, 63, 66, 69, 72, 74, 79, 81–82, 84, 86, 107–108, 118, 125–126, 140, 156, 162, 164
evolution 76–77, 84

faith 50–51, 55, 63, 66, 69, 72, 81–82, 84, 94, 113, 116, 118–120, 123, 127, 145, 156, 162–163
Fall of Man *See* original sin
fiqh 130, 141
Formula of Concord 71
freedom 9–11, 38, 49, 54, 57, 66, 68, 71, 73–80, 82–83, 85, 98–99, 125–126, 130, 133, 145–146, 151, 153, 157–159, 164–165, 167

grace 11, 28, 61, 63–64, 66, 68–69, 71–72, 74–75, 80, 82, 84, 89–94, 96–97, 159, 161
grave sin *See* major sin
guilt 1, 49–50, 52, 54, 60, 62, 64–68, 73, 77–81, 83, 89, 91, 99, 151, 157–158, 160

ḥadd 106, 108–109, 134–137, 139, 141, 162, 165
halakhah 4–5, 18–19, 24, 26, 34–36, 38–40 43–44, 153–155
Ḥaside Ashkenaz 20–22, 37, 39, 154–155
Hasidism 26–27, 29–32, 34, 36, 39, 42–44, 154–156, 167
heaven 18, 20, 88, 114, 125, 160
Hebrew Bible 2, 4, 6–7, 9–10, 19, 39, 44, 52–58, 61, 76, 87, 152, 156–158
hell 88, 114, 123, 125, 128, 160
hereafter 108, 111, 114, 117–119, 123, 128, 134, 141, 145, 162–166
ḥeṭ 1–5, 152
ḥudūd See ḥadd

indulgence 91–98, 160–161, 168
intention 2–3, 15, 18–19, 152–153, 164–165, 167
Israel 14, 20, 22, 35, 53–55, 157, 167

justice 49, 73, 112, 115, 130, 142
justification 69, 71–72, 74–75, 89, 94, 96–97, 159, 161

kabā'ir See major sin
Kabbalah 13–15, 20, 24, 32, 34, 153, 167
Kharijites *See* al-Khawārij

https://doi.org/10.1515/9783111319452-007

al-Khawārij 123–124, 128, 164
Kingdom of God 54–55, 76, 79, 83–84, 86, 157, 160

Last Judgment 55, 83–84, 86–87, 89, 113–114, 160
law 5, 15, 18–19, 24, 26, 30, 33–35, 39, 43, 52, 55–57, 63, 69, 106, 108, 111, 114, 118, 130, 135, 153–158, 168
legal capacity 133, 165, 167

major sin 21, 58–60, 91, 99, 108–111, 115, 119, 123–125, 128–129, 137–139, 145, 157, 160, 162–165
mercy 54–55, 60, 105, 109, 121, 123, 125, 157, 164
minor sin 58–61, 98–99, 108–109, 128–129, 137–140, 157, 162, 164–165
Mishnah 2–5, 152
monogenism 67, 76–77
morality 50, 52, 98, 105–108, 110–111, 113, 140–145, 162, 166, 168
mortal sin *See* major sin
al-Murji'ah 123–124, 164
Mu'tazilites 124–126, 129–130, 164
mysticism 14–15, 20, 23–24, 29, 32, 34, 36, 154, 167
New Testament 53–57, 59, 67, 83–84, 87, 157–158

Old Testament *See* Hebrew Bible
original sin 10–13, 15, 19, 54, 61–70, 72–74, 76–83, 153, 158–160, 167
Orthodox Judaism 38, 41–44, 155–156, 168

paradise *See* heaven
peccatum originale See original sin
penance 21–22, 36–37, 58, 89, 91–96, 157–158, 161, 165
pesh'a 1–5, 152
punishment 8, 11, 50, 53, 59, 64, 66–67, 89–92, 94–96, 98, 106, 108–110, 114, 116, 118–120, 123–125, 127–130, 134–139, 141, 151, 156, 160–166, 168
purgatory 87–91, 160

qiṣāṣ 134–135, 141
Qur'ān 105, 107–116, 120–121, 138, 140, 144, 162–164, 166

Ramadan 137, 139
redemption *See* salvation
Reform Judaism 33–35, 38, 155, 168
Reformation 70–71, 159–161, 167
repentance 6, 20–21, 27–28, 36–39, 44–45, 55, 109, 115, 118–121, 123, 125, 128, 139, 145, 152, 154–155, 157, 161, 163, 167
responsa literature 22, 36–40, 154, 156
revelation 12, 116

Sabbatean movement 19, 23–26, 34–35, 44, 154–155
Sacrament of Penance *See* confession
ṣaghā'ir See minor sin
Ṣaḥīḥ Muslim 119
salvation 11, 13, 15, 23, 25, 49, 52, 55–57, 60, 62–76, 78, 80, 83, 85, 88, 93–94, 97–99, 119, 145, 153, 157–159, 161, 168
sanctification 72, 94, 97
satisfaction 94, 96
school of Izbica 27, 29–32, 155
Second Council of Lyon 88
Second Vatican Council 51, 60, 158, 161
sexuality 9, 12, 18, 39, 65, 112, 114, 137, 139–140, 158–159
sharī'ah 108, 130–131, 134–135, 140, 162, 164
shirk 109, 111, 114–115
social sin 81, 99
soul 11, 66, 68–69, 73, 87–89, 105, 115, 142–143, 159
Sufism 142, 145, 166–167
Sunnah 110, 115–116, 119, 128, 138, 141, 144, 166
Synod of Carthage 66–68, 73, 159
Synod of Orange 68–69, 73, 85, 159

Talmud 2–5, 8–10, 12–13, 15–17, 19–20, 24–25, 30–31, 36, 39, 41, 43–44, 153, 167
ta'zīr 134–137, 141

Ten Commandments 16, 111, 162
Torah 11–12, 18, 24–25, 31, 34, 37, 40, 43–44
Tree of the Knowledge of Good and Evil 7–8, 61, 152, 158
tsadik 27–28, 154
Tun-Ergehen-Zusammenhang 53, 57–58

Umayyads 122
uṣūl al-fiqh 130, 145

venial sin *See* minor sin
vice 59, 141–144, 166
virtue 57, 59, 70, 141–144, 166

Yom Kippur 2

www.ingramcontent.com/pod-product-compliance
Lightning Source LLC
Chambersburg PA
CBHW031834230426
43669CB00009B/1347
9783111303949